FROM SLAVERY TO WEALTH

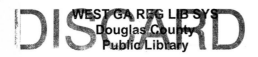

FROM
SLAVERY TO WÉALTH

The Life of Scott Bond

Edited with a New Preface and Introduction by

Willard B. Gatewood

PHOENIX INTERNATIONAL, INC.

FAYETTEVILLE

12 11 10 09 08   5 4 3 2 1

Designed by John Coghlan

Inquiries should be addressed to:
Phoenix International, Inc.
17762 Summer Rain Road
Fayetteville, Arkansas 72701
Phone (479) 521-2204
www.phoenixbase.com

Reproductions of the photographs from the first edition of *From Slavery to Wealth: The Life of Scott Bond,* by Dan. A. Rudd and Theo. Bond, are courtesy of Special Collections, University of Arkansas Libraries, Fayetteville.

Library of Congress Cataloging-in-Publication Data

Bond, Scott, b. 1853.
  From slavery to wealth : the life of Scott Bond / edited with a new preface and introduction by Willard B. Gatewood.— Reprint ed.
     p. cm.
  Originally published: Madison, Ark. : Journal Printing Co., 1917.
  Includes bibliographical references and index.
  ISBN-13: 978-0-9768007-6-7
  1. Bond, Scott, b. 1853. 2. African Americans—Biography. 3. Successful people—United States—Biography. 4. Slaves—Arkansas—Biography. 5. African American farmers—Arkansas—Madison—Biography. 6. African American businesspeople—Arkansas—Madison—Biography. 7. Madison (Ark.)—Biography. 8. Saint Francis River Valley (Mo. and Ark.)—Biography. 9. Saint Francis County (Ark.)—Biography. 10. Cross County (Ark.)—Biography. I. Gatewood, Willard B. II. Title.
  E185.97.B7A3 2007
  920'.009296073—dc22

                                                                    2007040722

Contents

Preface to the New Edition

The story of Scott Bond's life provided in *From Slavery to Wealth,* originally published ninety years ago, is very much in the tradition of African American biographical and autobiographical literature of the late nineteenth and early twentieth centuries. A classic example of such literature is Booker T. Washington's phenomenally popular autobiography *Up from Slavery,* published in 1901. Despite obvious differences, the lives and careers of Bond and Washington possessed many striking similarities. Both were born in slavery in the 1850s a few years apart, one in Mississippi and the other in Virginia; both had white fathers whom they never knew; and both grew to maturity in the South during the era of Civil War, Emancipation, and Reconstruction. Both were ambitious men who cultivated cordial relationships with prominent whites and espoused approaches to race relations that were virtually identical. Both pursued strategies that enabled them to succeed in the decades following Reconstruction when African Americans confronted a proliferation of legal and extralegal restrictions that stripped them of their civil rights and relegated them to an inferior status in American society. Washington became a famous and influential educator whom many blacks and whites considered the preeminent spokesman of black America, while Bond, on a much more limited scale, gained considerable recognition as a highly successful farmer and entrepreneur. Like his friend Washington, Bond also enjoyed the respect of both blacks and whites, but no one held him in higher regard than his sons.

It was not surprising, therefore, that one of his sons, Theophilus (Theo) Bond, and Daniel A. Rudd, a former editor of several black newspapers and long associated with Scott Bond's diverse enterprises, compiled a record of his life and achievements that was privately published in 1917. A contract for printing the book was first made with the Journal Printing Company, a small printing concern in Madison, Arkansas, but when the company proved incapable of performing the job, another contract was negotiated with the National Baptist Printing Board in Nashville, Tennessee, a modern printing outfit owned and operated by the nation's largest black

Baptist denomination. The product was a handsome and profusely illustrated volume with a gilt-lettered cover that has long been classified as a rare book. The book reveals not only much about Bond the man, but also about race relations in the South during almost a half century after the end of Reconstruction. In the process, the work sheds light on changes that occurred in the Arkansas Delta, the area of the South in which Bond spent his adult life, and especially those changes brought about by Bond and others of his generation who figured prominently in the transformation of the area from a swampy wilderness frontier into a highly productive and more densely populated agricultural region.

Sixty-three years old at the time the story of his life, reprinted here, was in progress, Scott Bond contributed his own recollections that were incorporated verbatim into it. At times these recollections appear within quotation marks and at other times the authors introduce lengthy sections, written in the first person, but indicate that they are in Bond's "own words." In brief, the authors produced a hybrid work consisting of as much, if not more, autobiography than biography that provides rich insight into an extraordinary individual as well as the place and era in which he lived and labored. As might be expected, this work does not claim to present an objective, balanced, or dispassionate account of Bond's life. It abounds in praise and admiration of the man and his success under daunting circumstances, beginning with a preface by James C. Napier, a well-known African American and a former president of the National Negro Business League. The authors' primary objective was to depict the difficulties that blacks confronted in the South during the late nineteenth and early twentieth centuries and to inspire black people to follow Bond's example, especially his work ethic and perseverance, in overcoming obstacles they were likely to encounter in their own pursuit of success. Bond's career is presented as a model for young, ambitious African Americans to follow.

From Slavery to Wealth poses certain problems for readers. One concerns its organization, which exhibits what may be described as its random quality—a hodge-podge of topics ranging from the significant to the trivial that convey little about the sequence and chronology of events. Many photographs appear to be located at random without regard to the text. Interspersed throughout the book, without much discernible rhyme or reason, are stories about bears, snakes, slaves' means of communicating, and the discovery of various "treasures," which are interesting and offer insight into the frontier wilderness in which Bond spent his early days, but they have little if any relationship to what precedes or follows them. The random insertion of such stories and other material seriously disrupts the continuity and flow of the narrative. Another problem is that specific dates appear only very rarely in the volume. The result is that it is difficult if not impossible to date with precision events mentioned in the story of Bond's life compiled by Rudd and Bond. In spite of its defects and limitations, this work is of immense value as a historical document. In the absence of any known collection of Bond papers, *From Slavery to Wealth* has been the source of most secondary accounts of his life.

The principal purposes of the editor's introduction are to place Bond's story in historical context and to provide, insofar as is possible, a chronological framework for the significant events in his life that are treated in the book. Although the basic text of the work has not been altered, the editor has corrected some obvious errors in printing and spelling and has added notes to help clarify the meaning of certain references and whenever possible to identify individuals mentioned but not adequately identified in the text.

Numerous individuals provided invaluable assistance in the preparation of this edition of *From Slavery to Wealth*. I owe special debt of gratitude to John Coghlan, who first suggested that I undertake this project and who has consistently provided encouragement and wise counsel along the way. My labors have benefited enormously by the extraordinary editorial skills of Debbie Self and by the help provided by Andrea Cantrell and other librarians and archivists at the University of Arkansas, Fayetteville. Finally, I owe a very large debt to Margaret Bolsterli, Tom Dillard, and Jeannie Whayne for their perceptive comments and criticisms.

W. B. G.
Summer 2007

Introduction to the New Edition

Among the large number of African Americans gathered for the annual meeting of the National Negro Business League in New York in 1910 was a well-dressed and very fair-complexioned representative from Arkansas.* Though seated toward the rear of the auditorium, he was recognized by the presiding officer Booker T. Washington, founder and life president of the League, who deviated from the printed program to summon his friend from Arkansas to the podium to comment on the conditions of black people in his state. The unscheduled speaker was Scott Bond, a highly successful farmer and wealthy entrepreneur from Madison, Arkansas, who delivered one of his provocative "heart to heart talks with his own people" in which he urged blacks to remain in the South and to focus on economics rather than politics as the best means of realizing their desire to achieve the rights and privileges of first-class citizenship.** His remarks clearly identified Bond as an adherent of Washington's formula for the progress of African Americans in an era of deteriorating race relations—a formula that ultimately divided the black community into Bookerites and anti-Bookerites.

---

*Material in the Introduction quoted from the book *From Slavery to Wealth: The Life of Scott Bond,* reprinted here, is not specifically documented, but the sources for other information and quotations are cited.

**Useful information on Scott Bond's life is found in Fon Louise Gordon, "Scott Winfield Bond," in *Arkansas Biography: A Collection of Notable Lives,* edited by Nancy A. Williams and Jeannie M. Whayne (Fayetteville: University of Arkansas Press, 2000), 31–32; Ulysses S. Bond, "Highlights of the Life of Scott Bond," *Arkansas Historical Quarterly* 21 (Summer 1962): 146–52; "Scott Bond," in *Era of Progress and Promise, 1863–1910,* edited by W. N. Hartshorn and George W. Penniman (Boston: Priscilla Publishing Co., 1910), 426; Tom W. Dillard, "Remembering Arkansas: Scott Bond Was the State's 'Black Rockefeller,'" *Arkansas Democrat-Gazette* (Little Rock), December 10, 2006; John W. Graves, *Town and Country: Race Relations in an Urban-Rural Context, Arkansas, 1865–1905* (Fayetteville: University of Arkansas Press, 1990), 78–79, 88–89; Robert W. Chowning, *History of St. Francis County, Arkansas* (Forrest City, AR: Times-Herald Publishing Co., 1954), 153; "Scott Bond," *Negro History Bulletin* 2 (1942): 41–43; "Scott Bond" in *The National Cyclopedia of the Colored Race,* edited by Clement Richardson (Montgomery, AL: National Publishing Company, 1919), 92–93.

Scott Bond was one of several African Americans who amassed considerable wealth in farming and various other enterprises in Arkansas during the late nineteenth and early twentieth centuries. Bond prospered in that section of Arkansas that lay in the Mississippi Alluvial Plain, commonly called the Delta, whose physical environment was characterized by incredibly rich soil, numerous swamps, virgin forests, lush vegetation, and abundant fish and wildlife, including dangerous snakes and mosquitoes. The Delta included a series of fickle rivers that meandered southward. According to one authority, the Delta was "a land of rivers, built by rivers, and defined by rivers."[1] The same waterways that enriched the land, nourished cotton agriculture, and served as the principal means of commerce and travel prior to the arrival of railroads and motor transportation were also the sources of various diseases and frequent floods that caused staggering economic losses, numerous deaths, and great human suffering.[2] Bond later recalled that when he first arrived in the Arkansas Delta it was largely a forested wilderness with scattered small clearings and "trails here and there but few roads."

Scott Bond's career was closely linked to one of the Delta's principal rivers, the St. Francis. He spent most of his life in the St. Francis River Basin in the vicinity of Crowley's Ridge, an unusual crescent-shaped landform sometimes described as a highland in the lowland because it rose up to five hundred feet above the flat alluvial plain. Here Bond established a highly diversified economic domain that included agriculture, stock raising, orchards, sawmills and lumber, cotton gins, a brickmaking plant, gravel pits, and a large mercantile establishment. The center of his operations was located in the town of Madison, Arkansas, located on the St. Francis River a few miles from Forrest City, the seat of St. Francis County. Notwithstanding threats posed by floods, malaria and other diseases, and a variety of environmental conditions that tormented Delta residents, Bond quickly recognized that this isolated and sparsely populated frontier area offered poor people opportunities for achieving economic independence. He concentrated his attention and energy on taking advantage of nature's many gifts in the region, including its mild climate with a long growing season, rich land, and prime timber. Throughout his career he never wearied of imploring African

Americans to seize the opportunities offered them in the South in general and in the Arkansas Delta in particular.

Although born a slave in Mississippi, Bond spent most of his life in Arkansas, in Cross and St. Francis counties. His earliest memories included those of his mother, described as a "bright mulatto girl named Ann." Bond's mother, a native of North Carolina, was among a group of slaves hired by William H. Goodloe, the owner of a large plantation located about twelve miles from Canton, Mississippi. These hired slaves originally belonged to the Mebane (misspelled as Maben in the text) estate and had been inherited by "the widow Bond," Mary Frances (Fannie) Mebane Bond, whose Mebane ancestors of Alamance and Orange counties in North Carolina had been prominent in public affairs since the colonial era. Fannie Bond appears to have been related to Goodloe's wife, probably through the North Carolina Mebanes. Over the years members of this Mebane family moved into Tennessee, Mississippi, and Arkansas. A settlement in St. Francis County, Arkansas, known as Mebaneville, was named in honor of William T. Mebane, a physician, postmaster, and planter, who was a relative of Fannie Mebane. Shortly after their marriage in 1851 Fannie Mebane and John W. Bond migrated to the Arkansas Delta and settled in St. Francis County near Mebaneville. John Bond does not appear to have lived long after their marriage. Although Goodloe referred to the slaves he hired from Fannie Bond as the "Mebane slaves," these slaves later became known as the "Bond slaves" and adopted Bond as their last name. Various members of the Mebane family figured prominently in the life of Scott Bond during and after slavery.[3]

There is inconsistency among published sources about the year of Scott Bond's birth. Secondary sources usually cite either 1852 or 1853 as the year of his birth, but the federal census of 1880 indicates that he was born in 1854. What is indisputable is that the place of his birth was Madison County, Mississippi, in a settlement called Livingston near Canton, where his mother was a hired slave, one of the hired "Mebane slaves," in the Goodloe household. Later these slaves, including Scott Bond and his mother, lived briefly in Fayette County, Tennessee, where Mebane relatives of their owner resided. In 1861 they were moved to Arkansas with their owner "the widow Bond" and lived on the Bond plantation located near Wittsburg,

Arkansas, on the St. Francis River in what was then St. Francis County. Wittsburg at one time was a thriving river port on the St. Francis but rapidly declined after the arrival of the railroad. The Bond plantation was in the portion of St. Francis County that became a part of a new county created in 1862 and named Cross County in honor of Colonel David Cross, a large landowner. Cross County was carved out of three adjoining counties, St. Francis, Poinsett, and Crittenden.[4]

As a child, Scott Bond road horseback seated behind his mistress as she regularly inspected her plantation, which was enclosed by fences with numerous gates. Landowners fenced their land, because under the so-called fence law any land not under fence was open to public grazing. Young Bond's job was to "jump down and unlock gates she had to pass through" in her rounds over the plantation. Since he possessed keys to all the gates, he became known as the "key boy." His owner was especially attached to her young slave.

Bond had vivid memories of the impact of the Civil War on the residents of the newly created Cross County. It was a time when whites and blacks alike lived in continual fear of Union army patrols, Confederate army forays, and the activities of irregular military forces known as Jayhawks in the area. Bond as a young boy knew from firsthand experience how slaves were herded into hiding whenever word spread that military units were in the area. He never forgot the scarcity of food in these chaotic times and the hunger that he experienced as a child. The enthusiasm with which slaves greeted Emancipation also made an indelible impression on young Bond. His joy over the ending of slavery was no doubt mixed with his sadness over the mental deterioration of his owner by the close of the war. These two events marked the collapse of the only world he had ever known.

A significant figure in his youth was a slave named William Bond, also one of the hired "Mebane slaves" belonging to the "widow Bond," whom Scott believed to be his father since he was his mother's husband. He later learned that William Bond was actually his stepfather. His natural father was a white man, Wesley Rutledge, a nephew of William H. Goodloe and an overseer on the Goodloe plantation in Mississippi. After the Civil War, while living in Cross County, both Bond and his stepfather briefly attended a school for freedmen at a time when "the whole colored population [in the area] seemed to be crazy about education." Bond's education was cut short by his mother's death when he was barely a teenager, which meant that he had to shoulder much of the responsibility for his younger siblings.

It is uncertain how many half-siblings Bond had. The census of 1880 reveals that numerous African Americans by the name of Bond were residing in the vicinity of Madison, Arkansas, in St. Francis County.[5] Scott Bond appears to have had at least two African American half-brothers and at least one half-sister. The husband of the latter, Patrick Banks, was Bond's close friend. It is unclear whether Bond was related to Burrell Bond, an ex-slave who lived in St. Francis County in 1880 and for a time attracted considerable publicity because of his success in growing tea.[6]

By 1872 Bond, while still residing in Cross County, was share-cropping with his stepfather in adjacent St. Francis County where his stepfather had bargained to buy a farm. The farm was near the bustling town of Madison, located on the St. Francis River at the foot of Crowley's Ridge, and had twice served as the seat of county government prior to its transfer to Forrest City in 1874.[7]

Before the Civil War Crowley's Ridge had stalled the completion of the Memphis and Little Rock Railroad so that by the beginning of the war, its rail lines extended westward only to Madison, Arkansas, forty-five miles from Memphis. During the war Confederate general Nathan Bedford Forrest saw the possibility of cutting through the Ridge to complete the rail line and after the war negotiated a contract with the railroad company to cut a passageway through Crowley's Ridge. Almost a thousand Irish workers labored for months digging and removing dirt to complete the task ordered by General Forrest. The commissary and railroad camp that Forrest established a few miles from Madison became known as "Forrest's Town," which evolved into Forrest City after the completion of the Memphis and Little Rock Railroad. Incorporated in 1871, the same year that the first passenger train from Memphis to Little Rock traveled over the newly completed rail line, Forrest City grew rapidly and was noted especially for its businesses related to cotton and lumbering. In an age of railroad consolidation and the emergence of large railroad systems, the Memphis and Little

Rock Railroad was first absorbed by the Choctaw, Oklahoma, and Gulf Railroad and still later by the Chicago, Rock Island, and Pacific Railroad, commonly known as the Rock Island.[8] As Bond's recollections make clear, the Rock Island played a significant role in the development and expansion of his economic empire during the early twentieth century.

As Reconstruction in Arkansas was winding down in the early 1870s, Bond ventured forth on his own. With no money but "lots of will power" he rented twelve acres. By 1876 he was tending thirty-five acres with the help of one hired hand. He then rented a large farm located near the base of Crowley's Ridge that belonged to Celia Mebane Allen, who at the time lived in Knoxville, Tennessee. Celia Allen was the widow of John Abijah Allen, a native of Louisiana and a first cousin of Bond's former owner. When Mrs. Allen moved away from St. Francis County, her son, John Mebane Allen, managed her 2,200-acre plantation located there. After renting this plantation for about a decade Bond decided that it was far more profitable to work for himself than to pay cash rent to someone else. He notified Celia Allen that he would no longer rent her plantation. However, her son John persuaded him to purchase the farm in partnership with a highly respected white Republican officeholder, T. O. Fitzpatrick.[9] Bond later sold his half interest in the "Allen farm" to Fitzpatrick for cash with which he purchased a series of small farms to add to the 300 acres he had already purchased near Madison from a saloonkeeper in Forrest City. For years thereafter he continued to buy land, especially parcels of swampy wilderness land that he could acquire cheaply. His intention was ultimately to drain the swamplands and plant them in cotton, corn, and other crops.

Over the years Bond acquired considerable acreage for a few dollars per acre at delinquent tax sales. He first learned about such sales from a white friend in Wittsburg, Raphael Block, a native of France and a prosperous merchant. At Block's urging he purchased eight hundred acres sight unseen for sixteen dollars at a delinquent tax sale. Later after he and Block visited the land that he had purchased, Block described it as "800 acres of the finest virgin timber I have ever seen and just one-half mile from the river." This purchase would one day figure significantly in Bond's sawmilling and lumber enterprise.

Transforming this swampy domain into tillable land required much time and arduous labor because it involved digging drainage ditches, clearing away dense thickets of vegetation, and cutting large trees and removing their stumps. His purchase of a powerful Hercules Stump Puller in 1915 greatly facilitated the latter task. After buying several tracts of farmland, Bond made it a practice to purchase a farm or at least additional acreage about every year or so until his holdings amounted to thousands of acres, including some of the choice farmland in St. Francis County. Throughout his early years he bought and sold property, including town lots in Madison, experimented with various crops, and managed to survive a succession of disastrous floods and price fluctuations in cotton and his other crops.

In 1877 an event occurred in Forrest City that was to figure significantly in Bond's climb to wealth and prominence: It was his marriage to Magnolia Nash, known as "Bunnie" or Maggie, a native of Virginia and a former house slave belonging to Leila Nash, a well-to-do spinster. Miss Nash, other white friends, and one "colored woman" of Forrest City provided Magnolia with her wedding attire and with the cake and "maple biscuits" served after the wedding ceremony. The bride not only had been exposed to some education but also had learned much by her long association with educated and "highly cultured" whites both in slavery and freedom. No less than her new husband, Magnolia Bond possessed much energy and "lots of will power." The two functioned effectively as a team in realizing their ambitions. Bond often gave credit to his wife for their success.

They started their married life as a desperately poor couple, so poor in fact that Magnolia "hardly had a change of clothes."[10] They lived in a primitive log cabin furnished with a few items that had been borrowed or given to them. Bond obtained a cow in exchange for his fancy wedding suit. In the early years of their marriage Magnolia Bond worked in the fields alongside her husband. Though sharecropping, the couple managed to save small amounts of money, in large part because they lived frugally and grew most of their food. Bond never went to town with an "empty wagon." He usually filled it with fresh vegetables and smoked meats that he sold, but when these items were not available he loaded the wagon with stove wood or with fresh fish that he had caught in the St. Francis River with his trotline. He kept the fish in a "live box" submerged in the river until he made his next trip into town. In these ways he earned enough cash "to pay for his needs between harvest times."

According to the federal census of 1880, the couple still resided in that portion of Cross County that had previously been a part of St. Francis County. Here their first two children were born, Waverly Thomas Bond, in about 1878 and Theophilus (Theo) Bond, in 1880.[11] In the early years of their marriage the Bonds moved around from one farm to another until they purchased and restored his "old home," presumably a reference to the "big house" on the Bond plantation that the Bonds named "Cedar Hill," often referred to as "The Cedars." In time they were able to afford more amenities and employ servants. Their commodious residence was located in a dry, healthy place on a knoll overlooking Madison with a view of the St. Francis River and the railroad. Here Magnolia Bond efficiently managed a household, which included their eleven children—all sons. Bond was devoted to his industrious wife, and both he and his wife took great pride in their sons.

At the time that the Bonds began housekeeping, African Americans in certain Delta counties including St. Francis still participated in Republican Party affairs, and some occupied government offices at both the local and state levels. A total of eighty-four African Americans, primarily from the Delta, served in the Arkansas General Assembly between 1868 and 1893. Numerous others were elected to local offices. Factionalism within the Republican Party, the intimidation of black and white Republicans by Democrats, and the enactment of a new election law, a poll-tax measure, and a segregation statute in 1891 combined to solidify the political dominance of white Democrats and resulted in a drastic decline in the participation of African Americans in Arkansas politics. The rising tide of radical racism that emerged in the state during the 1890s ultimately produced a succession of Jim Crow measures and extralegal stratagems at both the local and state levels designed to eliminate African Americans from the political arena and to confine them to an inferior place in society. The persistence of Jim Crowism with its practices of discrimination, segregation, lynching, and other acts of violence dealt a devastating blow to the newly freed slaves' hope of achieving the rights and privileges of first-class citizenship that for a brief time after the Civil War had seemed to be within their reach.[12]

Although Bond made no secret of being a Republican, there is no evidence that he played a conspicuous role in local party affairs. He focused his attention almost single-mindedly on acquiring land and wealth and on maintaining cordial relations with prominent whites, regardless of their party affiliations, who could aid him in achieving his economic objectives. Bond demonstrated great skill in navigating the treacherous terrain of race relations. Prominent whites including bankers, merchants, lawyers, businessmen, and railroad officials appreciated his integrity, work ethic, keen intelligence, and ability to back his word with ample collateral. Undoubtedly, they also were impressed by his knowledge of economic and financial matters and his modesty and deferential manner. Among those whom Bond considered his friends were Captain Jesse W. Wynne, a former officer in the Confederate army who served as the first president of the National Bank of Eastern Arkansas in Forrest City; Captain James Fussell, another Confederate veteran who succeeded Wynne as president of the bank; and other equally prominent business leaders in the local white community with whom he had frequent dealings. As a result his requests for loans, advice, and various kinds of assistance in expanding his agricultural and entrepreneurial enterprises were almost invariably granted.

Among Bond's closest white associates were the Rollwage brothers, Louis and Otto, the sons of German immigrants in Cincinnati, Ohio. Following the Civil War the Delta attracted a sizable number of migrants from the Midwest and other regions outside the South. The Rollwage brothers settled in Forrest City where they established a large mercantile firm in 1874 and figured prominently in the social and political life of the town for years thereafter.[13] Bond was especially close to Otto Rollwage, who was prominent in city government and served for a time as a progressive and popular mayor of Forrest City. He quit the mercantile business in 1902 and became a lawyer whom Bond frequently consulted. It was Otto who had assisted Bond in selecting his wedding suit in 1877 and who insisted that he wear his own white silk vest and gold watch and chain at the wedding. When Bond protested, saying that it would constitute too serious a breach of racial etiquette in the view of local whites, Rollwage responded: "I am willing to do anything I can for you."

Bond enjoyed an enviable reputation among blacks as well as whites. This reputation ultimately extended far beyond his local community to prominent blacks throughout the South and elsewhere, especially after he gained wider exposure as a conspicuous figure in the National Negro Business League in the early years of the twentieth century. Most blacks in St. Francis County and the surrounding area, consisting of hundreds of black sharecroppers, tenants, and day laborers, no doubt stood in awe of his achievements and his cordial relationship with powerful whites. His relationship with those blacks employed in his gins, brickyard, sawmills, and farming operations, including several hundred black sharecroppers on his farms at the peak of his career, appears to have been essentially paternalistic and similar in many respects to that of white employers and landlords.

Bond was a demanding but fair employer. He paid good wages and expected a full day's work for a day's pay. His advice to ambitious young African Americans was: "It is always best to hunt the job, not the salary. Master the job and the salary will surely come and nine times out of ten the amount will be larger than expected." He demanded that those working for him carefully follow his instructions and especially his example by working hard. He lectured to them about the virtues and rewards of tasks executed properly and on time. He did not tolerate malingering or shoddy work. Those who fell short of his expectations were promptly fired. As a "hands on" employer, Bond set the pace for his employees by often working alongside them and showing them how to perform tasks rather than telling them how. He apparently never demanded more of those who worked for him than he demanded of himself. In his timber-logging operations, for example, he often personally led his teams of hired hands into the swampy forests.

Bond was what today would be described as a workaholic. A restless, slender man whose weight varied between about 85 and 115 pounds, he appeared to possess boundless energy, great physical strength, and incredible stamina, despite bouts of severe headaches, probably migraines, and other health problems. By all accounts he was not only an engaging conversationalist who did not hesitate to express strong opinions on a wide variety of topics, but was also a superb raconteur always ready with a story to drive home his point. In addition to his definite ideas about what he considered the proper methods of farming and crop diversification, Bond also discoursed frequently and at length about the South as the region that offered African Americans the greatest opportunities for achieving economic success. He never denied that blacks in the South confronted a host of racial barriers or what he termed "bitters," but he insisted that such barriers existed elsewhere, especially in the urban North. "The sweet of the South is so much greater than the bitter for the colored man," he once remarked. "It convinced me that the South is really our home." As a result he consistently opposed the migration of blacks out of the region.

Bond conveyed the impression of being a genial, even-tempered individual possessing far more than ordinary intelligence despite his lack of formal education. Those who had dealings with him recognized that in matters that he considered important he exhibited an unmistakable tough-mindedness. While he generally maintained good relations with his renters, sharecroppers, and employees, he was capable of displaying a fiery temper toward those who repeatedly disregarded his instructions, and on occasion even physically threatened them. If they failed to correct their ways, he summarily fired them. His dealings with whites, especially prominent businessmen, were of a wholly different character. With such whites he proved to be a master of the art of indirection in which his tough-mindedness was masked by his skillful mixing of graciousness, deference, and flattery. In situations in which he disagreed with bankers or businessmen, Bond argued his position forcefully but always politely. In such exchanges he made effective use of his large repertoire of stories by choosing one with a moral that clearly supported his viewpoint. His technique usually worked, but if he felt strongly that he had been shortchanged or somehow wronged, he did not hesitate to resort to legal action.

Throughout his adult life, Bond was always on the lookout for new endeavors that would turn a profit. For example, when he read about the cultivation of artichokes in a farm journal and discovered that they would thrive in the Delta, he planted a small plot of

Jerusalem artichokes that flourished, but rather than harvest and sell them he allowed his hogs to feast on the succulent tubers. Learning that frog legs were considered delicacies elsewhere and well aware that frogs existed in abundance in the swampy areas that he owned, he built a frog pond and harvested frog legs to sell in nearby cities.

Bond was keenly aware of his limited formal education, which he claimed consisted of no more than a few weeks in a school for freedmen. His own lack of education no doubt helps explain the high priority he placed on educating his sons who survived to maturity—Waverly Thomas, Theophilus (known as Theo), and Ulysses. Waverly and Theo were graduates of Roger Williams University in Nashville, Tennessee, and Ulysses was a graduate of Atlanta Baptist College (later named Morehouse College) in Atlanta, Georgia. It is unclear whether his son John attended college. All four sons entered the family business, which Bond organized into a partnership known as Scott Bond and Sons, in which he remained the dominant figure. By 1904 three of his sons occupied managerial positions in the partnership with his eldest son, Waverly, as secretary, treasurer, and manager of the partnership; Theo as general manager of the farms and ginnery; and John as a manager of the mercantile establishment. The youngest surviving son, Ulysses (the tenth son born to Magnolia and Scott Bond), later joined the partnership after graduating from Atlanta Baptist College and completing a course of study at Oberlin Business College in Ohio. Ulysses became the treasurer of the partnership and the manager of its gravel operation.

It is interesting to note that Bond's sons enrolled in colleges that emphasized the liberal arts rather than institutions such as Booker T. Washington's Tuskegee Institute, which focused on industrial (vocational) training. Because his sons grew up working in the family's various enterprises, Bond may well have decided that they had been exposed to enough vocational training under his direction and needed what he termed a "literary education." Their choices of colleges may also have reflected their father's desire that his sons acquire the culture and refinement that he so much admired in certain of his upper-class white friends and acquaintances.

Despite his own lack of formal education, Bond did learn to read, write, and figure, and apparently was especially proficient in handling complicated figures without resorting to the use of pencil and paper. No less important were his persistent efforts at self-education. By his own admission he was a "close observer," especially of those who possessed skills that he lacked and needed. He quickly mastered such skills, as in the case of brickmaking. His venture into brickmaking was the result of his need to replace the crumbling mud-and-stick chimneys of the sharecroppers' cabins on the large farm he and a partner had purchased from the Allen family. He wanted to replace them with brick chimneys but ascertained that transporting the bricks from the brickyard in Forrest City would make the cost prohibitive. To solve this problem he worked free of charge for a well-known brickmaker in Forrest City to learn as much as possible about all aspects of the brickmaking craft, then established his own brickyard that turned out products that rivaled the high quality of those produced by his mentor. Never lacking self-confidence, he once remarked that he could "do anything any other man could do." Because of the quality of his bricks, a white congregation in Forrest City used them in constructing the façade of its new church.

Bond kept himself well informed about recent developments relevant to his varied business interests. For example, through reading farm journals he kept abreast of changes taking place in agriculture. He became an early and enthusiastic advocate of crop diversification and different methods of cultivation, which he put into practice on his own lands. In referring to his use of modern methods and equipment, he observed about three decades after he started farming that he could make more money with less expense on fifty acres than he "used to make on five hundred acres."

While cotton always remained his main crop, Bond also produced large amounts of corn, potatoes, cane (for molasses), apples, peaches, and hay, as well as peas, clover, and other crops that replenished nutrients in the soil. He took especial pride in his orchard that was said to be one of the largest in eastern Arkansas. It covered many acres and included three thousand peach trees and two thousand apple trees of excellent and marketable varieties, as well as an assortment of other fruit trees. Once when asked what he produced on his farms, he answered: "I grow everything imaginable." He also used defective cottonseeds as fertilizer. His secondary crops augmented his income and enabled him to make payments on existing mortgages, purchase additional farms, and replace worn-out mules. He not only practiced crop rotation, but also carefully chose crops that were harvested at different seasons, especially times that did not coincide with the harvesting and ginning of cotton. Planting crops that were harvested at different times allowed Bond to have income throughout the year. He did not shy away from experimentation, as was evident in the case of artichokes, but if an experimental crop proved not to be profitable, he abandoned it for something else. In addition to his various crops, Bond was widely known as a "stock-raiser" who in time came to own numerous milk cows, cattle, mules, sheep, hogs, and chickens. Bond fed his large family on foodstuffs that he raised on his farms, and his smokehouse was sufficiently stocked with meats to "furnish" his sharecroppers and tenants from it prior to establishing his store in Madison.

In addition to crop diversification and rotation, Bond manifested great interest in various methods of cultivation. He became enthusiastic about "deep plowing," and given the acres that he wished to clear of swamps, thickets, and trees in order to put the land into crop production, it is not surprising that he focused much attention on how to expedite the cultivation of such "new ground," which was "the nightmare of farming life" in the Arkansas Delta. He developed and patented about 1910 a plow that reduced "the terrors of new ground cultivation." Known as the Bond New Ground Plow, it was longer and heavier than the traditional plow, which with a coulter fastener (sharp disk) attached to its beam made a vertical cut in the surface and permitted clean separation and effective covering of the soil and materials being turned under. Manufactured by Bond and Sons in Madison, the plow became a popular farm implement in Arkansas, Mississippi, and other states. Guaranteed to "do satisfactory work," the Bond Plow, according to one source, enjoyed phenomenal success.[14]

Bond continually sought to achieve and maintain high quality, greater efficiency and economy, and increased profits in all of his business and agricultural enterprises. The central office of Scott Bond and Sons, located in Madison, employed the latest bookkeeping and accounting practices and early possessed typewriters and other modern office equipment, electric lighting, and telephones. Telephones in particular expedited contact with wholesalers, bankers, cotton brokers, and others in Forrest City, Memphis, Little Rock, St. Louis, and other cities.

Also located in Madison was the Madison Mercantile Company that Bond purchased and transformed into a much larger concern. Housed in what became known as the Bond Mercantile Building, an imposing three-story concrete structure, the establishment attracted a large clientele of blacks and whites, including those whom Bond referred to as "the best people." Locally he was considered "a live wire" in the mercantile business. The Madison store was reputedly the largest mercantile establishment between Little Rock and Memphis. It employed from five to eight salespersons and possessed an inventory that included "nearly every commodity that the taste or the necessities of the people can desire" from wagons, buggies, farm implements, hardware, and furniture to dry goods, groceries, and notions. From this store Bond furnished supplies (on credit until harvest time) needed by the several hundred tenants who worked his farms. An African American observer in 1911 described the store as a "mercantile emporium" that catered both to "the man in grimy overalls" and "the man with kid gloves and patent leather pumps." The observer was especially impressed by the store's stock of high-quality shoes, including Frederick Douglass Shoes "manufactured by a colored shoe factory in Massachusetts." Bond clearly had benefited by an earlier unhappy experience as a partner in an undercapitalized mercantile establishment in Forrest City that proved to be of very short duration.[15]

No less impressive than Bond's large store was his Madison Gin Company, located near the town on the St. Francis River and easily accessible by wagons and boats. Convinced that too much time and money were spent transporting cotton to gins at distant places, Bond decided that the construction of a thoroughly modern gin at Madison, though initially expensive, would be a profitable investment. Despite the threatening objections raised by a white merchant and ginner to his plans to build a gin, Bond proceeded with the construction of the gin. After careful research, he contracted with the highly reputable Continental Gin Company of Birmingham, Alabama, to provide the equipment for his steam gin. Even in the short crop season of 1909–1910 the new Madison Gin Company ginned 2,485 bales of cotton. Encouraged by the success of his gin in Madison, Bond established a second gin there and either owned or operated others in the all-black village of Edmondson and in the towns of Widener and Cotton Plant. By the calculations of some contemporaries he was the largest cotton ginner in east Arkansas.

Early in his ginning career Bond manifested a special interest in cottonseeds that had long been considered a nuisance by ginners. He knew that the oil of cottonseeds had value and that he could make money by selling the tons of seeds produced by his gins to various cotton oil companies. He not only contracted to sell the seeds from his own gins to the Richmond Cotton Oil Company, but also set about buying up cottonseeds in the Delta until he became the largest cottonseed handler in a wide area. He became known as the region's primary "cotton seed booster." When Bond insisted that the oil companies pay higher prices for cottonseeds, the companies balked and, led by the Richmond Cotton Oil Company, boycotted Bond's seed business. Bond countered by selling his seed through a white commission agent in Memphis, which made it difficult if not impossible for the oil companies to identify him as the owner of the cottonseed. This strategy thwarted the oil companies' boycotting effort, and Bond ultimately received the "fancy price" he demanded. Recognizing that he had been outmaneuvered by Bond, an official of the Richmond Cotton Oil Company admitted: "Why, that nigger put me in the same ditch I dug for him."

Another facet of Bond's agricultural and business empire was his timber and lumber operation. Much of the land that he had purchased over the years contained hundreds of acres of virgin forests, many of which were located in swamps that he intended to drain and use the rich alluvial soil for growing various crops. But first Bond had to get the timber cut and then the more complicated problem was getting the logs to a sawmill by water, which required knowledge of currents and the location of what were called "float roads" in order to get them out of the swamps. Once the logs reached the St. Francis River, they were rafted to Madison where Bond constructed a sawmill that was operated in conjunction with his gin there. The sawmill produced thousands of feet of top-quality hardwood lumber that was in great demand and regularly shipped by rail to Chicago, Pittsburgh, and other distant cities.

His building of the sawmill sparked a controversy, led by disgruntled whites who injected the race issue by insisting that "this was a white man's country and white men were going to rule it." According to Bond, these white men were "carpet baggers from the north" who did "not represent the sentiments of aristocratic southern born democrats." It was this group, he contended, that secured an injunction against his building the sawmill. A court battle ensued, but the case against Bond was ultimately thrown out on a legal technicality, clearing the way for him to proceed with the construction and operation of his sawmill.

Because neither Bond nor his sons had any experience in sawmilling, he employed two African Americans from Mississippi who were veteran sawmill operators to oversee his newest enterprise. One of these men, Daniel A. Rudd, had a remarkable past.[16] He had been a widely respected journalist who was recognized as the preeminent black Catholic layman in the United States. He had edited several newspapers in Ohio and Michigan, including the *American Catholic Tribune* that focused on black Catholics, and he had organized five national black Catholic congresses between 1889 and 1894. For reasons that remain unclear Rudd abandoned journalism and had moved to Mississippi by 1910. Bond recognized that Rudd was not only a man of integrity, but also one who possessed many talents that would be useful to Scott Bond and Sons. Rudd remained a part of Bond's inner circle for years in the capacity of "supervising engineer." He was the coauthor, with Theo Bond, of the biography of the latter's father that was published in 1917 and reprinted here.

Not only did Rudd play an important role in assisting Bond in the establishment of his sawmill and lumber operation, he also figured significantly in the development of the gravel enterprise that Bond launched about 1913, which became one of the most reliably profitable components of his complex of businesses. Running through one of Bond's farms was Crow Creek, a stream that possessed what was described as "inexhaustible deposits" of gravel "unsurpassed for concrete purposes" and useful in railroad construction and maintenance as ballast to stabilize rails. The gravel project, however, posed serious problems for Bond. One was getting the gravel out of the creek and loaded on rail cars for shipment, a process that was difficult, labor intensive, and expensive. It was Rudd who devised a method for extracting and loading the gravel that made it a less difficult and less expensive task. He drew up blueprints for a system of cables and blocks, which Bond forwarded to a well-known cable company. Using Rudd's blueprints the company installed the needed equipment that made his gravel operation less labor intensive and far more efficient and profitable.

Another problem Bond faced was the refusal of the Rock Island Railroad Company that purchased his gravel to pay a price per carload that he considered reasonable. Throughout the protracted negotiations with the railroad, Bond held firm in demanding a certain price. Ultimately the Rock Island agreed to pay what he considered an acceptable price, but when he received the initial checks from the company, they were for amounts less than those agreed upon. The discrepancies were in time corrected, but only after Bond vigorously protested. In the process of their dealings with him over the gravel and other matters railroad officials came to appreciate him as an important shipper on their line and as a tough negotiator who would not tolerate cavalier breaches in the written contracts that he insisted on having with the railroad and all companies and individuals with whom he did business. The Rock Island officials no doubt were well aware that Bond retained excellent white lawyers and did not hesitate to go to court to rectify breaches in contracts and other wrongs. After the satisfactory settlement of the dispute over gravel, Bond and the Rock Island seem to have maintained cordial relations, and the gravel pits remained one of his most valuable assets.

By the first decade of the twentieth century the story of Bond's success was attracting considerable publicity. In 1905 the leading white newspaper in Forrest City included a sketch of Bond's career that characterized him as a "skillful and energetic farmer" who owned twenty-one hundred acres of prime farmland in the St. Francis Basin, a large, well-stocked mercantile establishment in Madison, a first-class cotton gin, and an extensive timber operation.[17] Six years later a lengthy sketch of his life appeared in a collection of essays on thirty-six prominent African Americans in the South, entitled *Beacon Lights of the Race* by Green P. Hamilton, a well-known black educator who was principal of Kortrecht High School in Memphis. Hamilton described Bond as "one of the most astonishing examples of success" in the history of the nation, a former slave who had "risen to sublimer heights in the world of success than millions of the dominant race who were blessed with a thousand years of freedom and opportunity to make the most of life." Bond's speech in 1910 to the annual meeting of the National Negro Business League in New York prompted extensive coverage in the nation's press that devoted attention to his career as a successful farmer and businessman. One journalist described him as "the black John D. Rockefeller of the South."[18]

Ironically, such publicity and accolades appeared on the eve of a period in which Bond confronted challenges that threatened his economic ruin. While he had suffered difficult years before, the challenges became especially acute in the period between 1911 and 1914, when the St. Francis River Basin experienced a combination of disasters. Among the most notable were a series of floods that inundated much of Bond's farmlands, destroying his crops and drowning his livestock. In the periods between the floods, cotton prices plummeted and an infestation of cutworms and blight destroyed his cotton crops. At one point when confronted with the responsibility of providing food for about eight hundred sharecroppers and his numerous livestock, Bond feared that he might lose everything. His problem was complicated by the fact that so many of his assets were in land and enterprises significantly affected by an economic slump in the agricultural economy. During the hard times he managed to stay afloat largely because of the income from his lumber operations and gravel pits and his ability to secure heavily collateralized loans from banks, insurance companies, and individuals. That he successfully weathered the crisis owed much to his past emphasis on diversifying his economic endeavors and to his extraordinary determination to persevere. Whatever his worries may have been, he "put up a good front" and as always maintained an optimistic outlook about the future. His survival of the economic crisis added luster to his reputation for perseverance and resilience.

In many respects Bond's background was similar to that of Booker T. Washington, the principal of Tuskegee Institute in Alabama. Certainly his career exemplified Washington's philosophy. Washington was the preeminent African American for almost two decades following the address he made in Atlanta during the Cotton

States and International Exposition in 1895. Delivered amid the rising tide of racist demagoguery in the South before a predominantly white audience and known as the Atlanta Compromise, his address was one of the most important and influential speeches in American history. It set forth a formula of race relations in which blacks would be guaranteed equal justice and equal opportunity and in return they were to acquiesce in segregation, eschew politics and any "agitation of questions of social equality," cultivate "friendly relations with the Southern white man," and focus on economic advancement that would ultimately bring the privileges of citizenship currently denied them. In the course of his speech Washington declared: "In all things that are purely social we [blacks and whites] can be as separate as the fingers, yet one as the hand in all things essential to mutual progress." He also urged blacks to forego migration and to cast down their buckets in "our beloved South" where "the Negro is given a man's chance in the commercial world." While he boasted of the progress of his race in diverse fields, he reminded blacks that in making the "great leap from slavery to freedom" they must disabuse themselves of any notions of beginning their new life of freedom at the top rather than the bottom and must recognize that the black masses would continue in the foreseeable future to live primarily "by the productions of our hands."[19]

The careers of few African Americans equaled that of Scott Bond in embodying the ideas articulated by Washington in his Atlanta address. What is no less obvious is that Bond had been practicing Washington's philosophy for many years prior to 1895. His later visits to the Tuskegee campus reinforced his admiration of Washington and his work, and like many other African Americans Bond came to view the so-called Wizard of Tuskegee as the "Moses of the race." Washington reciprocated the admiration and considered Bond's achievements as validation of the basic principles of his philosophy.

The association of the two men increased over time, especially after 1900 when Washington organized the National Negro Business League (NNBL) that promoted and showcased black economic progress. His organization also served as an important component of what was called the Tuskegee Machine, a nationwide network of Washington's lieutenants and allies that enabled the Wizard of Tuskegee to perpetuate his influence and reputation.[20] As a life member of the organization Bond manifested great interest in its yearly meetings and figured significantly in efforts that ultimately brought the annual meeting to Little Rock in 1911.

Two years earlier Bond had addressed the annual gathering of the NNBL in Louisville, Kentucky, on the subject of "Succeeding as a Farmer." Washington invited him to take part in the program of the 1910 meeting of the NNBL in New York City because he thought the Arkansan had been "the very spice" of all previous meetings he had attended. Bond declined the invitation ostensibly because of his lack of education. Such an excuse hardly seems plausible as he had spoken to large audiences earlier. Bond may have been intimidated by the site of the 1910 meeting, New York City, and knew it would attract many northern African Americans including those who would object to both the delivery and the contents of what he would say. Perhaps another possible reason for declining to deliver a formal address at the New York meeting was that he felt his time could be more profitably used in assisting John E. Bush and other African American leaders from Arkansas in persuading the organization to select Little Rock as the site of its next annual meeting. As it turned out, however, Bond did give a speech in New York. In the process of the 1910 meeting Washington disregarded the printed schedule of events when he recognized Bond in the rear of the convention hall and summoned him to the podium to "tell the audience about Arkansas."

In what one observer described as his "unique and purely Southern method of expression," Bond delivered an extemporaneous speech that pursued some of his favorite themes. One theme was that African Americans had "no more business than a rabbit" living in New York or any other large northern city, where whites made it abundantly clear that they neither wanted nor needed them. Bond declared that with very few exceptions northern blacks, no matter how well educated, could find employment only as janitors, coachmen, and other dead-end jobs, while in the South their opportunities for jobs and economic advancement were virtually unlimited, especially those related to farming. As usual, Bond downplayed the significance of the restrictions imposed by whites on African Americans in the South, noting merely that "a few white people (in the South) from time to time cause trouble and friction." Even so, he insisted, many "broad-hearted" whites in the region understood that it was impossible to keep a man in a ditch without staying in the ditch with him, meaning that such whites recognized that any effort to retard the progress of blacks also retarded the progress of all southerners, white as well as black. To demonstrate that the South was the place for African Americans, Bond called attention to those blacks in the region who occupied prominent positions in government, professions, businesses, and agriculture. Describing himself as "an old one-gallused farmer who never went to school but two weeks in his life," he supported his claims about the South by outlining his own success in acquiring wealth, status, and an enviable reputation in Arkansas. As Bond no doubt expected, a few northern African Americans did voice strong objections to both the contents and tone of his speech, but it was enthusiastically received by a vast majority of both blacks and whites in the audience. His speech was frequently interrupted by vigorous applause, received glowing compliments in the northern white press, and prompted Washington to promise Bond that the next meeting of the NNBL would be held in Arkansas.

The annual meeting of the National Negro Business League took place in Little Rock, as Washington promised, on August 16–19, 1911. The meeting, hosted by the Arkansas chapter of the League headed by John E. Bush, a prominent black businessman and Republican officeholder, received the full support and cooperation of Little Rock's city officials. At the end of the meeting the League arranged for a special train to take the delegates on an excursion to Hot Springs.[21]

Long desirous of having Booker T. Washington visit Madison and St. Francis County, Bond set about to arrange such a visit. Unwilling to allow Washington to ride in a Jim Crow railroad car, he contacted his acquaintances in the Little Rock office of the Rock Island Railroad who readily agreed to have a special car attached to the end of an east-bound "fast train" to accommodate Washington and his party. The train was to make an unscheduled stop in Forrest City, where the special car was to be sidetracked and later attached to another "fast train" that would speed Washington and his party to Memphis in time to make connections to Chicago. Although Washington insisted that he would not object to traveling in a Jim

Crow car, he was both pleased with Bond's arrangement and profoundly impressed that the railroad company complied with his request for a special car. In his opinion few whites anywhere in the South had such influence.

A throng of people lined both sides of the road as Bond, Washington, and several officers of the NNBL traveled in a chauffeur-driven automobile from Forrest City to Madison. There Bond provided a lavish barbeque for the occasion to which all spectators and visitors were invited. It seems likely that Bond gave his employees time off to have the opportunity to see and hear Washington and to participate in the festivities. While in Madison, Washington made a speech, then toured the town, including the offices of Scott Bond and Sons, various Bond enterprises, and some of Bond's nearby farms. Washington also visited "The Cedars," where he was photographed with Scott and Magnolia Bond and their family. After a day-long visit Washington and his party returned to their special railroad car in Forrest City that was attached to a train that sped them to Memphis, as planned. If Bond had been impressed with Washington's Tuskegee Institute, Washington was no doubt equally impressed with Bond's business enterprises and home. The day after leaving Madison, Washington wrote a friend: "We spent yesterday, Sunday, at the home of Scott Bond where I spoke to an audience of seven thousand white and black people. Old man Bond stands for much more than I realized. He is in many ways a great man."[22] In 1913 Washington returned to Arkansas for his last visit, but there is no evidence that he again visited St. Francis County. Following Washington's death two years later, Bond was among those African Americans who continued to broadcast and practice Washington's philosophy.

Throughout his life Bond expressed strong opinions about race and class. He was fully aware that his fair complexion clearly revealed his white ancestry, but he knew, too, that despite his light complexion, he was considered black according to the prevailing "one drop rule" in the South.[23] This rule held that no matter how fair a person's complexion if he or she possessed even a minuscule amount of "Negro blood," he or she was classified as black and therefore subject to all the proscriptions, legal and otherwise, endured by African Americans. Since Bond was often mistaken for a white man, he on occasion had arguments with railroad conductors who, convinced that he was white, tried to force him out of Jim Crow cars into those reserved for "whites only." On one occasion when a conductor tried to force him to leave a Jim Crow car and move to a white only car, Bond vented his frustration. "What in the name of the Lord shall I do?" he asked the conductor. "The law says I shall not ride in the other car (for whites) and you say I shall not ride in the car with the niggers. What shall I do?"

After Bond learned that his father was a white man, he undertook a search in the hope of finding him. Aware that many prosperous whites had been impoverished by the Civil War, he intended to help his natural father if he "was in need." In his search he visited the plantation in Mississippi where he had been born while his mother was a hired slave employed there. Assuming that he was a young white man from Arkansas, William H. Goodloe, the plantation owner, and his wife greeted him cordially and entertained him in their well-appointed parlor. Goodloe's wife well remembered Scott Bond's mother, a favorite house slave, who had a baby while residing with the Goodloes. The baby had been given the name Scott Winfield. Bond learned that his white father had later married and moved to Texas where he had died. When he discovered that his father had white children living in nearby Canton, Mississippi, he visited them on some pretext but never identified himself in any way other than as "Bond of Arkansas." He allowed them to assume that he was white and never mentioned to them that he was their half-brother. In reflecting on his own racial background Bond noted that the fact that mixed-bloods vastly outnumbered the relatively few "full-blooded Negroes" in the colored population of the country, which he interpreted to mean that race-mixing had been going on a very long time especially in the South. In a reference to whites' claims about the immorality of African Americans, he observed that the sheer number of mixed bloods offered ample evidence that whites by no means had a monopoly on "moral rectitude."

While Bond objected to being referred to as "colored" and insisted on being identified as a Negro, he did on rare instances pass for white or at least did not correct those who mistook him for a white person. In the United States and especially the South during the late nineteenth and early twentieth centuries, whites expressed great concern about "racial purity," and there was much discussion of fair-complexioned blacks passing as whites.[24] There were several varieties of passing designed to allow fair-complexioned African Americans to escape the restrictions placed on all blacks. One form of passing involved those blacks who cut all ties with the black community and disappeared permanently into the white world, and another was convenience or occasional passing such as that involved in gaining admission to decent restaurants, hotels, and theaters that excluded black patrons. One of those most notable incidents of Bond passing as white was his attempt to secure medical treatment.

Bond suffered from malaria, severe headaches, and a variety of other maladies. By his own admission he was "never a healthy person." At one point he became so ill and emaciated that he had to be transported about on a mattress in a wagon in order to look after his various enterprises. None of the prescribed remedies brought improvement, and he continued to lose weight until he weighed only eighty-five pounds and was largely bedridden. Finally, a physician in Forrest City recommended that he go to Ravenden Springs, Arkansas, near the Missouri border where the spring water was reputed to have miraculous healing powers. William Bailey, a Methodist minister who had suffered many years from a stomach ailment, discovered the spring deep in a canyon on Hall's Creek in Randolph County. A dream supposedly led him to the site of the spring. Drinking large quantities of the spring water restored Bailey's health. News of his miraculous recovery quickly circulated. One of those fascinated by the news was R. D. Welsh, a conductor on the nearby Iron Mountain Railroad's route between Little Rock and St. Louis. Welsh resigned his job with the railroad, organized a stock company in St. Louis, and laid out a town near the spring that he called Ravenden Springs. One of the town's earliest buildings was a forty-room hotel named the Southern Hotel that provided lodging for visitors who flocked to the area to partake of the healing water of the spring discovered by Reverend Bailey.[25]

Accompanied by his brother-in-law Patrick Banks, who also possessed a very light complexion, Bond traveled by train and stagecoach to the village of Ravenden Springs (around 1890) and checked into the Southern Hotel. Located in the hill country,

Ravenden Springs was an all-white village. Because Bond and his brother-in-law were assumed to be well-to-do whites from the malaria-infested St. Francis River Basin, they were graciously received by the hotel's all-white management and staff. Other guests welcomed them to the hotel's dining room. Bond allowed the guests and staff to assume that he was white. He told his brother-in-law: "They (whites) have made a mistake (in thinking the two of them were white men). We did not intend it. We will put the best foot forward and do the best we know how. We will not put ourselves on them and will not entertain them any more than we have to." Bond credited their success in passing for white not merely to their color, but also to the fact that both he and his brother-in-law as young slaves had spent much time in the presence of upper-class whites, he as a houseboy and his brother-in-law as a coachman, and as a result knew the behavior and manners associated with such whites.

The physician who treated Bond during his stay in Ravenden Springs ordered him to drink generous amounts of the famous local water and prescribed "good whiskey" to be used in making a weak toddy that he was to drink each morning before breakfast. Bond rejected the latter because he was a teetotaler. As an alternative his doctor recommended that the whiskey be used to bathe his swollen feet every morning. Bond ordered a gallon of "good whiskey" from Memphis for that purpose. Bond's brother-in-law had a toddy each morning and the doctor himself had a drink or two of the premium whiskey on each of his frequent visits to Bond's hotel room.

Carefully following the doctor's orders, Bond rapidly improved; he regained his energy and strength, added weight, and was soon walking about the village. It is uncertain whether the mineral water from the spring or the enforced rest was responsible for his recovery. As he was recovering Bond spent time inspecting the few businesses located in the village, and as always he was on the lookout for opportunities to make money. When he noted that the grocery stores displayed excellent locally produced eggs and sold them cheaply, he contracted to have nine barrels and twenty-four cases of eggs shipped express to Madison where he sold them for enough profit to more than cover the cost of his hotel bill in Ravenden Springs.

Despite his white appearance and occasional passing for white, Bond expressed pride in being "a Negro." He enjoyed a reputation as a strong "race man," a term that African Americans commonly applied to one of their own who defended black people and promoted their welfare. As a dedicated prohibitionist Bond urged African Americans to avoid the evils of liquor and "engaged actively in eradicating whiskey" from St. Francis County.[26] All the while, he continually delivered homilies counseling them to take advantage of their "latent power" to rise in the world and "be somebody." He assured them they could best do so by pursuing his formula of hard work, sobriety, perseverance, virtuous living, and self-improvement, attributes that had enabled him to achieve success. Such success, he insisted, was the best means of combating the racial prejudice that was taking a heavy toll on the economy and efficiency of both the region and the nation. He often described himself as a former slave, uneducated and without any worldly goods or influential connections, who through diligence and perseverance in applying his brain as well as his brawn had achieved both status and wealth. He rarely missed an opportunity to emphasize the importance of a formal education, which he lacked, and to assure young African Americans that the business and commercial world tended to be colorblind. What counted in that world, he argued, was not the color of one's skin but rather a person's possession of a clean character, "a good bank account," and sizable real estate holdings. In brief, his view was that the path to both personal success and racial progress was for individual blacks to acquire reputations for integrity, hard work, and honesty backed by ample economic collateral. African Americans in the vicinity of Forrest City and Madison who regularly sought Bond's counsel on a wide variety of issues were likely to receive this message or a variation of it.

Given Bond's strong conviction that the South, more than any other region in the United States, offered African Americans opportunities to realize their potential, it is not surprising that he opposed various efforts in the late nineteenth century that advocated the migration of southern blacks to other parts of the United States in order to escape the escalating racial oppression in the South. He was even more resolute in opposing the Back-to-Africa movement that waxed and waned throughout the last quarter of the nineteenth century and that culminated in focusing on migration to Liberia. Poor black sharecroppers in Arkansas and elsewhere in the South, mired in debt and ignorance and subjected to discrimination and violence, undoubtedly found it difficult to accept Bond's rosy view of the region as a "paradise" for African Americans.

Many blacks, especially those in St. Francis County, including Forrest City and Madison, viewed the "promised land" as a place outside the United States. Bond considered the Arkansas Delta, with all of its natural resources and opportunities for economic advancement, as the black man's "promised land." In his view local blacks had been misled by the migration advocates and had become "Africa struck." Hundreds in the county rallied to the banner of those advocating Liberia as offering the best prospect for a brighter future. The African republic was described as a place that promised emigrants free land and an escape from white racism. In addition, it was said to be rich in valuable natural resources, including gold and diamonds. Lured by such propaganda, many blacks in St. Francis County prepared to return to their African "homeland," especially during the first half of the 1890s when Arkansas witnessed a dramatic increase in lynching and the proliferation of laws regarding segregation and other measures that further diminished the rights of black citizens.[27]

Like the vast majority of well-known black leaders, Bond viewed the idea of blacks migrating to Liberia as sheer nonsense. He believed that poor African Americans were being deceived into believing that instant riches awaited them in Liberia and that good food in the country was everywhere bountiful. Bond witnessed the activities of Dr. Anthony L. Stanford, who toured St. Francis County recruiting members for his emigration clubs. Stanford was a flamboyant minister in the African Methodist Episcopal Church, a politician who had been elected to the Arkansas legislature from Phillips County, and a physician with credentials from a dubious medical school in Philadelphia. Although Bond considered Stanford a windbag who "could talk the horns off a frozen cow," the latter's recruitment efforts in Madison, Forrest City, and other places in St. Francis County were nonetheless successful. For example, the *Forrest City Times* reported early in 1896 that a large group of St. Francis blacks gathered at the Iron Mountain Railroad Depot in Forrest City to board a train that was to take them to Savannah, Georgia, on the first leg of their journey to what the newspaper termed their "dreamland" in Liberia.[28] Some who left the county for Liberia such as Bond's friend, Harry Foster, did prosper in Africa. Others were stranded in American port cities and never reached their destination; still others who actually settled in Liberia confronted an environment that bore little resemblance to what they had been led to expect. The number of African American settlers in Liberia who died from malaria, fevers, and other illnesses shortly after their arrival was appalling.

It is, of course, difficult if not impossible to ascertain with precision all of the considerations that figured in Bond's vocal opposition to the migration of blacks from the South. It is worth noting, however, that his success owed much to the availability of an adequate labor supply made up of landless, poor blacks who worked on his farms and in his cotton gins, gravel pits, and timber and sawmilling operations. The issue of Liberian migration, as Bond no doubt realized, had serious implications for his own welfare. In this respect he resembled prominent white planters and businessmen in St. Francis County who forthrightly opposed the migration of local blacks to Liberia because of their fear that it would deplete their own labor supply.

Regardless of the motives that prompted Bond to oppose any exodus of blacks to Liberia, mounting evidence tended to confirm his stand on the issue. Such confirmation was provided by the testimony of at least two individuals from St. Francis County who settled in Liberia. One was Gilbert Dean, who had settled in Brewerville, Liberia. Dean wrote home about conditions he had encountered there. In a letter published in a Forrest City newspaper, he wrote that while the soil in Liberia was good, the country's government was "bad." He warned other African Americans to "stay away." Messages from Liberia sent by Taylor Swift and his wife were no doubt more important in convincing Bond that his strong opposition to Liberian emigration had been altogether justified. Swift had been a tenant on one of his farms, and Bond obviously thought highly of him. If Bond knew of Swift's intention to migrate—and he may not have because much of the migration activity was secret—he probably urged him as he did others not to be swayed by the propaganda being broadcast about Liberia. At any rate, Swift sold his livestock and other belongings and traveled with his family to Liberia in 1895. Thoroughly disillusioned, he was back in St. Francis County the following year, renting fifteen acres from Bond, who gave him a mule and aided him in getting started over. Swift became a highly vocal critic of Liberia as a poor, backward place unfit for civilized people. He provided a vivid description of the destitute condition of African American settlers there, and claimed that the country was anything but free because it was virtually owned and controlled by the British. All the while, Bond remained adamant in his view that the South, even with all of its problems, was the best place for African Americans.[29] He no doubt looked upon the version of the Back-to-Africa movement championed by Marcus Garvey in the 1920s with the same hostility he had earlier manifested toward Liberian emigration.

Bond's efforts on behalf of blacks included deeds as well as words. He was inclined to lend assistance to those who were attempting to help themselves and those who were victims of racial prejudice and natural disasters such as floods. One African American contemporary wrote: "As a friend of the race, he (Bond) is constantly lending a helping hand to the worthy and deserving."[30] For example, when whites gained control of the cemetery in Madison where both blacks and whites had been buried "promiscuously" for a half century, they excluded blacks. Bond responded by giving land for a black cemetery. He aided blacks in nearby communities in their efforts to establish their own cotton gins and at great personal risk assisted those whom he believed had been mistreated by a racially prejudiced legal system. By posting bond for a black man accused of killing a white man, he aroused the ire of the white community and strained his relations for a time even with some whites whom he considered his friends. The incident revealed the limits of white tolerance of any actions by African Americans, regardless of their good character and wealth, which they perceived as challenges to the racial status quo. Bond rarely found himself in such a predicament because of his knowledge of and adherence to the fine points of prevailing racial etiquette.

Despite his own encounters with racial prejudice and frequent exposure to the use of racial slurs by whites, Bond persisted in being an enthusiastic booster of the South and often made extravagant claims about the opportunities available to blacks in the region. Such claims were all the more remarkable in view of the steady proliferation of laws and practices in the South that thwarted the aspirations and ambitions of African Americans. In 1896, the year after Washington made his famous Atlanta Compromise speech, the Supreme Court of the United States issued its decision in the *Plessy v. Ferguson* case, which put the court's stamp of approval on racial segregation by laying down the so-called "separate but equal" doctrine. This decision, as well as others that followed, permitted separate facilities for the two races so long as these facilities (the *Plessy* case involved railroad accommodations) were equal. The doctrine as actually applied in the South came to mean separate and "unequal." Nowhere was this more evident than in educational opportunities for the two races; they were indeed separate but black schools were grossly inferior in every way to those of whites.[31] Many white southerners continued to subscribe to the notion that to educate a black person was to ruin a field hand. In the era of Jim Crow when the practice of separate and unequal prevailed, African Americans were disfranchised, stripped of many, if not most, of their civil rights, burdened with debt, and regularly threatened with violence, often in the form of lynching.

Bond shied away from direct and vocal opposition to the steady advance of Jim Crowism. His apparent acquiescence in the prevailing "separate and unequal" practices relating to race in the South may have resulted in part from his conviction that protesting was futile and would only jeopardize his cordial relationship with whites of the "better class" and in part from his rationalization that such legalized segregation actually benefited blacks by uniting them and forcing them to become self-reliant. At any rate, Bond seems to have concluded that the best policy for African Americans at the time was to avoid politics and agitation, take advantage of whatever opportunities they possessed, and go along in order to get along economically. He may also have convinced himself that if he had been able to overcome many of the hurdles imposed by racial prejudice to achieve status and wealth so could other African Americans who possessed a strong work ethic and a "clean character."

Bond also possessed strong convictions about the role of class in both the black and white communities. He looked with disdain on "low class, degraded" people of both races, and believed that they were the sources of much of the racial prejudice so abundantly evident in the South and elsewhere. In his view "low class" people lacked initiative and possessed scant education and little ambition for themselves and their children. Bond was convinced that the most reliable white supporters of black progress were those "broad minded" individuals whom he repeatedly referred to as the "aristocratic, refined, and cultured" element of society, composed primarily of native southerners. He often noted that as a youth he had been closely associated with such whites, especially the white Mebanes, Bonds, and Goodloes, and therefore had had ample opportunity to observe the attitudes, manners, and values of upper-class whites. Even though Bond over the years established relationships with a variety of respectable, educated whites from various parts of the country who could help him realize his ambitions, he identified most closely with those white southerners whom he considered cultured and aristocratic; he found them more trustworthy than uncouth, lower-class white southerners and many of the "smooth, slick Yankees" who had settled in the South after the Civil War. His frequent references to "aristocratic, refined and cultured" white southerners suggest that Bond may well have internalized at least some of the traits he attributed to such whites.

Upper-class white southerners may well have been responsible for introducing the term "Uncle Scott" in referring to Bond. In the South whites and many blacks often addressed elderly black people as "aunt" and "uncle" to indicate their respect for them. Since prevailing racial etiquette prohibited whites from addressing blacks of any age as Mr., Mrs., or Miss, whites in St. Francis County apparently chose to indicate their respect for Bond by referring to him as "Uncle Scott" long before his age warranted references to him as "uncle." Bond did not object to being addressed in such a manner; in fact, he encouraged it. He obviously preferred "Uncle Scott" to the denigrating terms applied to blacks by many whites. On first meeting Bond, the superintendent of the Rock Island Railroad, a northerner, referred to him as "Mr. Bond." "This is not Mr. Bond," Bond replied. "This is Uncle Scott Bond. I have my doubts as to whether you mean the word Mr. or not, and if you do, you can not afford it here in the South, so will you please call me Uncle Scott." Clearly, Bond's advice on the manner in which he should be addressed was aimed no doubt at protecting himself as well as the white railroad official.

Within the local black community Bond and his wife appear to have pursued a limited social life but they did socialize with their family members and with African Americans of the "better class" in the area. As for Bond himself, he apparently had little time for an active social life. The Bonds belonged to the local black Baptist church, and Bond assured strangers that the black church in general was making great progress as evidenced by its riddance of ignorant preachers and by developing "a higher, holier, and more spiritual conception and practice of Christianity." Magnolia Bond may have been more active in church affairs than her husband, but the church does not appear to have been the center of their lives. Theirs was a home- and family-centered social life. They did entertain distinguished African Americans who on rare occasions visited St. Francis County, where the Bonds occupied a distinctive and largely separate place in the social hierarchy of the local black community.

In his travels outside the county Bond made a point of socializing with African Americans of prominence and high social status. When, for example, he was in Kansas City for two weeks to undergo surgery to remove a "cancerous growth" on his face, he had dinner and a long visit with Bishop Abraham Grant of the African Methodist Episcopal Church. Grant was one of the most influential African American churchmen in the country. After dinner Bond discoursed at length about the virtues of the South as the best home for African Americans in responses to questions posed by the bishop regarding racial conditions. The South more than any other region, as he often noted, provided blacks with the greatest opportunities to advance themselves individually and the race collectively. Similarly, in his visits to Nashville, New Orleans, and New York as well as Little Rock and Hot Springs he rubbed shoulders both with the old black elite and with many African Americans who were conspicuous in the emerging new black middle class. Bond's association with the National Negro Business League provided greater opportunities for him to become acquainted with numerous African American leaders outside Arkansas.

Scott Bond remained active in various aspects of his economic empire in the St. Francis River Basin throughout the 1920s and opening of the 1930s. Over time two of his sons, Theo and Ulysses, assumed increasingly important roles in the management of the family's twelve thousand acres of fertile land, store, lumber business, cotton gins, gravel pits, and other enterprises. At the time of his death the empire that Scott Bond created survived largely intact despite the post–World War I slump in the prices of cotton and other agricultural products, the devastating Mississippi River flood of 1927, the severe drought in the following years, and the stock market crash of 1929. Bond died on March 24, 1933, twenty days after the inauguration of Franklin D. Roosevelt as president. The eighty-year-old Bond died as a result of an injury he suffered while attending to one of his registered bulls. Ulysses Bond said of his father's death: "Scott Bond went down swinging and died among the things he loved."[32] Hundreds of citizens, both whites and blacks, mourned his death and paid their respects. Few failed to mention his remarkable career. His wife, Magnolia Nash Bond, died a decade later.

The two surviving sons, Theo and Ulysses, continued the tradition of their father by expanding and further diversifying the family's interests.[33] In addition to extensive landholdings and various enterprises bequeathed to them, they added, among others, a modern, well-appointed motel for African American travelers located on a main highway between Little Rock and Memphis, the Funeral Directors Exchange that dealt in caskets and funeral supplies, and Bondol Laboratories that manufactured embalming chemicals. All three enterprises had national markets. In addition, the Bond sons followed in their father's footsteps by assisting African Americans in creating and operating their own businesses and in devoting both their time and resources to various philanthropies.

Scott Bond's contemporaries, both blacks and whites, considered him an extraordinary individual, one who had risen from slavery to wealth and status in an era in which African Americans were oppressed and deprived of many of the rights and privileges of citizenship. He was widely known and respected for his integrity, prodigious energy, and strong work ethic. In the words of a contemporary, Bond was universally respected as a man whose word was "as good as a government bond."[34] Frank W. Chowning, author of a history of St. Francis County published in 1954, characterized Bond as a legendary figure and "one of his race's most inspiring leaders." Seldom in the eventful history of the county, Chowning observed, had one individual accomplished "in his life's span as much" as did Scott Bond.[35]

Notes

1. Thomas Foti, "The River's Gifts and Courses," in *The Arkansas Delta: Land of Paradox,* edited by Jeannie M. Whayne and Willard B. Gatewood (Fayetteville: University of Arkansas Press, 1993), 30.

2. See Willard B. Gatewood, "The Arkansas Delta: The Deepest of the Deep South," in ibid., 3–25.

3. The genealogy of the Mebane family is the subject of numerous websites, see especially http://www.sallysfamilyplace.com/Wheeler/mebane and *Biographical and Historical Memoirs of Eastern Arkansas* (Chicago: Goodspeed Publishing Co., 1890), 331, 351, 373, 380, 389; see also U.S. Census Records (1880) on microfilm for Cross and St. Francis counties, Arkansas. Mebane is consistently spelled incorrectly as Maben in the original work on Bond's life reprinted here.

4. On the area detached from existing counties to create Cross County in 1862, see *Biographical and Historical Memoirs of Eastern Arkansas,* 321; compare a map of Arkansas, published by J. H. Colton, New York, 1855, with a map of Arkansas published after the creation of Cross County (1862), noting especially the location of Wittsburg to ascertain an approximate location of the Bond plantation; for a brief history of Wittsburg, see Robert L. Harkness, *Wittsburg, Arkansas: Crowley's Ridge Steamboat Riverport, 1848–1890* (Little Rock, AR: Rose Publishing Company, 1979), especially the mention of Scott Bond on pages 51 and 80.

5. U.S. Census of 1880 (microfilm), St. Francis County, Arkansas.

6. On Burrell Bond, see *Forrest City Times,* November 8, 1895.

7. *Biographical and Historical Memoirs of Eastern Arkansas,* 455.

8. Robert W. Chowning, *History of St. Francis County, Arkansas,* (Forrest City: Times-Herald Publishing Co., 1954), 153-154.

9. On Celia Mebane Allen, her husband, and her son, see http://www.sallysfamilyplace.com/Wheeler/mebane.

10. Thomas O. Fitzpatrick, born in Tennessee in 1849, was county surveyor of Cross County and a schoolteacher there until 1871 when he launched the *Wittsburg Gazette.* Active in Republican politics, he was elected judge of the circuit court in Cross County.

He later moved to St. Francis County and in 1883 was appointed postmaster of Forrest City. In 1886 he was elected county clerk of St. Francis County. He also engaged in farming and operated a cotton gin. See *Biographical and Historical Memoirs of Eastern Arkansas,* 470.

11.　Magnolia Bond quoted in "Them Dark Days—The Arkansas Slave Narratives," in http://www.oldstatehouse.com/exhibits/vitual/narrativeDetail.asp/nid=51.

12.　U.S. Census (1880), Cross County, Arkansas.

13.　On the post-Reconstruction decline of the Republican Party and deterioration of black participation in politics, see Graves, *Town and Country,* chapters 7–12; Carl Moneyhon, "Black Politics in Arkansas during the Gilded Age, 1876–1900," *Arkansas Historical Quarterly* 44 (Autumn 1985): 222–45; Carl Moneyhon, *Arkansas and the New South, 1874–1929* (Fayetteville: University of Arkansas Press, 1997), 58, 72–73, 90–91; Blake Wintory, "African-American Legislators in the Arkansas General Assembly, 1868–1893," *Arkansas Historical Quarterly* 65 (Winter 2006): 385–434; Fon Louise Gordon, "From Slavery to Uncertain Freedom: Blacks in the Delta," in Whayne and Gatewood, eds., *The Arkansas Delta,* 98–127.

14.　On the Rollwage brothers, see *Biographical and Historical Memoirs of Eastern Arkansas,* 489.

15.　On the Bond New Ground Plow, see Green P. Hamilton, *Beacon Lights of the Race* (Memphis: F. H. Clarke and Brothers, 1911), 158–59; Bond, "Highlights of the Life of Scott Bond," 148–49.

16.　Hamilton, *Beacon Lights of the Race,* 157–58.

17.　Peter Schilling, "Daniel A. Rudd," *Encyclopedia of African American Culture and History,* edited by Jack Salzman et al. (New York: Simon and Schuster, 1996), iv, 2368–69.

18.　*Forrest City Times Souvenir Edition, 1905 Excerpts* (article published in September 29, 1905, edition of the *Times,* 120.

19.　See Green, *Beacon Lights of the Race,* 153; quoted in Tom Dillard, "Remembering Arkansas: Scott Bond Was the State's 'Black Rockefeller.'"

20.　For the complete text of Washington's Atlanta speech, see Louis R. Harlan, ed., *The Papers of Booker T. Washington* (Urbana: University of Illinois Press, 1974), iii, 583–87.

21.　On the Tuskegee Machine, see Louis R. Harlan, *Booker T. Washington: The Making of a Black Leader, 1856–1901* (Urbana: University of Illinois Press, 1972), ch. 13, 254–71.

22.   Booker T. Washington to Robert Russa Moton, August 21, 1911, in *Booker T. Washington Papers,* edited by Louis R. Harlan and Raymond W. Smock (Urbana: University of Illinois Press, 1981), xi, 297.

23.   On the Little Rock meeting of the National Negro Business League in Little Rock on August 16–19, 1911, see the *Arkansas Democrat,* August 16, 18, 19, 1911; *Arkansas Gazette,* August 19, 1911.

24.   On the "one-drop rule," see Joel Williamson, *New People: Miscegenation and Mulattoes in the United States* (New York: Free Press, 1980), 108.

25.   On "passing" as white, see Willard B. Gatewood, *Aristocrats of Color: The Black Elite, 1880–1920* (Bloomington: Indiana University Press, 1990), 175–76; William M. Kephart, "The Passing Question," *Phylon* 10 (Fourth Quarter, 1948): 336–40; for an excellent analysis of the long history of racial passing in the United States, see Randall Kennedy, "Racial Passing," *Ohio State Law Journal* 62 (2001), http://moritz law.osu.edu/law/journal/issues/vol62.

26.   On Ravenden Springs, see Lawrence Dalton, *History of Randolph County, Arkansas* (Little Rock, AR: Democrat Printing and Lithographing Co., 1946?), 231–34.

27.   Hartshorn and Penniman, *Era of Progress and Promise,* 426.

28.   For a superb account of Liberian migration in late-nineteenth-century Arkansas, especially the Delta, see Kenneth C. Barnes, *Journey of Hope: The Back-to-Africa Movement in Arkansas in the Late 1800s* (Chapel Hill: University of North Carolina Press, 2004); see also Adell Patton Jr., "The 'Back to Africa Movement' in Arkansas," *Arkansas Historical Quarterly* (August 1992): 164–77.

29.   Barnes, *Journey of Hope,* 16–19; *Forrest City Times,* January 17, 1896.

30.   Barnes, *Journey of Hope,* 170–72; "Letter from Liberia," in *Forrest City Times,* August 8, 1896.

31.   Hartshorn and Penniman, *Era of Progress and Promise,* 426.

32.   See Louis R. Harlan, *Separate and Unequal: Public School Campaigns and Racism in the Southern Seaboard State, 1901–1915* (Chapel Hill: University of North Carolina Press, 1958).

33.   Quoted in Ulysses Bond, "Highlights of the Life of Scott Bond," 152.

34.   Hamilton, *Beacon Lights of the Race,* 165.

35.   Chowning, *History of St. Francis County,* 153–54.

FROM SLAVERY TO WEALTH

FROM
SLAVERY TO WEALTH

THE LIFE OF

SCOTT BOND

THE REWARDS OF HONESTY, INDUSTRY, ECONOMY
AND PERSEVERANCE

BY

DAN. A. RUDD AND THEO. BOND

WITH PREFACE BY HON. J. C. NAPIER
President National Negro Business League and Ex-Register of U. S. Treasury

PUBLISHED BY
THE JOURNAL PRINTING COMPANY
MADISON, ARK. 1917.

CONTENTS.

(Note: The Contents listed below are the same as in the original, but the page numbers have been changed.)

ILLUSTRATIONS.

(Note: The Illustrations listed below are the same as in the original, but the page numbers have been changed.)

ACKNOWLEDGEMENT.

The Journal Printing Company's plant at Madison, Ark., was not large enough to print this book and in order to have the work done by Negroes the National Baptist Publishing Board at Nashville, Tenn., was awarded the contract for printing and binding.

How well the work was done is attested by the appearance of the book.

The magnitude of the plant of that great concern must be seen to be appreciated. With its large batteries of linotype machines, presses and cutters, and complete bindery with all the latest mechanical devices it is indeed an establishment for the race to be proud of.

Tuskegee Institute furnished the photographs illustrating scenes in Mr. Bond's visit to that school. The portraits, as well as the photographs showing some of Mr. Bond's activities and farms, were made by Hooks Bros. of Memphis. The engravings from these pictures were made by the Bluff City Engraving Co. of Memphis.

The generous courtesy of all these people merits our highest praise.

PREFACE.

I have known Mr. Scott Bond since 1905. He is unassuming and progressive and while lacking in what men generally term education, I regard him as highly intelligent. To value him at his true worth, one must become thoroughly acquainted with him; upon such acquaintance, his motives, purposes and aims in life become more highly appreciated. By intuition, he is naturally a merchant, a conservative trader, and a man who at a glance sees the advantages and disadvantages of any proposition made to him.

During the sessions of the National Negro Business League, he has been the very spice of all meetings he has attended. Dr. Booker T. Washington, founder and lifetime President of this League, was always insistent upon his being present at these gatherings, because of the life he always threw into their proceedings.

His unique and purely Southern method of expression always added, not only to the material and interesting side of the League's deliberations, but also presented a most exemplary phase that increased the inspiration of the many young men who have heard him and known of his life and work.

On the occasion of the League's meeting at Little Rock, Ark., in 1911, a special visit was made to his home and place of business at Madison, Arkansas. There we found him surrounded by every comfort of life, domiciled in a beautiful home, presided over by a devoted wife and surrounded by a happy family of children whose loyalty and devotion to him were made manifest by every action and movement. His place of business was perhaps the largest in Madison, every part of which showed method, order and intelligent direction.

The people of his community were unanimous in their praise of the manner in which he conducted his business and of his life among them as a citizen. At a recent meeting of the National Negro Business League, at Chattanooga, Tenn., Mr. Bond was really the life of every proposition presented before that body; and while he did not fail to express himself on every question that came before the

League, he at no time failed to make good his point and to impress his views thereon, firmly and intelligently.

I regard Mr. Bond as one of the most substantial, exemplary and really meritorious men produced by our race.

Scott Bond at 40.

Mrs. Magnolia Bond.

INTRODUCTION.

The world of unrest in these days is but the harbinger of better things. This is a crucial period in the history of mankind. Whatever may be the efforts of men to force certain unholy conditions, history proves that in the end right will triumph over wrong. Truth and justice will at last prevail.

In offering this biography to the public, it is our purpose to show some of the many disadvantages that must be overcome by the Negro in his way upward. We also want to impress the idea that the Negro will be measured by the white man's standard; that he must survive or perish when measured by that scale. The Negro must "find a way or make one." His goal must be the highest Christian civilization. His character, his moral courage, his thrift and his energy must be in excess of the difficulties to be surmounted. He must use his own powers to the limit, then depend upon God and the saving common sense of the American people for his reward in years to come.

To the white friends of the race and to the progressive, earnest Negroes of all our country this book is especially dedicated by the authors.

SCOTT BOND.

SIXTY-FOUR years ago there was born near Canton, in Madison County, Mississippi, a slave child that was destined to show the possibilities of every American-born child of any race. It was a boy. His mother was subject to the unhallowed conditions of that time. That her son was to be numbered among the leaders of his generation was not to be thought of; that he should become the largest planter and land owner of his race and state seemed impossible; that as a merchant and all-round business man, owning and operating the finest and one of the largest mercantile establishments in his state was not to be dreamed of; that at the advanced age of 61 he would erect and operate successfully the largest excavating plant of its kind in Arkansas and one of the only two in the entire southland was beyond conception. Yet, these things and many others equally remarkable have been accomplished by the little Mississippi-born slave boy whose history these pages recount.

The illustrations in this book show some of the many successful enterprises owned and managed by Scott Bond, and also some interesting incidents in his still more interesting life. This is the story of one, who started to lay the foundations of his career at the age of 22, with a bed quilt, a clean character and a manly determination to do something and to be somebody. Today he is one of the largest land owners, merchants and stock-raisers in Arkansas.

Mr. Bond credits much of his success to his charming wife, who has been his helper and his comforter in all his struggles. We offer this as an inspiration to the young men of the race and of all races. No race that produces men who can build and operate such works as these needs have any fear for the future.

At the age of eighteen months, little Scott, removed with his mother to Collierville, Fayette County, Tennessee, and at the age of five years removed with his mother and step-father, William Bond, to the Bond farm, Cross County, Arkansas. The question of "States' Rights" was uppermost in the mind of the American people. Mighty things were to happen that would settle forever this vexatious question. The south was drawing farther and farther from the north. The north was declaring "union forever."

Bleeding Kansas! Forensic battles in the Congress of the United States! John Brown's Raid! Then in April, 1861, the first shot of the civil war crashed against the solid granite walls of old Fort Sumpter [Sumter]. What has all this to do with some little obscure mulatto boy, born on an obscure plantation somewhere down in Dixie? Just this: Had these tremendous events not transpired and ended as they did, the country would have still kept in bondage a race of men who have in fifty years—years of oppression and repression—shown to the world what America was losing. Booker T. Washington would not have revolutionized the educational methods of the world. Granville T. Woods would not have invented wireless telegraphy.[1] There would have been no Negro troops to save the rough riders on San Juan Hill. There would have been no Negro soldiers to pour out their life blood at Carrizal.[2] There would be no black American troops to offer to bare their dusky bosoms in the fiery hell beyond the seas today in the mighty struggle for world democracy. Scott Bond would have had no opportunity to prove to the world that if a man will be may.

There were many things in the life of the slave to break the monotony of daily, unrequited toil. At no time in the history of slavery in America was there more rapid change of scenes than during the years of the civil war. It was in these years little Scott had his ups and his downs, enjoying as others the bitters and the sweets of youthful slave life. As the fratricidal strife neared its close, and the dawn of freedom appeared upon the horizon, slaveholders were put to their trumps to keep their human chattels. When the union soldiers would be nearing some big plantation the slaves were hurriedly secreted in some out-of-the-way place to keep them out of sight until the apparent danger had passed. It was an occasion like this in 1865 that the overseer on the Bond farm was ordered to hurry the Negroes to a hiding place in the swamps. News that the Yankees were coming had spread abroad. Teams were hitched to the wagons and some provisions for camping were loaded and the Negroes, some seventy-five in number, were started for the hidden camp ground. This was great fun for these poor people. The overseer had some of the slaves make brooms of brush and spoil out the

Flood in the Mississippi River.

mule and wagon tracks to keep the Yankees from following. They were headed for the big blue canebrakes on the banks of the bay and Morris pond, a great fishing ground, where little Scott joined the others in fishing and frolicking. They had not been long at this place before the cry was raised, "The Yankees are coming." Soon a troop of union cavalrymen came upon the scene. They ordered the slaves to surrender. A few knew what this meant and threw up their hands. The lieutenant in command ordered his troopers to dismount. Then all fell to fishing, singing, dancing and feasting. Skillets, pots and frying pans were called for. Mr. Bond says he never saw men eat fried speckled perch as did those soldiers. This was a picnic for the slaves. "The only thing," says Mr. Bond, "that threw cold water over my pleasure was that my good mother could not be with us; she being the house maid had to remain with the mistress while all the other slaves were sent to the bottoms."

"When the dinner of fish was finished, the lieutenant ordered us to gather up our things and load them into the wagons. This was done. He got upon a stump and said: 'This war will certainly end successfully for the union. Every Negro under the stars and stripes will be free.'

"Right there," says Mr. Bond, "was one of the greatest events of my life. Old gray-headed women with children clasped in their arms; old, feeble, decrepit, worn-out men, all shouting—Hallelujah! Hallelujah. The officers stood quiet until the hysterical demonstration had subsided. He then continued: 'I am going to take you back home to the farm from which you came. Don't leave home and run from place to place while the war is going on. Stay at home and be good and obedient servants as you have been, until the war is over.' The drivers mounted their seats, the children climbed upon the wagons, and men and women walked behind, the soldiers bringing up the rear started back home. When they reached the Bond farm, they came as they went through the middle of the field down the turn row. I saw things happen up and down that turn row, young as I was" says Mr. Bond, "that I thought were very wrong and think so to this day. The hoes and harrows lay along the turn row. Some of the Negroes in the crowd took axes and broke every one of these farm implements."

When they reached the great house, Mrs. Bond,[3] the mistress, walked out on the front veranda and with her little Scott espied his dear mother. The lieutenant introduced himself and said: "I have come to restore to you about fifty head of mules and seventy-five colored people. I regret very much to know that you thought that we as union men were coming down here to destroy the south. I want to congratulate you upon the skill with which you had your colored people hidden. It required some skill to find them but we had more fish to eat than we have had since the war began."

The madam replied: "I am so much obliged to you for your kindness and generosity. I was not indeed looking for union soldiers; I was expecting the jayhawkers, that was my reason for sending them down there." The soldiers then rode off.

One of little Scott's duties was to ride behind the madam and carry her key basket, for in those days when she would be absent from the house she would turn the keys in the locks, then put the keys in a basket kept for that purpose.

> "But they change as all things change here,
> Nothing in this world can last."

Sheep and cattle. Unloading hay in the back ground.

SCOTT BOND'S MOTHER DIES.

Not long after this Scott Bond's mother died leaving him yet a little boy with his step-father. They laid her to rest on a beautiful spot on the side of a towering hill overlooking the Bond farm.

STARTING A NEGRO SCHOOL.

In 1866, a northern gentleman, Mr. Thorn, was renting the Bond farm. He was very kindly disposed toward the colored people. He wrote to Memphis for a teacher for a colored school. The parties to whom he wrote, referred him to Miss Celia Winchester. She accepted the school.

There were no railroads in this part of the country at that time. The only method of transportation was from Memphis, by steam boat, down the Mississippi and up the St. Francis rivers to Wittsburg.

When the boat arrived at Wittsburg, Mr. Thorn, not knowing the customs of the south, secured a room at the hotel for Miss Winchester, who was an Oberlin, Ohio, graduate. She had attended school with the whites at that famous seat of learning. She too, was ignorant of the customs prevailing in the south.

When the proprietor of the hotel learned that Miss Winchester was colored, he went out and bought a cowhide. He met Mr. Thorn on the street, held a pistol on him and cowhided him.

Mr. Thorn stood and cried. He said that he was seventy years old and had never done any one any harm in his life. What he had done was not intended as a violation of custom.

We lived about sixteen miles out from Wittsburg. The next day a wagon met Mr. Thorn and Miss Winchester and took them to the farm.

Thus was opened the first school for Negroes in this part of the country and the first school I had ever seen. In the school my stepfather and myself were classmates in the A B C class.

Later on, Mr. Thorn's wife came from the north to visit her husband. She opened a night school for those old people who could not attend the day school. The hours were from seven to nine.

It was a curiosity to me to see so many people, some of whom were gray-headed, trying to learn to read and write. They were enthusiastic and very much in earnest.

This condition held good for the whole neighborhood. In the daytime, the children would gather pine knots to make light at night. All about the country one could see lights in the homes and people trying to learn their lessons.

Coal oil and electric lights were unknown. The white people, in the great house, used candles. The colored people used pine knots and little flat iron lamps filled with grease; and used a rag for a wick.

When the weather grew warm, people would collect pine knots and at night they would gather in great crowds in the open, and then such singing of A B C's and a-b ab, you never heard. The whole colored population seemed to be crazy about education.

I remember an old lady seventy-eight years old, who was determined to learn to read, and in less than eight weeks she was reading the Bible. I know of another instance of a Negro, named John Davis, who in twelve months after he learned his A B C's, was elected Justice of the Peace. He had learned to read and write. He did not know enough to prepare his docket and papers, but the kindly disposed white people for whom he worked, would fix up his documents for him. He would sign them "John Davis," J. P. These white people were southern born democrats.

Scene on Gray farm, looking south.

There was a Mr. Brooks, a white democrat, who was John Davis' predecessor in office, who would frequently prepare Davis' docket and warrants. The docket went regularly before the grand jury and was favorably passed upon. Davis served out his term and was eventually married. He lived respected by all who knew him.

It must be remembered that at that time the southern white man was largely disfranchised.

As Mrs. Thorn advanced with her educational work, it was very encouraging to see the good results of her efforts.

As the season drew to a close, it was common to hear the old people spelling at their exercises. When they reached "baker" in the old blue back speller, it was b-a ba, k-e-r ker, baker; l-a la, d-y dy, lady; s-h-a sha, d-y dy, shady; at the wash tub, over the cook pot, in the kitchen, at the mule lot and in the cotton patch, it was "baker," "lady," "shady," from sun-up to sunset, and way into the night.

Had that enthusiasm kept up until to day the Negro would be the best educated race in the world.

What the Negro needs today is more of the eager enthusiasm of the years just after the close of the Civil War. From this cup we must quaff deeply and often from the cradle to the grave.

There is no place for drones in human society. The lazy man, the listless man, the passive, happy, go-lucky man is a real curse to his race.

"Up and at them!" is the command that comes ringing down the ages. "Up and at" the obstacles that stand athwart the pathway of progress. Think! Work! Get results!!

If one would study German history of the last fifty years, he would find out what it means to be thorough; what results come from intense application in developing human efficiency.

Yet, after all that is said and done concerning the Negro race in America, we must admit that they are a great people. If the Negro has plenty, he is happy; if he has nothing, he is happy. He can come about as near living on nothing as any other race and still be happy.

This philosophic tendency to be happy under all conditions and in all circumstances is characteristic of the race.

Before the war a Negro's rations consisted of three pounds of meat, a peck of meal, and a pint of black molasses; and they lived to be one hundred and one hundred and ten years old and would still be strong men to the day of their death.

It was a rare thing before the war, to hear of a Negro having tuberculosis.

He is as proud as a peacock. The jolly good nature of the race has been its salvation. In fact, the Negro is the only race that can look the white man in the face and live.

Better still, the white man does not want to get rid of the Negro.

MAKING A SLIP GAP.

"I remember," says Mr. Bond, "once when I was quite young, one of my tasks was to look after the calves. When the cows came up to the cow pen, I would let them in. Then I would drive the calves half a mile to get them into the lane and back through the lane to the cow pen.

I thought I would make a slip gap. I got some rails and dragged them up. I was not big enough to carry the rails, so I would move one end ahead, then I would go back and move the other end. When I got ready to put it into place, I would take a rail and by prizing, managed to get the rail in.

Scott Bond's sheep at home.

The overseer came by one day and asked me who made the slip gap. I told him I made it. He had a paddle with a strap on the end. He said he was going to whip me for lying to him. I told him I had not lied. He said he would like to see me make another. I then showed him how I managed to make it.

DEER FOR DINNER.

In the time of the Civil War, the high cost of living was as much in evidence as it is today.

I can remember that when I was a little boy, living on the Bond farm on the Bay road in Cross County, Ark., that anything like a square meal was a thing of the past. There was neither meat nor bread to be had. We had a little wheat that would be ground in an old-fashioned corn mill. From this we would make mush for breakfast and cush and greens for dinner.

On one occasion my step-father killed a quail with a clod. My mother prepared and cooked the bird with dumplings. It made a meal for seven people.

One morning as we were going to the field we heard the hounds in the distance. As the sun rose higher the hounds seemed to be getting nearer. About nine o'clock the dogs were running around the north end of the farm. This was not unusual, as there were plenty of deer and panther in Arkansas, so we paid little attention to the hounds. To our surprise a big buck jumped into the field where we were at work. It was about a mile and a half to the next fence. Mr. Cook, the overseer, had his horse tied to a bush near where the deer jumped into the field. The overseer being like the rest of us, half starved, mounted his horse and gave chase. The deer that had been running for six or seven hours was practically run down. So when the overseer overtook the deer, he leaped from the back of his horse to the back of the deer and cut the throat of the fleeing animal.

That was meat in the pot. There was no more work that day. It was deer for dinner, deer for supper and deer for breakfast.

SITTING ON A SNAKE.

There was a woman named Julia Ann on our plantation, who, one day at dinner time, went to a tree where she had hung her dinner bucket. She reached up and got the bucket and backed up to the tree and sat down between its protruding roots to eat her dinner. When she got up, she found she had been sitting on a rattle snake. The snake was killed. He had fifteen rattlers and a button on his tail. Ann fainted when she saw the snake. She said that she had felt the snake move, but thought that it was the cane giving way beneath her.

Snakes of that size and variety were numerous in Arkansas in those times.

I heard of an instance where a man built a house on a flat, smooth rock on a piece of land that he had bought. It was in the autumn when he built his house. When the weather grew cold he made a fire on the rock. There had been a hole in the rock, but the man had stopped it up.

One night he had retired, and late in the night, his child, which was sleeping between him and his wife, became restless and awakened him. He reached for the child and found what he supposed was his wife's arm across the child. He undertook to remove it and to his consternation, found he had hold of a large snake. He started to get out of bed, to make a light, and the whole floor was covered with snakes. He got out of the house with his wife and child.

The next day the neighbors gathered, burned the house and killed hundreds of snakes.

The house had been built over a den of snakes.

When I first came to Arkansas as a little slave boy, things were different from what they are today. Arkansas was on the western frontier. The clearings were small and far between. There were trails here and there, but few roads.

Wild game of all kinds was abundant. Deer, turkeys, bears, raccoons, o'possums and all varieties of small game were so plentiful that one only had to look about him to see some one or more kinds of game.

It was next to impossible to make a corn crop unless there was some one to hunt at night and guard the fields of ripening grain. If this was not done, the farms would be stripped of their corn.

There was a man named Slade, whose duty it was to hunt all night. He slept in the day time. He could not bring in all the game he would kill, hence the hands on our place would divide themselves into squads and take time about hunting with Slade at night until he had killed a load of coons, and they would then carry them home and go to sleep, leaving Slade to make the rest of the night alone.

The meat secured in this way would last several families for some time. The next night another squad would accompany Slade on his hunt.

One night a party who had been hunting with Slade, started for home. The night was dark and cloudy. They lost their way. They finally came to the bank of a lake they had never seen before. There was a boat moored where they came out. They saw a light across the lake, so they got into the boat and rowed across to see if they could get information as to the direction home.

One [On] their way back across the lake—it was by this time nearly sun-up—they ran their boat upon something which began to move. Upon investigation, it proved to be a large turtle. They secured it and sent for a mule to haul it out. When the shell was removed they had one hundred and forty-eight pound of turtle meat.

Such was the abundance of wild life in those days that whole families could subsist on game if they so desired.

SCOTT BOND MOVES TO MADISON.

Scott Bond moved to Madison, St. Francis County, Ark., with his step-father, who had bargained to buy a farm, in 1872, and remained with him until he was 21 years of age. He then undertook to vouch for himself. His step-father contracted with him to remain with him until he was 22 years of age. His pay was to be one bale of cotton, board, washing and patching. He thought the pay was small, but for the sake of his little brothers, that they might have a home paid for, he remained that year. The next year he walked eighteen miles to the Allen farm, having seen the possibilities in the fertile soil of that place in the two years he had worked on it with his step-father. He decided that would be the place to make money. He rented 12 acres of land at $6.50 per acre. He had no money, no corn, no horse, nothing to eat, no plows, no gears; but all the will-power that could be contained in one little hide. In 1876 he rented 35 acres and hired one man. In 1877 he married Miss Magnolia Nash[4] of Forrest City. The Allen farm, as stated elsewhere, contained 2,200 acres. The proprietor[5] lived in Knoxville, Tenn. She sent her son over the next autumn, who insisted on Scott Bond renting the whole place. This he refused to do on the ground that he was unable to furnish the mules, feed, tools and other stock sufficient to cultivate it. Mr. Allen[6] took a letter from his pocket that read: "Now, Scott, I have told Johnnie to be sure and do his uttermost to rent you this place, and as I am sure it would be quite a burden on you financially, you may draw on me for all the money that is required to buy mules, corn and tools." And at the bottom: "Scott, I think this will be one of the golden opportunities of your life." This lady was near kin to Scott Bond's former owner. He grasped the opportunity. There were all sorts of people living on the Allen farm. Some half-breed Indians, some few white families and some low, degraded colored people. The whites were no better than the others. The first thing Scott Bond had to do was to clean up the farm along those lines. He then secured axes, cross cut saws, and built a new fence around the entire farm—something that had not been done for 20 years. When the

Cattle just after dipping.

crops were gathered and disposed of, Scott paid Mrs. Allen and everyone else for the rent and all other obligations. He received from Mrs. Allen, the owner of the farm, who lived in Knoxville, Tenn., a fine letter of thanks and congratulations for the improvements on the farm. The net profits, all bills paid, were $2,500, in addition to the gains on cotton seed. This farm is situated right at the east base of Crowley's Ridge, 42 miles due west of the Mississippi river. There were no levees in this county at that time, and when the overflows came we had a sea of water spread out from the Mississippi to the ridge. Mr. Bond said the next winter there came the biggest over-flow he had ever seen. He took his boat and moved all the people, mules, cattle, hogs and horses to Crowley's Ridge. He lived about a mile and a half from Crowley's Ridge and owing to a deep slough or bayou between him and the ridge he was compelled to use a boat. There was perhaps no more exciting time in Mr. Bond's life than when with his boat he would brave the dangers of the murky flood and with the help of his crew scout the country over hunt-ing out and rescuing people and stock from the rising, rushing waters. It is said by those who know, that Scott Bond saved the lives of hundreds of people, white and black. In this particular overflow he had 7,000 bushels of corn and 10,000 pounds of meat that he had killed and cured. He saved all this by putting it in the lofts of the different buildings on the place. Having secured his own people and property, he spent his time looking out and helping his neighbors. He lived in the great house on the Allen farm. He took flour barrels, placed planks on them for a scaffold to put his cooking stove and bed on. The next day he ran his dugout into the house and tied it to his bed post. Three days later he was compelled to get another set of barrels, to raise his scaffold a little higher. On the third evening he arrived at home between sundown and dark with all his boatmen in dugouts. It was impossible to get in the door on account of the water. They ran the boats in through the windows, each man to his sleeping place. Every one of them was as wet as rats. They would have to stand on the head end of their boats to change their wet clothing before getting into their beds. The cook and his helper, who looked after things in the absence of the boats, were brave to start in with and promised to stay with Scott Bond as long as there was a button on his shirt, but when they saw the boats coming in through the top sash of the window their melts drew up. They said, "Mr. Bond, we like you and have always been willing to do anything you asked us to do, but this water is away beyond where we had any idea it would be. We are going to leave tomorrow morning."

They had all changed and put on dry clothing, and as a matter of course felt better. The next call was supper and dinner combined. A big tea kettle full of strong, hot coffee, spare ribs, back bones, hog heads, ears and noses. There was some shouting around that table. Mr. Bond says he did not attempt to pacify the cook and hostler until after all had finished supper, as the time to talk to an individual is when he has a full stomach.

"The next day when we started out," says Mr. Bond, "I instructed my men to 'do as you see me do.' If a cow jumps over board, follow her and grab her by the tail and stick to her until you come to some sapling or grape vine; grab it and hold to it until help arrives. Any man can hold a cow by the tail or horn in this way."

All Mr. Bond's people were comfortably housed on Crowley's Ridge. In those days people did not need the assistance of the government to take care of them. They had plenty of corn, meat and

"The Cedars" Scott Bond's home at Madison, Ark.

bread they produced at home. Six months later you could not tell that there ever had been an overflow from the looks of the corn and cotton.

"But to return to the boys who were getting frightened at the ever-increasing flood," said Mr. Bond, "we all loaded our pipes and you may know there was a smoke in the building. 'Twas then I said, 'Boys, all sit down and let's reason with one another. The water will be at a standstill tomorrow evening. I really know what I am talking about, because the stage of the river at Cairo [Illinois] always governs the height of the water here. That is a thing I always keep posted on. While this, the great house, is two-thirds full of water, you must remember that this is the eddy right along here, and anyone of you take your spike pole and let it down to the floor and you will find from 8 to 10 inches of sand and sediment.'

"One man said, 'I know he is right, because whenever an overflow subsides I have to shovel out from ten to twelve inches of sand. This house is built out of hewn logs, 46 feet long and the biggest brick stack chimneys in the middle I ever saw. Now, boys, with all this meat and other things piled on this scaffold you are perfectly safe. I am feeding you boys and paying you well. I am asking you to do what you see me do. This satisfied them and we stuck together."

Mr. Bond rented the same farm for eleven years. In that time he had paid for rent $16,000. He then wrote Mrs. Allen at Knoxville in the month of August for her to be sure and try to get a tenant for the next year, as he had bought a farm of 300 acres of land at Madison on the St. Francis River, and he would be compelled to go and develop it; that he had seven boys and he really felt that he would be doing them an injustice to have them renters the balance of their days. He received a letter from Mrs. Allen in reply. The offer she made was hard to turn down, but looking around at his wife and beautiful boys, there was a longing for home sweet home and while he regretted to have to do so, he refused the offer. Mr. Bond says: "I paid $2 per acre for 320 acres and today I am offered $85 per acre for every foot of it. If one had seen it before I bought it and would see it now with all its improvements, with splendid roads around it, over which automobiles pass every few minutes, they could hardly realize that it is the same place."

The south seems to be the only place on earth for the Negro, with its fertile soil, its mild climate, its sunshine and its flowers, it does seem that nature had left this fair land in which to raise the Negro to the highest state of civilization.

Mrs. Allen asked Mr. Bond to recommend to her the best tenant he could find. He could only think of two colored men whom he thought had the ability to take and manage the place, Richard Miller and Henry Anderson. They were so placed at the time that they said it would be impossible for them to take hold. His next thought was of a white man named Newt Johnson, who had been his neighbor on the Allen farm for ten years. Mr. Johnson was proud of the chance. The next year there came another overflow, Mr. Johnson was unable to employ the right kind of hands and made a failure. He told Mrs. Allen his troubles with the overflow and he agreed to try it another year, that he thought he would succeed. I don't know what per cent of the rent young Mr. Allen collected that autumn. Mr. Johnson and others told young Allen that those two big over-flows had literally ruined the farm. They took him around and showed him the different sand bars that had accumulated on the place. Mr. Allen, a gentleman as he was, not being posted about these conditions, said: 'Gentlemen, I have heard of just such things." No

Scott Bond's birthplace.

sprouts had been cut nor ditch banks been cleaned off for two years. The place really did look desperate. Mr. Allen returned to his mother at Knoxville and explained things to her just as he found them. They held a consultation. Mrs. Allen said: 'Johnnie, what shall we do with that farm? I would not have you go back and live there for anything. You know that the Boyd Manufacturing Company promised that if I would not take your wife back to Arkansas to give you a half interest in the manufacturing concern. Now, Johnnie, I had rather for Uncle Scott to have that place than anyone I know. Get your pen and I will dictate a contract to Uncle Scott. It read thus: 'Uncle Scott, if you will pay the taxes which amount to $136 and then pay me $1,000 every November until you pay me $5,000, I will make you a warranty deed to the whole 2,200 acres.

"When Mr. Allen arrived with the contract in his pocket," Mr. Bond says, 'he found me ginning cotton to beat the band on gin on my new farm that I had cleaned up. The sun was about three hours high the morning Mr. Allen came to me. He seemed to be full of glee. His aristocratic breeding and training showed in his every movement. He grasped my hand and said, 'Howdy, Uncle Scott, mamma sends her highest regards to you and your family.' I was proud to have the pleasure of meeting Mr. Allen at my new steam gin with all the modern improvements and last but not least, it was built on my own land. I showed him my new brick kiln that I had just blown out. I made everything around the gin plant as pleasant for him as I knew how and looked every moment for him to say, 'Good bye, Uncle Scott,' knowing his quickness of movement and decision. I was at a loss to know what to do for him. At 10:30 o'clock I sent a messenger to inform my wife that Mr. John Allen of Knoxville would be with me for dinner. She had not much time to prepare, but when the boy returned he brought turnip salad, eggs and fried chicken. Knowing the customs that existed between the white man and the Negro in the south, I spread a cloth on the top board of the scales, fixed his plate, knife and fork and said, 'Mr. Allen, have a lunch.' Mr. Allen said, 'Uncle Scott, this is your gin and your property. As you used to belong to Cousin Mary Francis [Frances] Bond, who always felt dear to mother, now you come and let's eat together.'

"'You know a man feels best just after he has had a good dinner. Mr. Allen said, 'Uncle Scott, I have a proposition for you that will make you scratch the back of your head.' This, of course, took no effect on me, but when he drew from his pocket the contract his mother had authorized him to submit to me, I was struck with amazement.

["]When I came to myself I was standing on the front side of the scales scratching my head. I looked around and Mr. Allen laughingly remarked: 'I told you I would have you scratching your head.' I then began to figure. I had hundreds of acres of land already on hand that were already paid for, but I reasoned that if I could rent a farm and pay $1,250 a year rent until I had paid the proprietor $16,000, as I had done on that same farm, it looked to me like the proposition was a good one. I said, 'Where will you be tomorrow at 9 o'clock?' He said he could be at any place I would have him to be."

Mr. Bond agreed to meet Mr. Allen in Forrest City the next morning and close the deal. "The next morning," says Mr. Bond, "I rode over to Forrest City and met Mr. Allen and Mr. T. O. Fitzpatrick[7] on the sidewalk. As usual Mr. Fitzpatrick said, 'Good morning, Uncle Scott.' Mr. Allen said, "Uncle Scott, I have a better proposition to offer you than the one I offered you yesterday. I have a party who will take it at $5,000 and pay half of the money cash.'

Spring Creek Missionary Baptist Church of which
Scott Bond is a member.

Mr. Fitzpatrick said, 'Have you been talking with Uncle Scott about
this deal?' 'Yes,' I was at his gin plant yesterday all day and he promised to be here this morning at 9 o'clock to close the deal.' Mr.
Fitzpatrick remarked: 'Now, I take down my proposition and have
nothing to do with the deal. There stands one man, Scott Bond, that
I always thought to be a gentleman.'"

Mr. Bond said: "Mr. Fitzpatrick that is all O. K. Now in order to
help Mr. Allen out and also better your condition we will buy the
farm in partnership." Mr. Fitzpatrick said: "That would suit me better than buying it by myself, provided you promise me that you will
superintend the farm for five years, with the understanding that T. O.
Fitzpatrick will allow you big wages for superintending the farm."

Here, again, Scott Bond showed his ability and foresight. He says:
"I grabbed like a trout at a troll. I sold my new gin plant on my
place and moved back to the Allen farm. The only thing invested in
the farm to start with was a pair of plug mules and 180 bushels of
corn." He says when he got on the good old farm he felt like he
was the big dog of the bone yard. We here again repeat Mr. Bond's
word without quotation: When I was on this farm as a renter I

thought I had a big melt. When I looked around and seeing there was a probability of me becoming proprietor I felt that I could do four times the amount of work I could do before. There was immediate demand for axes, hoes, plows and people. In four years' time there was over 100 additional acres of land brought under cultivation; fourteen new houses with brick chimneys, a new steam gin and a kiln of brick; the farm was stocked out with work stock and tools and the farm all paid for. I then turned everything over to Mr. Fitzpatrick and rented to him my interest in the farm, gin, mules and horses. I moved back home with my beautiful wife and children and began clearing and improving my big farm at Madison. Some years later the colored people all around Madison, where I live, became Africa struck. I begged them not to sell their farms and go to Africa, but first go and see for themselves. All my begging and advising did not avail. I owned at that time 320 acres in that immediate locality and saw there was another opportunity. I sold my interest in the Allen farm to Mr. T. O. Fitzpatrick and received every dollar in cash. This money bought in seven other little farms adjoining mine. I told Mr. Fitzpatrick that he and I could get along in perfect harmony all the days of our lives but after our days our boys might not agree as we had done; that I thought it good policy as well as profitable to myself to sell. When I got the seven little farms attached to my main big farm, I found there was room for the little bull dog to grow larger and stronger as there was plenty of room for work and improvement. All these years cotton was only 5 cents a pound. My larger children were all in college. One can readily see there was plenty of room and reason for the little bull dog to raise his bristles. All this land was high-class, fertile land. I came to the conclusion that I would go into the Irish potato business. Potato growing was something new to me, but I always felt I could learn to do anything any one else could do. I paid $500 for seed potatoes the first dash out of the box and planted fifty acres. We made a very good crop, shipped about 20 car loads and made a nice profit. Seeing this was the thing to do, I next year planted 110 acres. I got a good stand and by digging time I found a tremendous crop of potatoes. I had everything arranged, about 75 hands, buckets, baskets, barrels and teams ready to start digging potatoes on Monday morning. I awoke at 3 o'clock and said to my wife in the bed, "Just listen to

Scott Bond landing logs at his saw mill.

the rain." This of course knocked potato digging in the head. I thought, however, that it would be all right in a day or two, but it rained a solid week and when I started digging the ground was really too wet, but I thought I had to do something but the next day it rained again. I finally made up my mind to continue digging but it was a bad old go. As fast as I would load one end of the car I could smell the potatoes rotting, in the other end of the car.

I shipped about 30 car loads, many of which when they reached their destination the consignee would write back, "Please remit $5 or $10 to pay balance of freight." One can see that I had the land and had the potatoes, there was no reason in the world why I should not have shipped 65 or 70 car loads of nice, clean, commercial potatoes, but the rain did it all. Instead of making a profit I lost $5,000. I soon learned to realize that this was an unavoidable accident. There was no negligence on my part. The little bull dog raised his bristles again and remarked to himself, "The place you lost it is the place to make it." I prepared the land again for a fall crop, got a good stand, built a potato house, dug and housed the potatoes and saved them for seed potatoes on the Texas market the following spring. I had about 10,000 bushels, which by holding until February brought $1.25 per bushel.

I got back all the money lost on the first crop to pay all the expenses of the second crop and leave me a neat margin.

Cotton was still selling for four and five cents a pound and as a matter of course I continued to grow potatoes. There is perhaps no vegetable that is more palatable and more nutritious than the humble potato. The next year I grew seventy-five acres of potatoes as the seasons came right and I had learned to prepare the land to cultivate a potato crop. All this gave me a wonderful yield. We began digging about the 10th of June. The market opened up at $1.10 per bushel, but this only held good for a few car loads and the prices took a downward trend. Chicago and Pittsburg were my best markets. My commission men in those two cities kept writing me, telling me to rush my shipments as the price would go sky high in a few days. I had not much confidence in their predictions. Potatoes had fallen to 75¢ a bushel. I was not able at that time to keep up with interstate commerce. I made up my mind to try some good horse sense concerning the market. Two of my southern friends came by to view my potato crop and to see the manner in which I was selecting potatoes for the market, as they were strictly in the potato business and had handled several hundred car loads from this community. They insisted that I should let them handle my potatoes for me. I told them I could not do it. I was taking at that time a paper that was devoted especially to potatoes that were grown in all parts of the United States. This gave me a chance to see and learn something of the market. I had already decided to close out my entire crop to some other people who understood the market better than I did, so I remarked to them: "Gentlemen, I cannot let you take this crop and handle it for me, but I have a proposition to make you; that is, I will sell you these two cars we are now loading for 75 cents per bushel, and then I will close out the balance of my crop to you for 65 cents per bushel and will gather, sort and load them, that is, deliver them to our station for 65¢ per bushel." They were both perfect gentlemen. They conferred with each other a short time, then turned to me and said, "Uncle Scott, we will take your proposition if you will allow us to put two inspectors to see that potatoes are selected and loaded properly." This I agreed to. It was about the 11th of June. I further agreed to get the crop loaded by 12 o'clock midnight, June 16th. I had worlds of potatoes to dig. Then and there I got busy. We finished those two cars that day, ate

Mr. Bond and Mr. Bridgeforth discussing hogs in the
Mulberry Orchard at Tuskegee.

supper and that night I jumped into my saddle and rode over the
entire community. The next morning at sun up I had 125 hands in
my potato field. I sent eighteen miles to my upper farm to get more
mules and wagons to double my capacity. I figured that I only had
five days in which to dig and load this crop, but if I got 10 days out
of five days by working day and night I could complete my contract.
Business picked up, but the price of potatoes continued to fall. This
inspired me with more ambition to hustle. We would begin in the
morning as soon as it was daylight. I had my teams arranged so as to
give each one of them rest. We would dig and barrel all day and at
sundown have fresh teams and a fresh crew and load cars all night.
This enabled me to load from two to four cars a day. On the 16th I
had finished digging my entire crop with the exception of one small
car. I dug that next day and it netted me only 15 cents a bushel. From
the day I sold the two cars at 75 cents and the balance of my crop at
65 cents a bushel the market continued to go down every day, so you
can see that it was to my interest to push things and get through by
the 16th. Just think about it! I had no written contract with these
gentlemen. The contract was only verbal. The names of these

gentlemen were Mr. Eugene Rolfe, now county judge of our county, and Mr. Eugene Borrow. Both of them were southern born, aristocratic gentlemen who always stand upon their honor. They paid me every dollar they agreed to like heroes. I wound up that year by making a handsome profit on my potato crop. Cotton advanced that year to 8 cents per pound. This brought about quite a change as cotton had been four and five cents for years. I looked over the situation and concluded that on account of the advance in cotton it would be hard to get hands to handle a potato crop. I knew the potato to be a leguminous plant. Then considering the amount of plowing I had to do to make two potato crops, I concluded that that land would grow a good crop of cotton. I planted that land to cotton. I never had in all my days such cotton crops as were grown on that land for the next two or three years[.] Cotton sold that year for 10 ½ cents and by Texas going into the potato business on account of the boll weevil, I decided to stop potato growing while times were good. Cotton has remained at a fair price from that time until the European war, when in 1914 the bottom again fell out of the cotton market. I then began to diversify my crops in earnest. I planted wheat, rye, oats and alfalfa and began in a small way to accumulate cattle and hogs. I saw the prices on that class of farm produce was up and going higher. During all these years I kept my children in college and managed to buy another farm every year.

One of the greatest mistakes people make is when they take their children out of school in the very years they should be in training. It is false economy to think they are of more permanent help in the field than in the school room. More children are cheated out of an education in this way than in any other.

SCOTT BOND'S FIRST MERCHANDISING.

In this age of specialization, it is unusual to find a man who does many things well. A saying that "a jack of all trades is good at none," is certainly not appropriate in relation to the subject of this sketch. It may be that the exception proves the rule: If this be true then, the life of Scott Bond is the exception. Mr. Bond not only did many things, but he also made a success of everything he touched.

In 1876, the records show that he was the first of his race to do

Corner of bedroom [in the Bond home]. Showing fire place where can
was found supposed to contain $500.

merchandising in the then little town of Forrest City, which has
since become the county seat of St. Francis County.

At that time, Mr. William Bond, Scott Bond's step-father and Mr.
Abe Davis, proposed to him to open a store. They agreed to go each
one-third share and share alike; each to invest $200 dollars and Scott
Bond to be in charge to handle the business. Each was to pay one-
third of the expenses, rent, clerk hire, etc. So about the 15th of
December, Mr. Scott Bond insisted that business should be started
in order to get the benefit of the Christmas trade. He therefore
invested his $200 and his step-father and Mr. Davis agreeing to come
in with their share a little later. January, February, March and April
came and still they were not ready. The business was a success for
the capital invested, but the capital was not large enough, so May
3rd Mr. Bond decided to pack up and store his goods. He stored
them with Mr. Abe Davis, and on May 4th, went back to the Allen
farm to make a crop.

About this time he was engaged to be married to Miss Maggie
Nash of Forrest City. The night before he went to the Allen farm,
he called on his fiance. She was living with a white family, one of

whom a young lady was also named Miss Maggie Nash. Mr. Bond told his future wife that he was going to the Allen farm and promised her a box of stationery and stamps, that she might write him. The next day he purchased a nice box envelopes, writing paper and stamps and sent them to her by a young colored man, who marched up to the front door and delivered the package.

The young white lady received it, thinking it was for her. At this time Mr. Bond's future wife entered the room and noticing the package claimed it and told Miss Nash to look at the name on the box, which she did and found it from Scott Bond. After a jolly laugh in which all joined, the present Mrs. Scott Bond was allowed to take her stationery.

It was in the time of the old horse gin, and the conveniences of the modern gin were undreamed of. The cotton was hauled to the gin and unloaded in baskets, then fed to the gin by hand and pressed into bales with the old wooden screw.

So when Mr. Bond had picked all his cotton he and his wife hauled it to the gin house and unloaded it up into the gin. He had two ponies and two borrowed horses. His wife, to save 75 cents a day insisted on driving the ponies for the week and his cousin Ananias drove the borrowed horses and it took all week to gin 12 bales. At noon they would go home to dinner of left overs from breakfast.

One of the most delightful southern dishes is baked raccoon. Mrs. Bond, a past mistress in the art culinary, would often get her husband to visit a famous trapper who was camped not far away to procure a raccoon, which she would proceed to cook after a fashion that would delight an epicure.

Upon one of these visits, the trapper had no coons, and offered Mr. Bond a beaver. Mrs. Bond had always said that she would not eat a beaver. The trapper skinned a beaver and persuaded Mr. Bond to take it and not tell Mrs. Bond it was a beaver. When he arrived at home, his wife remarked that it was the largest and fattest "coon" she had ever seen. She cooked it and both ate very heartily of it. Some time later she told Mr. Bond to bring her another "coon" large and fat, just like the other one. Mr. Bond then told her that what she had before was a beaver. Well it was excellent and that he had better get her another beaver.

Gin with cotton ready for shipping.

Mr. Bond swapped a mule for a yoke of small steers and he would load two bales of cotton on a little ox cart and drive 16 miles to Forrest City and get home again late in the night.

The next year he increased his acreage, procured more stock and took on some share croppers. By this time his wife was compelled to stay at home, to use Mr. Bond's own words, "because we had gone into the baby business."

With three share croppers he cultivated 75 acres in corn and cotton and gathered 67 bales of cotton and all the corn, hay and potatoes needed. He would never tell his hands to go on but would say "come on and let's go." He never knew what it was to get tired; and he never allowed any one about him to get tired. He was a close observer. Whenever he would find his hands becoming fatigued he would start joking and make them forget that they were working.

It was actually fun for him in those days to take an interest in what is now called diversified farming. Cotton, corn[,] peas, vegetables, calves and pigs each had a share of his interest and in each line he was unusually successful. And the things that encouraged him most was when he saw that his two boys were growing. This fired his ambition for greater effort, as he knew they would soon be ready for college.

One of his families of share croppers had worked with Mr. Bond's step-father while Mr. Bond was quite a boy. The old man's name was Bill Thomas. Another man, named Albert Banks, with Thomas and Mr. Bond were picking cotton for Mr. Bond's step-father. The rumor got out that Mr. Bond's step-father was going to give up the farm they were working, and move to a farm he had bought. Old man Bill Thomas was tongue-tied, hence could not speak very plainly. The three were picking cotton, side by side in cotton taller than themselves. Bill Thomas said to Banks:

"Suppose you and I rent this big farm next year and hire Scott to feed horses and do chores, and we will grease his mouth every day with a 'eatskin (meaning meatskin)."

Scott remarked you had better learn how to talk and not say 'eatskin, 'eatskin.

It would make the old man exceeding angry for anyone to mock him, because he was tongue-tied. He grabbed his sack and leaped across the rows after Scott exclaiming: "You stinkin' booga! I'll lick you if it is the last thing I do!"

The cotton was higher than one's head on horse back. Scott was so small he could run under the cotton and out run the old man. He chased Scott for some time and finally gave up, saying to Scott, "I'll git yer."

Time rolled on and Scott grew to manhood and finally bought the farm where they had this controversy, and the old man, Bill Thomas came to Mr. Bond and offered to work on shares with him. Knowing he was a good hand and easy to get along with, his proposition was accepted. Mr. Bond fed all the hands out of his own smoke house.

One Saturday evening all of the people came up to the smoke house to get their weekly rations, and to use Mr. Bond's words again:

"I locked the door and started into the house. All had their meat and were sitting under a large shade tree in front of the smoke house. Old man Thomas called and said, 'Bond come back here.'"

"I turned and went back to see what he wanted."

He said: "Boys, listen and let me tell you something. Some five or six years ago, I chased that ere man you see standin thar all over dat ar cotton patch over yonder, for mocking me when I said I would grease his mouf wid a 'eatskin. Little did I think at dat time, dat some day he would be greasin my mouf and my wife's mouf and my child's mouf wid a 'eatskin and heres de 'eatskin under my arm."

SCOTT BOND PAYS HIS FIRST CASH RENT.

While money in one sense of the word is no more than chips, yet it has a great power. The first money I ever had in my hands to amount to anything was $1,250.00. This money was to pay the rent on the farm I had rented. I had paid out this amount for several successive years before that. But as it was the custom and habit in those days, the Negro would give the land owner an order to his merchant and the merchant would pay the rent.

Toward the last it appeared that my merchant and my landlord did not agree pleasantly, when she went to collect her rent. I had paid out seven or eight thousand dollars for rent by giving orders in this way. So my landlord wrote me a note, telling me to go and get the money and bring it over and pay it to her, and she would give me my rent note. I was very busy at the time and thought this was working a hardship on me. But seeing this was the proper thing to do, I saddled my horse and proceeded at once. I had to go six miles to get to the merchant, and then nine miles to the landlord.

The merchant asked why I did not give an order as I had been doing.

I replied: "You Dutchmen have insulted my landlord, and you know she don't have to come after it. It is my place to carry it to her, so get it out."

As I had money there to my credit of course they proceeded to count it out.

I had made thousands and thousands of dollars up to this time, but I had never allowed the money to go through my hands. My business had all been done through orders and checks.

When Mr. Block, my merchant counted out this money, there was $500 in bran[d] new $10 bills, $500 in $5 bills, pinned in two different packages, then $250 in $1 and $2 bills. He looked at me and said: "Here is your money."

I took the money and placed it in the inside pocket of my overcoat. This gave me a new idea of the difference between handling the money and handling orders. I used great precaution in buttoning up my overcoat, bounced into my saddle and rode off to my landlord. Once in a while I felt like hugging this money. After I had gone about two miles I stopped my horse in the road and said to myself. I must take this money out, look at it and count it.

Another thought came to me, that no, I must not do that, some highwayman might come along, see it and rob me. I rode off into the woods until I came to a log. I dismounted, tied my horse to a brush, went up to the log, pulled out my money, unpinned it and scattered it all up and down the log. After I had this money all scattered up and down the log, it seemed that I could not view the money standing right over it so I stepped back from it a piece and walked up and down by the log. I said, "This is product of labor of my own hand. Here is $1,250 which I am giving the landlord to let me cultivate her land." And at that point, when I could realize how hard I had strived and struggled, to make this money, and as far is I was concerned it was just like taking that much money casting it into the fire or throwing it into the well so far is any good it would do me. Then I could look and see what it was to own a farm.

Now when I looked ahead of me down the lane of time, seeing what a hill I had to pull, by way of educating my children and also buying a farm, I was compelled to shed a few tears. But I soon looked on the bright side and said, "Others have accomplished those things and so can I, and I said then and there if I live, some day I will have others bringing it to me this way." I can say today, if I would sit down and demand it, I could have more than ten times the amount brought to me for rents.

I gathered up my money. I was not able to get it in as neat a package as when I started from town with it. Off I went to my landlord.

The landlord of whom I speak and my mistress were first cousins. They frequently visited each other. I was a little servant boy. When my mistress would visit the lady of whom I speak, of course I would at meal times, take my meals in the kitchen with the other servants. When I reached there with this money, it was then I learned another new lesson in the difference between orders and real money.

It was a little after 11 o'clock when I arrived at the lady's front

Wheat shocked on side of field. Land being prepared for peas.

door. I pulled off my hat and laid it on the steps which was customary for Negroes at that time. I rang the door bell. Mrs. Allen came to the door and said good morning Uncle Scott, how do you do. Walk in. "I replied, howdy, I have come to bring you your money."

She said, "That is all right." I took out the money and placed it on the center table and asked her to please count it and if correct to give me my rent note.

This she did in a few minutes. The money was all right. She hunted up the rent note, marked it paid and handed it to me, and said "Scott, I am much obliged to you for the rent money and your promptness in paying same."

"Mrs. Allen you are perfectly welcome, but I realize the fact that I am the dependent party. I have no property of my own and I am the one that is much obliged."

I turned around and said good bye Mrs. Allen. She said no, no, you can't go home until you have dinner. You have to ride 7 miles and now it only a few minutes to 12 o'clock. Take this seat and sit down and I will go and see Maria and have her to rush dinner. She soon returned and got a chair and sat down and asked how was "Bunnie" (nick name for my wife) and the two boys.

Then she asked me hundreds of questions and entertained me in a way that I had never been entertained before in life. She was cultured and refined and had the ability to entertain any body.

In a little while she had the servant to bring a small table. They used nothing but linen table cloths, silver knives and forks, and napkins. The servant was sent to the pantry and set all sorts of preserves on this little table. Dinner was brought in and I was asked to sit up and eat dinner. Mrs. Allen said, "I will sit and entertain you while you eat."

I want to say that this was an unusually fine dinner for a man like me. I ate very heartily, but I could not really enjoy this wonderful dinner. My mind ran back to the time when I was glad to eat in the kitchen among the cook pots and slop buckets, and at the time enjoyed the meals in the kitchen better than I did the feast set before me by Mrs. Allen. Instead of enjoying my dinner, I took all my time to figure out what had brought about this great and wonderful change. Now to solve this problem and entertain Mrs. Allen all at the same time was quite a job for a fellow who was uneducated, but by the time I got through eating and entertaining Mrs. Allen I had worked out the problem; that was this, the $1,250 paid it all.

I mounted my horse and arrived at home about sun down. This day's trip caused me to look and see differently from what I had ever seen in all my life. After supper I sat down with my wife and talked the whole thing over. I said, "wife I am going tomorrow and buy 300 acres of land. I have learned today what it is to own a farm."

SCOTT BOND BUYS HIS FIRST FARM.

There was a man in Forrest City, a saloon keeper named Pritchard, who had offered me 300 acres of land and made me two propositions. One was $800 in two payments and the other $600 cash.

The next morning I got on my horse and started to Forrest City, eighteen miles from where I lived. I found Mr. Pritchard very busy, but walked up to him and said:

"Is the deal still open on the piece of land that you spoke of, 300 acres on the Little Rock and Memphis R. R., right close to Madison?["]

View on Stevens farm looking north.

He said, "Yes."

"I think I understood you to say that you would take $800 in two payments or $600 spot cash."

"Yes, that is what I said."

"I will be here Friday next with the money."

["]I suppose you will be ready to make me a deed on that date."

"Yes, that is a trade and I will be here."

I returned home that evening went to Wittsburg and told my merchants, R. and B. Block, that I wanted $400. They asked me when I wanted it. I told them I would call for it Thursday evening at 6 o'clock. At this time I walked in. Mr. Ralph Block[8] said to his partner:

"Ben here is Uncle Scott. He wants $400."

Mr. Ben Block said "What are you going to do with it."

I said: "I am going to buy a piece of land."

"How much will the land cost you?"

"Six hundred dollars."

Mr. Ralph Block said: "You told me you only wanted $400.["]

I said: "Yes, sir, but I have $200 in my pocket."

Mr. R. Block said: "How will this suit you, you give us your $200 and we will give you a check on M.Y. Myers, New Orleans, for $600."

"I said: That is all O. K., if that will answer the purpose."

I paid over the $200 and got the check for $600. Went to Forrest City the next day. Found Mr. Pritchard very busy in his saloon.

I stepped up to him and said: "I am ready for the deed."

He said: "Have you got the money?"

"Yes, sir."

All right I will go and see Mr. Wilson, J. P., and have him write the deed.

We walked over to the Justice's office.

"Mr. Wilson I want you to write a deed to this man, Scott Bond, for a piece of land that I own on the Little Rock R. R., close to Madison. Here is my deed from which you can get the description of the property."

"All right I will have the deed ready for you in a few minutes. But I want to know what is the consideration."

Mr. Pritchard said: "Let's see I made him two propositions, one was $800 in two payments, the other $600 cash, which one are you going to take?"

I told him I would take the one for $600 cash.

Mr. Wilson said all right and started writing.

Mr. Pritchard looked at me a few minutes and said: "Nigger I am very busy and I have no time for foolishness. I want to know if you have the money."

"Yes sir. I will hand you a check from R. and B. Block at Wittsburg, Ark., payable by M.Y. Myers and Co., N. O."

He took the check and looked at it and said, "Wilson what do you think of that?"

Mr. Wilson said, "R. and B. Block at Wittsburg are all right I know. M.Y. Myers at N. O., has a fine rating and I think the check is all O. K., but carry it down stairs, L. Rollwage and Co.[9] and they can give you the information you want."

Mr. Pritchard took the check to L. Rollwage and Co., and they told him the check was as good as gold and they would be glad to cash it for him as soon as it was in his possession.

In a little while, Mr. Wilson had finished the deed. After the deed was signed and the check paid over, my appearance showed a fel-

Near view of fruit farm.

low that lived away back in the sticks, had not been to the barber shop for some time. My hair was long, my clothing were patches. I had been working at the gin and was full of cotton and really looked pretty tough.

Mr. Pritchard looked at me and made an oath and said: "Nigger, where did you get all this money?"

"You can readily see from the check that I got it from R. and B. Block at Wittsburg."

"I want to know how you got the prestige to get that much money?"

"From the day that your action drove me from Mrs. Maloney's hotel, where I was a waiter boy, I have learned to realize that all the money, gold and silver has been dug from the bowels of the earth. I am glad to say to you that I made 156 bales of cotton last year and I will get something over 175 this year, so you can see where the Negro got the money from."

SALE OF THE ALLEN FARM.

The incidents of Mr. Bond's life are all very interesting, but perhaps none will portray the financial foresightedness and ready ability of the man more than the sale of the Allen Farm. First the method in making the sale, second the look ahead for breakers that in time of prosperity and general contentment would not be thought of by the ordinary mind.

The attempt to sell a bunch of cattle caused him to find a ready buyer for the Allen farm.

He was in partnership in this farm with Mr. T. O. Fitzpatrick and had been superintendent of the farm for four or five years for himself and Mr. Fitzpatrick. At this time Mr. Fitzpatrick was superintending the Allen farm for himself and Mr. Bond.

On a certain day Mr. Eugene Rolfe a prominent white gentleman who is now County Judge of St. Francis County, wanted to buy a bunch of cattle Mr. Bond had at that time running on the Allen farm. Mr. Bond says:

"I agreed to sell these cattle and the day was set to go and look at them. Mr. Rolfe and he went up in a two horse rig. This was about the middle of November."

Mr. Bond says: "To get to where the cattle were we had to pass a gin I had built but was then being operated by Mr. Fitzpatrick. Prior to this time Mr. Fitzpatrick had agreed to turn over to me twenty bales of cotton as my interest as rent on the farm that year. This was one of the most notable farms in the county at that time, being situated on the St. Francis river, where the military road, built by Gen. Jackson, crosses that stream. There was a ferry boat there to transfer people back and forth across the river. It contained 2,200 acres of the most fertile land in Eastern Arkansas.

As Mr. Rolfe and myself reached the gin I asked Mr. Rolfe to stop a minute, and shouted, hello. Mr. Fitzpatrick came out on the platform. I said, "Good morning Mr. Fitzpatrick.["] Mr. Rolfe said good morning also. I said, "what day shall I send my wagons for the cotton?"

He said: "I have 18 bales ready for you now and expect to gin the other two bales this evening, so you can send your wagons tomorrow morning."

"All right sir." Mr. Rolfe and I drove on. Mr. Fitzpatrick was one of the most noted and influential white citizens of the county, was a Republican and had been County Clerk for a number of years.

Laying by corn with cultivators.

Mr. Rolfe was also a very noted gentleman in the county, being honest and upright.

We had been boys together and threw rocks on the creek on Sundays. This grew into manhood friendship. Mr. Rolfe remarked to me: "Scott you ought to feel mighty grand."

"Why so, Mr. Rolfe?"

"Just think of you driving up to a steam gin and hailing a man like Mr. Fitzpatrick, who is finely educated, who has a reputation equal to any man in the county and also having a man like myself driving you in a double rig."

"Mr. Rolfe it is a long lane that never turns. You must realize that Mr. Fitzpatrick has used me this way for several years."

(At the same time I was on his bond for $5,000.)

"So far as you are concerned it would be a real pleasure to me to drive you or wait on you in any way."

We drove on up to what was known as the big house. There we unloaded and took it afoot all over the farm, hunting up the cattle, I had agreed to sell to Mr. Rolfe.

Mr. Fitzpatrick and Mr. Rolfe were friends morally and socially. Mr. Rolfe being a very shrewd trader, Mr. Fitzpatrick was somewhat shy of him along these lines. After we passed the gin, Mr. Fitzpatrick began to wonder what Scott and Rolfe were up to. So he sent a boy out on the farm to see what Mr. Rolfe and I were doing.

The boy returned to Mr. Fitzpatrick and told him he really could not tell what we were doing. He saw us go up the river bank and then along the levee, thence south to the old mill yard; that we had left the double rig at the big house and gone afoot.

Mr. Rolfe and I found all the cattle. I closed the deal and sold him the cattle. We both got into the rig and started back to Forrest City. As we passed the gin Mr. Fitzpatrick was out marking some cotton. We raised our hands and waved him good bye.

This was 18 miles from my home place. I arrived home about 7 o'clock, which at that season of the year is after dark. Wife as usual had a hot supper waiting for me.

Right here I want to say something that a very few men can say. My wife has never turned me out from home, regardless of the time of night, without a warm breakfast or waiting supper for my return, in all our forty years of married life.

About 9 o'clock that same evening I heard some one speak at the front gate.

I remarked to my wife that, "that is Mr. Fitzpatrick. I wonder what is the matter? I just left him about five hours ago on the Allen farm." I walked to the door and said, "Get down Mr. Fitzpatrick and come in. I have a good fire. I will have a boy unsaddle and put up your horse and feed him."

He walked in. I gave him a chair and he sat down by the fire.

"I am sure you have had no supper."

"No, but it is too late now to think of supper."

"Yes, but it is never too late for a hungry man to eat."

"Well, as you insist, I will have a snack, for your wife can cook the best biscuit I ever ate."

My wife got busy and then the conversation started.

"Now I see that you and Rolfe were today on the Allen farm looking over and inspecting the farm. I don't intend to have any-thing to do with Rolfe as a partner on the Allen Farm. It is a part of our contract that when either of us take a notion the other should have the refusal of buying, and I am here tonight to say to you that I demand that refusal."

Bird's eye view of Madison from "The Cedars."

I dropped my head and began to think that the time had presented itself for me to sell out to a good advantage. I had several times thought of selling, but had decided that it would be a hard matter to find a man with the cash money to buy.

Mr. Rolfe had never said anything to me about buying the Allen farm, nor had I said a word to him about selling the Allen farm. I thought for a few minutes, that it would not do to mislead Mr. Fitzpatrick as we had always been friends and on the other hand I did not feel guilty of doing so.

I raised my head and said, are you willing to buy?

"Well, yes. What do you want for your interest?"

"I want $5,000 all cash."

"That is really more cash than I have, but I am sure I can raise the balance provided that you take my note 90 days for $500."

["]I will be able to close the deal with you, Mr. Fitzpatrick I think by 9 o'clock tomorrow."

Now he said, "I am not going to have a thing to do with Rolfe."

"All right, the chances are we can get together at 9 o'clock and close the deal."

He had supper and remained all night at my house. Next

morning we were in town, and by this time I had figured the thing out clearly that this was the best chance for me to sell. I met Mr. Rolfe in town and he said, "I suppose our deal is all right," but he meant the cattle deal.

I remarked, "Yes that is all O. K."

This made Mr. Fitzpatrick more anxious to close the deal so he proposed to give me $100 as earnest money. He gave me a written description of the farm and the conditions of purchase and paid me the $100 earnest money, and allowed himself 10 days to get the deed ready.

This I said to myself is all right. "Mr. Fitzpatrick I want you to know that I really believe that we could get along as partners in this farm for forty years, but as you have boys and I have boys, after our days, the boys might not get along as well as we have. For that cause I think this is the proper thing to do."

When the ten days had passed the deed was ready and the money paid over. I took the same money and bought seven other farms and added to the three hundred acres I had at Madison. This gave me a large and beautiful farm. These farms were fresher and hence far more fertile than the one I had sold to Mr. Fitzpatrick.

A CROP OF ARTICHOKES.

At the time of the aforementioned incidents I was living on a farm, which I had bought near Forrest City known as the Neely farm. It was also known as a fine fruit farm. The land being upland was of a poor nature. I bought the farm mainly on account of the health of my wife and children. I paid old man Neely $900 for 120 acres. This farm was two and a half miles from my main bottom farm. After moving on the Neely place and getting straight, looking over the farm and finding that the land was far from fertile, I decided to sow the whole farm in peas, knowing peas were a legume and hence fine to put life in the soil. I excepted several small spots that I planted in corn. I got a fine stand of peas, and looked as if I would make worlds of pea hay. When the peas were ripe I took my mower and rake to harvest my hay crop. This was the first time I had undertaken to cultivate this class of land. I prepared to house the hay and after the hay was cut and raked, I only got one-tenth of the amount of hay I

View of Fishing Lake Farm.

counted on. I prepared the land that fall and sowed it down in clover.
I got a fine stand. The clover grew and did well. The next year I took
two four horse wagons and hauled from the Allen farm large loads
of defective cotton seed. I turned all this under and planted the land
the next year in corn. I made and gathered a large corn crop that year.
I was at that time taking a paper known as the "Home and Farm." I
would usually sit at night and read my farm paper and entertain my
wife, while she was sewing. I read an article, where a party in Illinois
had claimed that he had gathered 900 bushels of artichokes from one
acre of land. That did not look reasonable to me at that time. I said
to my wife: "Listen what a mistake this fellow has made. He claims
to have gathered 900 bushels of artichokes from one acre of land."
This seemed impossible to me.

In the next issue of this paper, I read where another man claimed
to have raised 1,100 bushels to the acre. This put me at a further
wonder as to the artichoke crop. I decided to try a crop of artichokes. I had a very nice spot of land that I thought would suit for
this purpose. I prepared it as I would prepare land for Irish potatoes,
knowing that artichokes were, like the Irish potato a tuber. I took
a four horse wagon and hauled one and a half tons of rotten cotton

seed put a big double handful every 18 inches apart in the drill, then dropped the artichokes between the hills. I cultivated first as I would Irish potatoes. The plants grew luxuriantly and were all the way from 8 to 12 feet tall.

About the 10th of August I noticed the plants were blooming it occurred to me that there must be artichokes on the roots. I got my spade and began to dig. I could not find a single artichoke. I took my spade back home and decided within myself that both parties were mistaken when they claimed to have grown so many hundreds of bushels to the acre. After a few days I went to my lower farm and started picking cotton, and was busy as busy could be all that fall gathering and housing my cotton crop as usual.

Just before Christmas I promised my wife that I would be at home on Christmas Eve in order to accompany her to our church conference. I was on time according to my promise, helped her to get her household affairs straight and the children settled. I had bought my wife a beautiful cape. She took the cape, I took my overcoat and off we went. In order to take a near route we decided to climb the fence and go through the artichoke patch. As we had none of the children along and I helping her over the fence, made me recall our old days when we were courting. I remarked to her:

"Gee whiz wife, you certainly look good under that cape!"

She said: "Do you think so?"

"Yes, I have always thought that you looked good."

By this time we had gotten to the middle of the artichoke patch. I grabbed an artichoke stalk and tried to pull it up. I made one or two surges and it failed too [*sic*] come, but in bending it over I found a great number of artichokes attached to the tap root. I asked my wife to wait a few minutes. She asked me what I was going to do. I told her I would run back and get the grubbing hoe and see what is under these artichokes. She said, "don't this beat the band? Stop on your way to church to go to digging artichokes."

"All right I will be back in a few minutes."

I came with my grubbing hoe and went to work. I dug on all sides of the stalk, then raised it up. I believe I am safe in saying there was a half bushel of artichokes on the roots of this stalk. I then noticed that the dirt in the drills, the sides of the rows and the middles were all puffed up. One could not stick the end of his finger in

Bird's eye view of fruit farm.

the ground without touching an artichoke. I found that the whole earth was matted with artichokes. And really believe that had I had a full acre in and could have gathered all the artichokes, I would have gotten at least 1,500 bushels of artichokes.

I told my wife that now I could see that those people had told the truth when they said they had gathered 900 and 1100 bushels to the acre.

When I returned from church, I at once turned my hogs into the artichoke patch. I then climbed up on the fence and took a seat to watch the hogs root and crush artichokes. I looked around and saw my clover had made a success, the little artichoke patch had turned out wonderfully. The little poor farm, I said to myself: "Just think of millions and millions of dollars deposited in all of these lands both rich and poor soils. And just to think how easy this money could be obtained if one would think right and hustle."

SCOTT BOND SWAPS FISH FOR MEAT.

He said to the writer:
The first time I ever undertook to make a crop for myself and

manage it, I had an experience that has been a lesson to me all through life.

I did not own a horse but my aunt owned a little pony and she loaned him to me.

I secured a piece of land. I had no money to start with.

I sold a gold ring for which I had swapped a pig, for $5.00. With this I bought twenty pounds of meat and three bushels of meal.

I prepared the land and planted it. I then secured a trot line and set it. I would feed my horse as soon as I got up in the morning. Then I would run my trotline, take off the fish and re-bait the hooks. This task would be completed before sun-up. I would put the fish in a slatted box in the river. At noon when I came from the field I would go through the same process. In the evening this would be repeated. By Saturday I would have a nice lot of fish. These I would take out and sell.

I was too small to fill my sacks and put them on my horse, so I got two cotton seed bags and fastened them together. I put one fish in each bag and threw them across my saddle. I would then put a fish in one bag and go around my horse and put one in the other bag, continuing in this way until I had all my horse could carry. I would lead him along the road and dispose of my fish.

Sometimes a customer would have no money and would swap me eggs for fish. Another would give me a chicken for a fish. These I would leave until on my return home. Many of my neighbors passing along the road on the way home from town would trade me a piece of meat for a fish. I never refused a trade. Meat then selling for twenty-two and twenty-three cents a pound. In this way, when I reached home on Saturday night, I would have enough meat, eggs and chickens to do my aunt's family for a week or two: besides some little money to pay the blacksmith and buy other things.

Times were very hard that year. Corn sold for $1.75 a bushel. There had been a drought, and everything was literally parched. Hence meat and everything else was unusually high.

A quart of corn was my pony's noon feed. While he was eating I made it my business to keep the chickens away and pick the grains from the cracks with a little stick, that he should get every grain.

I made and gathered the crop without making a cent of debt; paid my rent and cleared $200.00 in money.

BRICK FOR ALLEN FARM.

The year I bought the Allen farm, Mr. Fitzpatrick and myself in partnership, and knowing that we had to build houses with brick chimneys, these brick had to be bought and hauled eighteen or nineteen miles, which would make the hauling cost as much as the brick. So I decided to burn a brick kiln on that farm. Mr. Fitzpatrick refused to do so, claiming that the soil would not make brick, and furthermore he was not willing to risk his money on my judgment in burning brick.

"Now this is all right Mr. Fitzpatrick, but this will not change my decision. I intend to make and burn this kiln at my own expense. When they are burned and proved to be O. K. I expect to charge Fitzpatrick and Bond the customary price for the brick at the kiln plus what the hauling would be from Forrest City, which will be about $18.00 per M. I really believe Mr. Fitzpatrick that if soil will make brick for one man, with the same precaution and attention, it will make brick for the other man. There are signs of brick that were burned on that farm forty years ago and they are as fine brick as I ever saw.["]

With the experience I have as a brick man now, I am sure I can make and burn as good brick as anybody. So I bought my wheelbarrows, sent down to my home place and got my old brick molds, wrote to Kerr Station again for Mr. Brown. I did not hire Mr. Brown, because I did not understand the brick business myself. It was because I had so much other business to look after that it was impossible for me to be there at all times.

I learned one thing when I was quite young, and that was, at any time when a black man applied art and skill to things with proper precaution, he would get the same results that a white man could get. I have found this to be true all along the lane of time.

We made and burned 125,000 brick. Mr. Fitzpatrick came up just as we were ready to fire the kiln, and said: "You may charge me up with one-half of all these expenses. I see that you are a better brick man than I had any idea that you were."

"No, Mr. Fitzpatrick you can't afford to trust your money against my judgment, so I have decided to take all the risk and keep all the profits."

"Yes, but I have other farms joining this farm on which I will need a large number of brick."

"Yes, you are right about that, but that will just make my profit the larger."

Of course all this was said in a joking way, because I felt that I had already been paid. Whenever I could strike a man and surprise him as to my ability, I always felt that that alone was big pay. We completed our kiln, got a fine burn and Mr. Fitzpatrick said the brick was as good as he had ever seen burned. We repaired all the old chimneys on the place and put up chimneys to fourteen new houses. Furnished Mr. Fitzpatrick all the brick he needed for his other places and had a few to sell the neighbors.

BUYS BACK OLD HOME.

At this time opportunity had presented itself by which I would buy back the old home place, situated on an eminence on the east side of Crowley's Ridge, overlooking Madison; giving a fine view of the St. Francis river and the Rock Island R. R., a nice dry healthy place surrounded by a nice garden and orchard. This was the second place I had ever bought. I paid $975.00 for it. This was deeded to my wife. A party came to see me and wanted to buy the place. I told him it belonged to my wife and I had promised her I would never ask her to sell it. The man offered me $1,150 for the place.

Wife heard of this conversation and said to me: "I would be glad if you would sell the place as I want to be with you every day in the week and I will have you to move me down on the farm with you."

I sold the place for $1,150 and moved my wife and children on to the river farm. We soon found that this was not healthy for either my wife or children. This compelled me to buy the Neely farm in order to conserve their health.

The man to whom I had sold was a white man and unfortunately for him he had gotten into trouble and was in jail. This man sent his brother-in-law to me to sell the old farm back to me. "I said to the gentleman, I own the Neely farm which is about 120 acres and that is enough grave yard land for one man to own, I don't think I really need the old farm back.["] The gentleman came back the next day

View of Section Twelve on Military Road.

and told me that his brother-in-law was in jail and in trouble and was compelled to raise some money, and if I would give him $550 that he and his wife would deed me the farm. I said: "I will let you know tomorrow morning.["] We were then living on the Neely farm. I talked the matter over that night with my wife and asked her what she thought of the trade. She said: "It is all up to you."

"Wife I believe it is a good bargain that will put us back on our old home place one and a half miles closer to our farms in the bottom, which will be much more convenient all the way round, as we will be able to stand on our porch and view our many farms in the bottoms, and we will really be making money in the deal. We are getting back a place that we got $1,150 for, for $550, and it really suits us better than the farm we are now living on.["]

The next morning the gentleman was on hand. I told him all right, I will pay you the $550 as soon as you make me a deed to the place. This seemed to please him very much. The deed was soon prepared and the money paid over.

I then went to work and had the house rebuilt, gardens and barn repaired, set out new orchard and today it is a lovely old farm and we have named it "Cedar Hill."

In the summer time wife and I often sit on the front porch and view the lovely landscape, stretched out before us to the east with the beautiful St. Francis river flowing like a silver ribbon for miles through the valley at our feet, the mountainous, verdure clad hills to the north, with our sheep, our pigs, our chickens, our cattle and other domestic animals about the place. Then look back over the road we have traveled and think of the time when as a boy I worked on this same place for 20 cents a day, ate what I could get in the kitchen and we sing the song, "Home, home, sweet home."

It must be remembered that all this time, my children, who were large enough were in school, the older ones in college. When they left home for college at Nashville, Tenn., we were living on the Neely farm. The houses on that place were typical southern cabins built of logs with open shutters for windows, the cracks chinked with puncheons and mud. When the boys returned from school, the following spring, they had not been informed of me buying back the McMurry place and started from the depot to the Neely farm, from which they left when going to Nashville. They met a man named Dick Sanford who had been working for me for years.

Dick said: "Hello boys, where are you going? You are going the wrong way. Your pa has bought back the old McMurry farm and has had all the old buildings torn down, rebuilt and painted and one would hardly know the old place."

The boys said: "This is really too good to be true, but as it is not far out of our way we will go by and see."

When they got in sight of the old home, Waverly looked and saw the house and said to Theo: "This really can't be true. See how pretty that house looks."

Theo said: "Yes, I see one of ma's quilts hanging in the back yard."

They both walked up to the front gate and stopped and looked with amazement. This is true because there is ma singing, back in the kitchen.

As they stepped on the porch, one said, yes, it is all right for I see the crib that we were all rocked in. They found their baby brother lying in the crib asleep. Theo picked up the baby. This awakened him and he began to cry. Wife ran to see what was the matter with the baby and behold there stood Theo and Waverly. Howdy mamma, howdy, howdy. How is pa and the rest of the children?

FROM SLAVERY TO WEALTH

At Tuskegee breeding farm.

"Ma, what in the world has happened? How did pa manage to get the old home place back?"

She replied: "I don't know. You know your pa is all the way around a great man and he has done many things that have been a mystery to me."

"Ma we are really proud to be back to our old home and see it so beautifully fixed up. I don't see why pa did not write and tell us of all these things that were happening."

"Your pa has always had a way of doing things in order to surprise us."

We had supper unusually early that evening and then I asked the children hundreds of things about college, their teachers and the progress of the school.

SHOWS BOYS THE NEW STORE.

I had bought out a firm known as the Madison Mercantile Co., the same year, all of this unknown to the children. Next morning bright and early we had breakfast and I said boys let's walk down town. I had not yet told them that we owned a store in town. We got into Madison and walked into the store. They saw their uncle in the store acting as though he was general manager, and also a young man named Ben Posey, who had been with me for years. These two were in charge of the store. This was the first and only Negro store that had ever been in Madison. The boys could not really understand what all this meant. They came to me and said quietly: "Pa whose store is this?"

"Why it is our store, yours and mine. It is ours. Not one but all of us."

This was another great surprise to the boys. It was not long until they were behind the counters and really all over the store. They finally said to me, "Pa is this true? Is this really our store?"

"It is true. It is really our store. Now if we will all take care of this store and look after things it will remain our store. If we don't do that, it will eventually belong to some one else. You can see now boys there is work for all of us to do."

I had at that time 24 or 25 families on my different farms, but had not attempted to furnish the families out of my store. The stock at this time only amounted to $700 or $800.

Waverly said: "Pa this is all O. K., we can put in $8,000, or $10,000 [worth of] stock and then we will be able to furnish all the people on our many farms."

"No son that won't do now. We must first learn how to buy goods and then learn how to sell goods, and also learn how to keep books. Your pa can correct a mistake of seven or eight cents easier than he can correct a mistake of $8,000 or $10,000."

"Pa, there is no excuse for mistakes."

"No son you are right. There is no excuse for mistakes, but there have always been mistakes made.

"You say that you have taken bookkeeping, but you will soon find out that taking bookkeeping is one thing and keeping books is another."

We dragged along in the mercantile business the next year until the boys finished up at college and came home. It was then we began to furnish the people on our different farms, and went more extensively into the mercantile business. I said then and there to the boys now for mistakes and vexation.

"The first thing that must be understood is this; our intention is

Scott Bond in orchard at Tuskegee with G. A. Bridgeforth.

to be honest and upright with all with whom we come in contact, in a business way. When you weigh a man out a pound of anything be sure to give him full 16 ounces. Then you must collect for 16 ounces. We are all comparatively green in the mercantile business and we must make as few mistakes as possible.["] I was sure mistakes would be made, although the boys said there was no excuse for mistakes and that they were not going to make any. I was uneducated so far as letters and figures were concerned, yet I was educated so far as books were concerned. I began to keep up with the books and could see mistakes being made every day, and would call the boy and say: "How is this?" He knowing that I was uneducated would always have a nice way covering his mistake by saying thus and so is the case. Yet no argument he could produce would change my decision. And I would say to him son I told you these things would happen.

He would say in a careless way, "Pa, this is all right, but I just failed to charge John and credit Harry."

"Son that is right, that is what we call a mistake."

That spring we bought our dry goods from Wm. R. Moore and Co., a large wholesale house in Memphis. These goods were bought on 30 and 60 days time, which was considered cash. In 30 days one-half of the bill was due. This was the 30 day goods.

The boy said: "Pa we owe Wm. R. Moore and Co., a bill of $900 and over."

"All right son write him a check for it and I will sign it."

He wrote the check and laid it on the desk for my signature, the same was mailed to Wm. R. Moore and Co., He gave that firm debit for this check. At the end of 30 days more the balance was due. He called my attention to this saying the other bill we owe Wm. R. Moore is due. I said: "All right son, turn and see what you owe them in full. He turned to the account and saw that it was something over $1,800. He sat down and wrote a check for the whole $1,800 put it on the desk for my signature. This was early in the morning and my horse was standing saddled at the door and I was in a rush to get to my farm. I grabbed the pen and signed the check without viewing the same. Some time in the day while I was down on the potato farm it occurred to me that the boy might have made a mistake and wrote a check for the whole amount. I was on my way home, went by the store got down and went in. I turned to Wm. R. Moore's account and then reached and got the check book. I soon saw that he had paid Wm. R. Moore and Co., $900 too much. I called the boy and said, look what you have done. You have paid Wm. R. Moore and Co., nine hundred and odd dollars more than you owed them. Now what do you call this? Is it one of the mistakes that we spoke of so often? No pa this is an oversight."

I found this was the hardest hill I had to pull. That was to get the boy to agree that these were mistakes. He would always disagree with me and say these were not mistakes.

"Well you let it be what it may, I know we are out of over $900 that we really ought to have."

I could see that the boy was really outdone. I closed the books and walked to the door. It was about sun down. The boy came to me and said, "Pa what shall we do about that?"

"Now son, I ought really to ask you. You are the bookkeeper, been to college and claimed at the start that there was no excuse for mistakes. The thing is for me to ask you what shall we do?"

"Well," he said, "I don't know what to do." He looked really pale.

Scott Bond on the Tuskegee truck farm with Mr. Bridgeforth.

I mounted my horse and went on home, had supper, talked for a while to my wife and retired.

After we had retired, I said [to my] wife, "Waverly has made a mistake of $930."

She raised up in the bed and said, "He has? How did it happen?"

"He paid one man $930 more than he owed him."

She jumped up, went to the fire and began to dress. I asked her what she was doing.

"I am putting on my clothes."

"What for?"

"I am going down to the store."

"Well, what can you do when you get there?"

"Didn't you say he had made a mistake of $930?"

"Yes, but how are you going to correct it when you get there?"

The fire was burning brightly and she continued to dress. I told her to undress and get back into bed. She asked what I was going to do about the mistake. I told her I would correct the mistake. This satisfied her, she undressed and went to bed again. She finally said to me after being in bed for some time:

"Is not that boy very much worried over the mistake?"

"He is certainly worried over the mistake."

"You get up right now and go down and ease his mind."

"No, you just let him wallow and worry. I have struggled and worried to make the $900, and also to educate him. So now let him wrestle and worry to hold it."

We finally went to sleep. Next morning as usual my wife was up and had breakfast on time and followed me to the front gate where I got on my horse put her arms around my neck, kissed me and said: "Will you please go by the store and relieve that boy's mind this morning?"

"Yes for your sake, I will do so."

I arrived at the store, dismounted and walked in. The boy said: "Good morning pa."

"Good morning son."

I walked up to the desk and said son get a blank sight draft. Draw a sight draft on Wm. R. Moore and Co., for the difference between what you owed them and what you paid them.

The boy said, "Pa do you think this will get the $900?"

"I do not have to think about that[,] I know it."

This looked as though there had been a dark cloud wiped from the boy's face.

This and a good many other things that I have done along these lines almost ruined him. Because he thought that no matter how difficult the business problem I would be able to solve it satisfactorily. It really took from him his self-reliance and originality and encouraged him to rely upon me rather than upon himself.

As I have before told you I purchased the business of the Madison Mercantile Co., and up to this time had been doing business in a rented house. Mr. Walter Gorman who was one of the principal owners and also manager of the business at that time, met me one morning and insisted on me buying out his business.

I said: "No, Mr. Gorman, in the first place I have not the ability and am not prepared financially to handle a store."

He said: "Uncle Scott your boys will be graduated next spring and you will have a business prepared and can put them to work for you instead of putting them to work for some one else, and after you get rated in the commercial world you will be surprised to know how much cheaper you can buy the farming implements and

Visiting poultry yard at Tuskegee with Mr. Bridgeforth.

supplies you use on your many farms. Besides a man like you can not afford to spend thousands of dollars educating children in college and then bring them home and force them to take a ten dollar job. I will take an invoice and sell the goods at wholesale prices with a discount of 10 per cent which will amount to about $550 or $560, and will take as many notes for the stock of goods as you want and date them to suit yourself.["]

I realized that this would be a nice deal for me and hence I agreed to take the store. The stock invoiced $560. It was discounted 10 per cent of the cost price and when Mr. Gorman went to draw the notes he asked how many notes I wanted and how I wanted them dated?

I told him all in one note and make it payable July 10th.

"Why Uncle Scott you won't be selling any cotton by that time. I will extend this note as far ahead as you want it."

"That is all right, I have a potato crop and I will have it on the market by July 10th and will be prepared to take care of the note by that time."

This was like opening the door and entering into mercantile business without a dollar in the world. I owned no property in

Madison at that time and was then paying rent on the house in which I was doing business.

I succeeded in growing and marketing my potato crop. I cleared on the crop about $1,800 which I considered a little side issue to my other crops. I met the note and paid it promptly and had my mind made up that I would go to Memphis and buy a fresh stock of groceries and recruit the business. At this time I saw an article in our county paper, stating that Scott Bond had bought out the Madison Mercantile Co., and gone into the mercantile business.

I met the gentleman with whom I had been doing business for 20 years, Mr. Louis Rollwage and Co. He said:

"I see you have gone into the mercantile business."

"Yes sir, and what do you think of it?"

Mr. Rollwage stopped a few minutes and said:

"Uncle Scott, I believe the right man has struck the right thing. I have noticed you for all the many years of our past careers. You seem to have the ability to reason from one thing to another and you are one of the most considerate men I have ever met. For this reason and many others I really believe you will be successful in the mercantile business and at any time I can serve you in any way I will be more than glad to do so.["]

I was somewhat surprised at these remarks, knowing of the many thousands of dollars of transactions between us, he being a merchant and I a farmer, I really had expected to be advised differently, but said, "all right Mr. Rollwage I appreciate your kindness along these lines. I shall go to Memphis in the next few days in order to try to increase my little stock of groceries. I have the money to pay for them but really want you to advise me who is best to deal with, as I do not want to go there and fall into the hands of thieves, the first dash out of the box."

"I will be more than glad to do so," he replied. "When you get ready, let me know and I will go over with you."

"I thank you sir. I will certainly appreciate that."

The next day or two the porter was handling a keg of powder in Rollwage's store and unfortunately this keg by some means exploded, and Mr. Rollwage's son was badly injured. For that reason he was unable to go with me. He gave me two letters of recommendation, one to Mansfield Drug Co., as all little country stores

Scott Bond and Mr. Bridgeforth inspecting Tuskegee's prize jack.

at that time carried a per cent of their stock in medicines, and a letter to Messrs. M. Gavan and Co., who were large wholesale grocers
in Memphis.

I went into their place of business in Memphis and said, "I want
to see the boss," and when I was introduced to him, "Mr. Gavan,
this is Bond from Arkansas."

"Walk around Mr. Bond and take a seat."

I walked in and sat down and then he began asking questions. It
looked to me as though that he was a very large man and stuffed
full of questions.

I reached in my pocket and handed him the letter from Mr.
Rollwage, which he opened and read. He then said:

"I see that you are a colored man."

"No sir, Mr. Gavan, I am proud to say that I am not a colored
man, but I am a Negro. I am always proud of the word Negro, but
ashamed of the word colored man."

Mr. Gavan said: "That is the reverse of what most of the colored
people think and believe, but you are correct in saying what you
have."

"You see that door there Mr. Bond?"

I said "Yes sir," and thought to myself that as we had just finished discussing the word colored man and Negro that the next would be get out of that door, but to my surprise, Mr. Gavan said, from my many years doing business at this place, there has never been a man walked in that door who held a better recommendation than I now hold in my hand.

"Listen what he says:" 'You may sell him anything that he may want and as much as he wants and L. Rollwage and Co., will be responsible for his transactions.'"

"Mr. Bond: There have but few men come to me with this kind of a recommendation since I have been in business. You must really be a great man, or this kind of a recommendation would never have been handed you."

"Mr. Gavan, I have always made it a rule to go in the front door with everybody with whom I have done business. That is to always be honest, tell the truth along all business lines regardless of results. I have just bought out a little mercantile business at Madison. I am over here to buy a fresh stock of groceries to fill out our business. I have the money to pay for what I expect to buy, but I am surprised at the reputation given me by L. Rollwage and Co. Not as to my honesty along business lines but as to the ability that Mr. Rollwage has commended me for."

Then Mr. Gavan sat down and gave me some of the finest instructions I had ever heard fall from a gentleman's lips, relating to general business transactions. I had found out long ago that such information as he was imparting was of great benefit to those who received it and cultivated the spirit it called up.

To my surprise Mr. Gavan himself waited on me and advised me what to buy and how to buy.

I bought my goods and returned home. I met Mr. Rollwage a few days later, and he wanted to know how I got along. I told him very nicely but was very much surprised.

"In what way?" he asked.

"In the recommendation you gave me to M. Gavan and Co., I was not surprised at the information you gave them as to my honesty, but was surprised at the confidence you had in my ability to buy a stock of goods.["]

He said: "In the first place I knew you were all right Uncle Scott and in the second place the gentleman to whom I commended you I knew would advise you along the right lines."

"He certainly did and I believe he is one of the greatest men of the kind I have ever met."

SCOTT BOND VISITS NASHVILLE, TENN.

I want to stop here for a minute and compliment L. Rollwage and Co. for the many and really great things they did for me through a long course of years.

I really felt that I owed them for the education of my children. For, several times when my children were off at school, my financial way looked so dark and gloomy that I felt at many times that my finances were at such a low ebb that I would have to bring them home, and when Mr. Louis Rollwage would find this out, he would always say, "Don't stop your children from school. If you do you will nip their education in the bud."

I want you to know for your many years dealing with me you have helped me to make my business what it is now, and you must feel that as long as L. Rollwage and Co., have two dollars one dollar of this is yours.

I will never forget the time my boy was to graduate from Roger Williams University at Nashville, and at the same time the Centennial [1897] was going on in that city my son Theophilus wrote me a very interesting letter stating that he was "to graduate and you will not be able to see me graduate here again, and you can come now and go back on half fare and also see the Centennial something you will never see here again, I do think that if you can possibly get off it will certainly be the thing for you to do. And I will be so proud for you to see me graduate."

I got this letter while I was in town and blundered over it two or three times and was not able to thoroughly understand the meaning of his letter. So while I was in L. Rollwage and Co.'s office, he read the letter to me intelligently and explained all its points clearly, and said he was sure I would have a nice time.

I said: "Mr. Rollwage, you don't think for a minute I am going to Nashville?"

He said, "I don't see how you can refuse."

Mrs. Manning,[10] who was a lady of rare culture and refinement said:"Why Uncle Scott, what in the world are you living for? The very idea of seeing a boy like Theophilus graduate is a great thing within itself. He is one of the finest boys I ever saw."

"In the second place you go and come on half fare."

"In the third place you will get to see the Centennial, something that will not occur there again in 100 years."

I told Mrs. Manning that what she said was all true, but it had taken every dollar that I could rake and scrape to keep my children in school, and the overflow has just come and gone and my crops have all been planted and are coming up nicely; I have a good stand and all worked out and I am rushed for time to repair my fences and to take care of my crop. I have no money to go on, nor have I a suit of clothes fit to wear to Nashville.

Mr. Louis Rollwage said:"Go and fit the best suit of clothes you can find in stock, and if they can't be found here go out in town and look until you do find one. Now I mean shoes, stockings, shirt, coat, pants and necktie. And Mrs. Manning hand him $65.00 and if you have not got it write him a check for it. Now we will make you a present of the suit of clothes out and out and will charge you with the $65.00 until next fall, without interest. If this is not satisfactory we will make you a present of the $65.00. Scott, this will be one of the greatest events of your life." And so it was. I went to the barber shop and got my hair cut and a shave, put on my new suit and lit out for Nashville.

Up to this time I had never seen the inside of a college. I had a fair idea as to how to meet and salute those with whom I came in contact. And when I arrived at Roger Williams [University] in Nashville, I had the pleasure of meeting all the faculty. Among whom were Prof. John Hope[11] and Hon. Wm. Harrison who is now a noted lawyer at Oklahoma City, and many young men students from all parts of the United States.

This was a great happiness to my son, Theophilus. He took great pleasure in introducing me to his many friends in the city of Nashville and to see the great Centennial, then being in full swing, which was the biggest thing of the kind I had ever seen. It then occurred to me that I would not have missed this for anything.

The ensuing year I had a chance to buy four lots in the heart of

Scott Bond's blacksmith shop.

Madison, and two small buildings on these lots for which I paid $500. One of those buildings had been used by Mr. Devine as a small store, I added another store on this building 38 feet wide and 40 feet long. I then moved out of the rented store into my own building in order to stop paying rent. I enlarged my stock and then began to furnish my many farms.

It was then that I learned the difference between buying farming implements from wholesale dealers and jobbers. My mercantile business at that time seemed to be a perfect success. Our trade was made up from all classes, both white and black. My object was to keep a clean house, morally and otherwise. By so doing I demanded the trade of the best people of the community. In a short time I was recognized by all my competitors as a live wire in the mercantile business.

BUYS HALF SECTION.

Perhaps the wonderful increase in the value of land in the St. Francis basin can be shown in no way better than the following story which we will let Scott Bond tell in his own inimitable way:

"I bought half of section 12, 320 acres at a tax sale for $16.50. I did not know where the land was nor what I had bought. Three or four months after I had bought the land a gentleman came to see me for the purpose of purchasing the land. I asked him what he was willing to pay for it. He said he thought $125.00 a good price.

"That was so much more than I had paid for it that I began to wonder just what I had bought.

"I told the man that I could not say on the spur of the moment what I would take for it, that I would go in a few days and view the land and would then likely be in position to give him an answer."

"A few weeks later another white man asked what I would take for the land."

"I asked him what he really thought the land to be worth."

"He said: 'Uncle Scott, I think $250 would be a good price for it.' This put me to thinking. I had as yet never seen the land. Now if the first gentleman had said, "I will give you $125 or $150 for the whole thing," I am sure I would have closed out with him. I paused a few minutes and said to myself: 'I certainly have bought a piece of land that is worth something.'"

"I informed the gentleman I did not care to sell it. I was very busy farming and did not, for the time being pay any more attention to the land."

"An overflow came the next year. There was a noted timber man in this part of the country at that time named Capt. Stearns.[12] He came and said he would like to cut some timber in my brake. He offered me $1.00 per 1,000 feet stumpage. I agreed to this. He put three men in the brake while the overflow was on when the timber was cut and floated out, and the water had fallen, Capt. Stearns paid me $225 for stumpage. I had as yet never seen the land.

"Two years later came another overflow, Capt. Stearns said to me: 'I want to make you some more money.'"

"I agreed that year, he cut and floated out timber. My stumpage came to $350.

"Three years later we had another overflow. I happened to meet Capt. Stearns on the train. He came and sat in the seat with me and said to me: 'There is going to be another big water and I hope to make you some more money.'

Scott Bond making a start in life.

"I replied, 'No Captain, I think I will go and cut the timber myself.'"

He asked me if I had ever cut and floated any timber?

"No sir, and I never saw a man stand in a boat and cut a tree in my life, and never saw a log floated in the brake."

"Capt. Stearns said: 'Now I have made money for you from time to time, right along. You are going into the swamps with a lot of inexperienced Negroes, and without experience yourself, you are going to loose all the money I have made for you from time to time and more on top of that. Now you can stay at home and sit down and make $400 or $500 where you are going to loose maybe twice that amount.'"

"Captain, why do you say this, I asked?"

"Because you don't know how to do it."

"Well Captain, I asked, how does a man learn to do things?"

"Go at it and try," he said.

"Well Captain, that is just what I am going to do; go at it and try. But if you will give me one experienced man to go along with me, I will give you half after all expenses are taken out."

He refused to do this. So bull dog like, I gripped my nerve, went to work got nine dugouts, hired nine men, telegraphed for two tents, axes, saws and complete outfit for sawing timber, including provisions enough to last a month.

Among the men that I hired there was one little Negro in the bunch named Sambo, who had large experience in cutting and rafting timber. When we all had our dugouts packed, I made my own paddle and each fellow followed suit. There was making and preparing spike poles. Each one had his own boat and when all were packed and ready to start to the swamp, I called the attention of the whole crowd and said, now Sambo, stand up on that log.

"Now boys, said I this little fellow is the captain of the whole squad. There shall not be a man in the whole crew who will be any more obedient, or honor him, more than I shall do myself. I am paying him $3.50 per day, while I am paying the balance of you $2.50. Whatever he says, right or wrong must be done by all of us. We then pulled out on our long journey to the swamp. We camped that night in an old house on the river bank. Next morning, Sambo rushed us into the brake. The water had just begun to come into the brake. Sambo took us all and said he wanted ten of the largest trees felled and sawed off 60 and 70 feet long. The water was coming in the brake so fast that we were compelled to use the stumps of the trees we had cut, to put our bedding and other camp equipage on to keep them dry. By this time we had water enough to float the logs we had cut. Sambo gave orders to get them together as quickly as possible. At the same time we put hands to cutting splicing. By dark all these were cribbed and toggled together, as we could not see to do anything else, we put our camp equipage and the dugouts on the raft and set up our cook stove. We managed to get supper and each fellow slept in his own dugout, all of which were placed side by side. The tent cloth was used as one quilt to cover the whole. All these orders were given by Sambo the great.

"After supper, I looked around and said to myself, "This is one of the greatest events of my life.'"

"We had a jolly crowd. All the work appeared to be perfect fun to me and the crew."

"We saw when we went to bed that the water was rising rapidly. Next morning, when we awakened, we found our new home on the raft was five feet higher than when we went to bed. We were

Miss Chism, milking.

able to float our raft over the stumps we had cut the day before. We had breakfast on time and by 10 o'clock you could hear trees falling in all directions.

Sambo's orders were for every cutter to be at least 100 yards from any other, in order to prevent accidents from falling timber and limbs. When we went to dinner we found the cook ready. Navy beans, onions, potatoes, bread and meat. I looked at my little band and realized the fact Sambo was capable—fully able to manage the situation, but for myself I caught it just after dinner.

"We had about 15 logs ready for floating. Sambo had given all the boys spike poles, and showed them how to float logs. He said to me: 'Mr. Bond, get your dugout and spike pole and come with me.'"

Recognizing him as our captain, I obeyed at once. He took me up to a fine cypress log and instructed me to get it out and put it in the float road.

"I mounted the log and in a few seconds it began to turn. I was at that time a good swimmer and very active so I thought 'Now Mr. log, I can move as fast as you can,['] but the faster I tramped the log, the more speed I imparted to its revolutions. All the while Captain Sambo stood looking at me. By this time the log was turning so fast that I was compelled to coonjine as they say, to keep up with it. My Captain Sambo said: 'You will go directly,['] and just then I went off into the water. I swam back to the side of my log. Sambo was still laughing. I tried to climb on, but the harder I tried, the faster the log would turn. Captain Sambo still watched and laughed. Finally he said: "Why don't you go to the end of the log." I did this and was soon riding the log again. I had learned two things, first how to fall off the log, and second how to get back on it.

The log lay north and south. As I had my face turned to the west when I was on it before, I thought I would correct my former error by facing the east. But it was the same old thing. The log began to turn and I was soon overboard again. I soon regained my position on the log. I was still turning to the right. Captain Sambo said, 'Turn your face up and down the log. Now bear down on the left foot.' The log soon stopped turning to the right and started back the other way. 'Now bear down on the right foot,' cried Sambo. Then I saw that I had learned how to keep the log from turning. I said, 'give me my spike pole Sam, I am off and gone.' I soon found myself the second best floater in the crowd.

Captain Sambo did not brag on me much, so I did not rest until I became the best. I found out afterwards that he had taken all the other boys through this same process.

After supper that night we were discussing the events of the day's work, I asked Sambo: "Why don't you tell a fellow how to do these things and save some of the trips overboard?"

He laughingly replied: "It is always better to show a fellow than to tell him."

The water did not stay up long that time, but in eleven days we cut and floated into the river 248,000 feet of timber and received for the same after paying all expenses $1,785 which was the quickest money that I had ever made in my life up to that time. I sold this timber to Captain Stearns.

At that time I knew nothing of the local prices for timber, so I took the first price that Captain Stearns offered me. I learned afterwards, that I could have gotten $2,785 for the same timber. That is all right however for we all felt that we had gotten $500 worth of fun apiece; and I thought the experience gained was more than the

Registered bull "Robert" at eleven months.

money I had made. Since that time I have floated logs from this same brake. I sold Mr. John Mosley, who is now my neighbor, something like $2,000 worth of white oak timber off of this same piece of land. I afterwards built a saw mill and sawed about $2,000 worth of gum, cotton wood, etc., I received $400 for the hickory and there is still only 40 acres of the land in cultivation. Today I have a standing offer of $50 per acre for the same 320 acres for which I paid $16.50 at a tax sale and for which I refused $125.00 and $250.00."

The above story, quoted in the words of Mr. Bond, is a reminder that the resources of Arkansas are hardly scratched. There are still standing in different parts of the state vast tracts of virgin timber, awaiting the woodman's ax, coal, kaolin, bauxite, oil, gas, diamonds and other minerals are to be found in abundance. The streams and lakes are teaming [sic] with fish. Rich pearls are found in great numbers in the rivers. The soil is unsurpassed in fertility, and fortunes await the energy and thrift of the husbandman. The south and especially Arkansas is the best place in the world for the poor man. Hence as the Negro is the poorest man in the world, it is the best place for him.

WORKING FOR NOTHING.

"At one time during the rainy season in the early years of my career," said Mr. Bond, "I was share cropping with a man named Route, who was managing a farm on which I lived. He came by my house one day with his team and wagon. I got on the wagon with him. He asked me where I was going. I replied, 'I am going wherever you are going.' He said, 'I am going to haul rails.'

I replied, "I am going, too."

I worked with him, making a trip about with him all day long. The next morning he came along bright and early and I bounced on his wagon. He stopped his team and said, "Scott, I am really glad to have you with me to help haul rails but I am not able to pay you and I don't want you to work unless I could see where I could get the money to pay you."

I told him that was all right. I was not charging him anything for my work. I was glad to be with him. The fence would help to protect the crop I expected to make with him.

This white man was cultured and refined and we kept up a conversation about farming. He was very entertaining and I could get something out of every subject about which he talked. At the beginning of the next day I found it dry enough to plow, and so I went to my field.

A few days later it rained again and as the wagon came by I jumped on ready for another haul of rails. Mr. Route stopped his wagon and said he was really glad to have my work, that I was good company and he liked to have me with him; but as he could not pay, he did not know how he could pay me, and for that reason he would rather that I did not work.

I told him that was all right. That I had rather be working with him than to be out fishing and hunting. I really enjoyed being with him.

We completed the fence and when the crops were all made, I had no wagon and team of my own. When it came to getting my wood and hauling my corn, Mr. Route voluntarily loaned me his team and wagon to haul my wood, my corn and my cotton, and did not charge me for their use. I thus received at least $5.00 per day for every day that I helped haul rails. I found out from this that one who works willingly to help his neighbor for accommodation, often gets more than the man who is always particular about how much he will receive for his day's work.

I should like to impress this thought: If one will get the job and master the situation, the salary will always come in doublefold. Hence, in working for nothing, in this way, we are generally gaining most.

BEAR STORY.

Mr. Bond tells this excellent "Bear Story."

"A year after the foregoing incident I had a new experience. I had never seen a wild bear. My corn was planted on black, sandy loam land. It was being destroyed and torn down by something, I did not know what. The ground was so loose I could not tell from the footprints whether it was horse, mule, cow or what, that was doing the damage. The land was very rich. There were several stumps standing about. I thought it was coons that were destroying my corn. One moonlit night I took my gun and seated myself on the fence alongside the field. There was a slight breeze stirring the blades of corn. I thought I heard a coon that had climbed up on a stalk of corn and broke it down. I slipped off the fence, cocked my gun and stooped, looking beneath the blades of corn I saw one of these stumps within fifty feet of me. I squatted, looking for the coon, and all at once what I thought was a black stump dropped down and I never heard such running and threshing in my life. When I realized it was a bear, I was really so weak I could hardly lower the hammer of my gun. I straightened up and I heard another bear running. When they reached the fence on the far side of the field they tore down the whole side of the fence getting out of the field. From this I learned that it was Mr. Bear that was devouring my corn.

The next day I saddled my horse and went across the river about seven miles to Mr. Patterson, the great bear hunter, who had a fine pack of hounds.

Mr. Patterson said it would be two or three days before the bear would return to my field, and that he would be over to my place in a day or so, and stay over-night; and strike the bear's trail before day.

According to his promise he came. About two hours before day, the bear-hunter asked me if I knew the exact place where the bears crossed the slough. I told him I did. He sent another man with me, telling us to get down next to the water and he would take his dogs into the field, and when the bear came to the water we could shoot him as he swam across. We started in a skiff, but got hung on a snag. When we got to the appointed place the bear was already in the lake. We made three shots at him without apparent effect. The hounds followed the bear across and in a few minutes there was as sweet music as I ever heard, from a chorus of dogs. They chased the bear three and a half miles to the St. Francis River and across it. They overhauled bruin about ten o'clock and captured him about seven miles from my field.

Mr. Patterson said the bear would tip the scales at 500 pounds.

I did not have the pleasure of helping to capture the bear, but I certainly had my fill of him at the dinner table. I learned the excellency of bear meat and that one could not possibly eat enough to hurt himself.

Mr. Patterson was broadly known as the "bear chaser" of the St. Francis bottoms, not only took pleasure in bear hunting, but also made plenty of money.

He usually killed from fifty to seventy-five every winter. The whole St. Francis basin was at that time full of all kinds of game. Wild pigeons were so numerous that they would darken the sky when they passed. No oak or walnut had been cut, hence most would be found washed up in enormous piles along the streams.

It is hard to realize that although a few years ago countless millions of pigeons would sweep north in the spring and southward in the autumn in their annual migrations, that not a single specimen is alive today, the last having died in captivity a few years since in the zoological garden in Cincinnati.

AN OFFER OF WAGES.

Mr. Bond relates this story of refusing an offer of employment on the ground that he could make more working for himself:

"Some years after I had become the owner of two farms, one of which I called my home place, Mr. W. S. Graham, an aristocratic

View on Stevens farm on St. Francis River—580 acres.

southern born gentleman, who owned a farm of some two thousand acres across the road from my farm, had been having a great deal of trouble in getting a suitable agent or foreman to handle his farm. It happened that every one he hired, was short one way by or another. If they were good farmers they would not be able to handle labor.

Mr. Graham was a cousin to my mistress.

Before the war when he would visit her, he would sometimes go hunting and take me along to carry the game. He would often, on these hunts, divide his lunch with me and was friendly to me in every way.

When he had grown to manhood, knowing my ability as a farmer and my capacity for handling labor, came to me one day and proposed to hire me to run his farm. He offered me $65.00 per month and a residence for myself and family, which was $15.00 per month more than he had paid any one else; in addition to this, a horse, bridle and saddle.

I told him that was all right. I could not ask him to pay me more than that, but I thought it was worth more to me to run my own farm.

"And you think," said he, "that you are worth more than $780.00 a year?"

"No sir; but I think I have earned more than that. Besides, what should I do with my own farm?"

"I will rent your farm, as it lays alongside of mine, and hire you to superintend it as well as my own."

He then got out his book and pencil and began to figure, saying, "I think I can convince you that $780 is more than you can make working on your own farm. And what you would get for rent and salary would amount to $1,500.00 a year."

"Yes sir, but I think I earned more than that last year. I will get you to figure it out for me."

"I went into the swamps in February and earned $550.00 cutting timber. I then planted and gathered a good crop of corn and cotton. I sold forty-eight bales of cotton at eight cents which amounts to $1,640.00[.] I made and burned a brick kiln; net profits were $600.00[.] Yet I have said nothing of the growth of my garden and chickens. I was ready at all times to go to my wife when she would call me, knowing I was my own boss. I was also in a position to improve my own farms during that year."

["]I had no objection to hiring to Mr. Graham if I could make more money working for him than any one else he had ever hired; this I felt sure I could do. Yet, I could not afford to work for him for $780.00 when I was making $3,000 working for myself."

SCOTT BOND HUNTS HIS FATHER.

When the writer asked Mr. Bond what he knew of his father, he related this story of his hunt for his father:

"My mother died when I was quite small, and had never explained to me who was my father. She married my step-father, who is still living, when I was eighteen months old.

"As I grew older and found that he was only my step-father, I began to inquire who was my father, and where he lived. My Aunt Martha told me I was born in Madison County, Mississippi, twelve miles from Canton, the county seat, at a little town called Livingston. That my father was a man, Wesley Rutledge, the nephew of Wm. H. Goodlow[13] [Goodloe].

View on Stevens farm looking north.

"After I had gotten started out in life and had accumulated a little spare money, I thought I would like to visit the place of my birth and, if possible, find my father, and if he was in need, help him.

"In ante-bellum days Mr. Goodlow was a very rich man. He owned five hundred slaves and thousands of acres of land.

"My mother had a large chest, which, in those days, was used as a trunk. I had often seen her going through the things in that old chest. She would take out her calico dresses, which we people called "Sunday Clothes." She would hang them out to air on Sundays. Among the things she would take from the chest was a pair of little red shoes and a cap, and would say to me. 'These are the shoes your father gave you.' Being only a child, I thought she referred to my step-father.

"I was married and we had two children and had rented a large farm, and I thought it a good time for this trip. [early in the 1880s]

"I purchased a nice suit of clothes, then paid a visit to the barber and got neatly shaved and trimmed up, and pulled out for Canton, Miss., where I arrived at night. The next day was a rainy, drizzly day. It was March, but the people were bringing into Canton onions, lettuce and other early vegetables. I was surprised to see this and thought they were being shipped in from farther south. I went to the livery stable the next day and introduced myself to the livery man as Bond from Arkansas. I told I wanted to drive to Livingston, sixteen miles away. The liveryman, thinking I was white, said 'All right Mr. Bond, the horse and buggy and nigger to drive you will cost you three dollars.'

"I told him I would be ready in about thirty minutes; and at the appointed time I paid him the money and started out for Livingston.

"We drove about two and one half miles and opened a gate to the enclosed farm of Mr. Goodlow. The old colored man who was driving was as active as a boy, although his hair was as white as cotton. This old gentleman took me to be a white man, and as he had never asked me I did not make myself known to him. He used these words:

"'White folks, I have been in the country since I was a boy, and since that time I saw the man you are going to visit, harness up a hundred and fifty mules to be used on this farm. In those days the water almost boiled in this country. When you went to bed at night you could hear the blood hounds, and in the morning when you would wake up, you could hear them running colored people. The white folks said the music they made was the sweetest music in the world. There was once a runaway slave who had been chased at different times for four years. At last a set of patrolers came in with their dogs and said they were determined to catch him. They ran him for two days. Once in a while he would mislead the dogs and make them double on their tracks and he would gain a little rest. Eventually they would again pick up the trail and you could hear the hounds as they ran; say, here he goes, sing-a-ding; there he goes, sing-a-ding. At last, finding he could not escape, he ran deliberately into a blazing furnace and was burned to death rather than be caught and suffer the tortures that awaited him.'

"He regaled me with many other stories of slave life that he had witnessed.

"He told me that many a time he would be so tired from his day's work that he would not wake up in the morning until the horn blew for work. He would not have time to cook himself any bread, and that he would run to the meal bowl and put a handful or two of meal in his hat and run with his bridle and catch his mule and while the mule was drinking, he would take water and mix the meal. Then when he got to the field he would go to a burning log-heap, when the overseer was not looking, and rake a place in the ashes and hot embers, put his cake in and cover it. Later, when chance permitted, he would take out his ash cake and eat it as he plowed. Thus he would work until dinner time.

"This old man was more than an average man.

"After telling me many other stories of the hardships of the slave, he said that after all, the things that looked hardest to him, were really blessings in disguise. These hardships had developed his self-reliance and resourcefulness, and now that he was a free man and a citizen, he could see a benefit, even in the hardships, he had undergone. He said that he knew he was a Christian and that he was respected by all his neighbors, black and white.

"This instance is but one of ten thousand, showing that the Negro in his long apprenticeship, has gained in adverse circumstances, that he has wrung victory from oppression.

"By this time we had reached an elevation. He stopped his horse and pointed to a house in the distance that looked no larger than a cow. He told me that was the house to which we were going.

"As the distance lessened, the house proved to be a great mansion with beautiful lawns.

"He stopped in front. I got out, and as I passed up the walk knowing this to be my birth-place, I felt that I was at home. I rang the bell. It was answered by a large gentleman, who had a perfect bay window of a stomach. He was so large that he was unable to tie and untie his shoes.

"I said, 'I suppose this is Mr. Goodlow?'

"'Yes; this is Goodlow.'

"'Mr. Goodlow, this is Bond from Arkansas.'

"'Come in, Mr. Bond.'"

"As I walked into the parlor over elegant brussels carpets, I could see myself reflected from the mirrors on either side of the hall. The furniture was rare and elegant, and was typical of the splendor of the old time southern mansion. I was invited to sit down and for the next hour answered a rain of questions about Arkansas.

"Mr. Goodlow was very much interested in the young state of Arkansas.

"At that time wild life in the state had not been much disturbed. Bears, wolves and panthers were plentiful. Arkansas at that time bore the reputation of being a paradise for murderers and other criminals fleeing from justice. Hence, Mr. Goodlow was interested to learn from me all he could about these things, as well as about the climate and country in general.

"After I had imparted to him all I knew, I was then able to ask him a few questions, and began by saying:

"Mr. Goodlow, can you recollect hiring some slaves from the widow Bond's estate in 1852?"

"To which he replied, 'Yes; I remember hiring some slaves from the Maben [Mebane] estate. Mrs. Bond was a Miss Maben [Mebane].'"

"I suppose you are right. Do you remember hiring a man named Alex, a woman named Martha and also a bright mulatto girl named Ann? Ann was said to be your house servant at that time."

"'Yes,' he said, 'I remember that very distinctly.'"

"I proceeded: 'Ann gave birth to a child while she was your servant. It is said that Mr. Rutledge, who was your nephew and manager of your farm at that time, was the father of this child. It is further said that Mrs. Goodlow dressed the child and called it Scott Winfield."

"'You are certainly right,' he said. 'All that is true.'"

"I then arose from my chair and, standing erect, said, 'I am the kid.'"

"I was at that time a young man, and from what I felt, and others said, I was a very good looking young man. I had not been married a great while, and I knew my wife was a judge of beauty.

Mr. Goodlow said, 'Wait a minute.' He stepped to the parlor door and called Mrs. Goodlow, telling her to come in, he wanted her to see some one.

According to custom it took Mrs. Goodlow sometime to dress and make her appearance.

As she entered Mr. Goodlow said to her, "Do you know this boy sitting here?"

"I got up and put on my best looks.

"'No;' she replied. 'Mr. Goodlow, I have never seen him before.'"

"Mrs. Goodlow was a typical southern matron, and with her

Harvesting alfalfa.

wealth of silvery hair, was the personification of womanly grace and dignity.

"'Yes you have,' remarked Mr. Goodlow. 'You put the first rag on him and named him 'Scott Winfield,' at the time our son James was a baby.'"

"'No, Mr. Goodlow. I do not remember.'"

"'Don't you remember Ann, our housemaid, at the time Wess was managing our business?'"

"'Yes! Yes!' she exclaimed. 'I remember now. You are Scott Winfield!'"

"She grasped my hand and said: 'I certainly dressed you and named you Scott Winfield.'

"It would be impossible to describe the scene that followed this greeting. Tears were shed, words were spoken that came from deep down in our hearts. A more touching and sincere greeting rarely comes to one in a life time.

"I was most hospitably treated and was urged to stay all night. I accepted and was given a nice room. The next day I was shown the place where I was born.

"Mr. Goodlow accompanied me. He had a man go into the

"plunder room"[14] and get out an old chair they used to tie me in, when my mother was about the duties in the house.

"One who does not know the south, can form no conception of the extreme hardships some of the slaves had to undergo; the many peculiar situations that would arise, nor can he have the faintest idea of the deep regard, and at times, even real affection that existed between the master and the favored slave. It is a reflex for this regard that is the basis of all the helpful things the better class of southern white people are now doing to help the Negro better his condition and rise to a higher plane of manhood.

["]The following day I found an opportunity to explain to Mr. Goodlow, privately, the cause of my visit, and to ask the whereabouts of my father.

"I told him that prior to the war, there were many people who were wealthy. Many of these were greatly impoverished by changed conditions. I had come to find my father, and if he was in need, to help him.

"I was informed by Mr. Goodlow that he was very sorry he would have to tell me that my father was dead. That he had moved to Texas twelve years before, and had died two years later. He also informed me that he had three children living and doing business in Canton, Miss.

"When I was ready to leave, Mr. Goodlow had me driven to Canton in his magnificent carriage. I called on the children in Canton and introduced myself as Bond from Arkansas. I congratulated them on their business but did not make myself known to them, so that all they ever knew of me was 'Bond from Arkansas.'"

This brings up a thought. It has been stated by some careful statisticians that there are not 10,000 pure-blooded Negroes in the United States. Without accepting or rejecting this estimate, we will say that there are enough of that part of our population mixed-blood to at least keep the pot from calling the kettle black, in point of moral rectitude.

A DEAL IN PEAS.

Mr. Bond tells this story to illustrate why the Negro so often fails to get ahead. He says:

"I have always tried to get my people to look and to think. There are many reasons why we do not succeed in accumulating more of this world's goods, one of which the following occurrence is an example.

"I hired a man named Gregory to work for me. He related to me how at one time he was farming and went to a merchant to buy some peas to eat. He paid ten cents a pound for them, planted them and gathered two bushels of peas. These he took to the merchant from whom he bought the seed and was offered six cents a pound for them which he refused. He took the peas home and fed them to the chickens.

"I asked him why he did this. Corn was only fifty cents a bushel. He could have bought two bushels of corn. He could have gotten $7.00 for his peas. He could have bought two bushels of corn for one dollar that would have done his chickens more good than the peas, and had $6.00 left. He said he had rather lose the peas than to let the merchant have them for less than ten cents a pound.

"I told him that he was unwise; that he had simply bitten off his nose to spite his face in trying to spite the other fellow. It is just such actions as these, that keeps him a hired man."

RENTING AN AXE.

"I was paying Gregory $25.00 per month and had instructed him to cut the undergrowth from a ditch bank. He asked me for an axe. I asked him if he did not have an axe at home with which to cut fire wood. He admitted that he had, but it was his axe.

"I told him that was true, but if I was not asking too much that axe would do.

"He went to work and cut off the ditch bank nicely and at the end of the month he came up for settlement. My son, Theo, who was cashier, settled with him for his work.

"I asked him if he had been settled with. He answered that he had except the pay for the use of his ax.

"He said he wanted fifty cents for the use of his ax.

"I asked him if I understood him to say that the use of his ax was worth fifty cents?

"He said to me that was what he wanted.

"I instructed the cashier to pay him fifty cents and told Gregory that I thought he had made a mistake, as in each year there are fifty-two weeks, and the rate I had paid him would make his axe rent for $26.00 per year. I further advised him to take this for a great lesson; that before many months he would find out that his position was all wrong.

"Some three weeks later we were running two-horse turning plows and finishing breaking a field near Gregory's house at 11 o'clock one morning. He was living on one of my places and I had given him a garden. He called my attention to the time and asked to have the team to plow his garden.

"I granted his request and told him he could get through by 12 o'clock. I took the other teams and went over in another field.

"At one o'clock Mr. Gregory was on time in the field, having finished plowing his garden.

"At the end of the month Gregory came for a settlement. I asked him how much time he had lost in the month. He replied:

"'Two days.'"

"I said to him, I owe you $25.00 and you owe me for two days lost time and $7.50.

"He asked me where the $7.50 came in.

"I told him he lost one hour plowing his garden.

"He asked if he understood me to say he owed me $7.50 for plowing his garden.

"I informed him I considered the money I had invested in the mules, plow and harness and the cost of their feed, that I was not charging him in proportion to its cost as much for the use of my mules and plow as he had charged me for his ax.

"I then told him I would knock off that charge, but to remember I was furnishing him a garden and team and paying him for his time. All I wanted was for him to be liberal enough to see clearly when he was making charges."

"The reader of these pages will readily see the uphill task it is for a Negro to succeed in large business enterprises, when it is considered that he must compete with white men of experience, education and a thousand years of training, as well as deal with a large class of his own race who are as ignorant as himself."

Potato crop ready for digging.

SETTLING A STRIKE.

Mr. Bond tells you in this chapter how he settled a strike:

"All my experience with gin machinery had been the old-fashioned horse-gin. But after reading and some travel, and seeing white men handle machinery, I came to the conclusion that I could learn to do anything that any other man could do.

"I bought a twenty-five horse power outfit, consisting of boiler, engine, gin stand and press. The rumor got out over the country that I was to build a steam gin. I had numerous applications from white men, in different places, to erect the plant for me. My answer to them was, 'Gentlemen, I am a Negro and a poor man. I have not got the money to pay for erecting a plant.'"

"Well," they would say, "Uncle Scott, it will be of no use to you if it is not put up right, nor will it render you efficient service."

I would say, "Yes, that is correct, but I am going to try to put it up myself."

"Have you ever had any experience with machinery?"

"No; this is the first one I have ever owned. I have never, so far as I can remember, had my hands on one; though I once saw a contractor who got $5.00 a day for putting in an outfit of this kind. I watched him very closely, and whenever he wanted to put up a building, he would use his level, his square and plumb bob. I believe the level, the square and the plumb bob will work for me the same as for him."

"I had a tenant on my place named Charley Dilahunty, who claimed that he knew how to lay foundations and set up engines. He agreed to work for me at $1.50 per day.

"When the machinery arrived, Charley and I started with our square, level and plumb bob and erected a plant that answered the purpose.

"We managed to make the plant pay for itself in two years.

"On one occasion Charley claimed on Monday morning to be sick. I went to the gin, fired up and attempted to run the engine myself. I had been watching Charley pretty closely in order to get an idea as to how to handle the engine.

"I raised steam, put on two gauges of water, oiled up and opened the throttle to start. The engine failed to turn. I closed the throttle and examined the engine to the best of my ability. I could find nothing wrong. I then turned on the steam slowly until I had the throttle wide open; still the engine would not move. I closed the throttle and had the boys help me turn the fly wheel over. Five men put on all their strength and yet they failed to move the fly wheel.

"I was then at a loss. I did not know what to do.

"By this time the steam gauge showed up one hundred pounds, and the boiler was popping off.

"I threw open the exhaust, raised the flue door and put on the water. I said what in the world do you think is the matter?

"I was afraid to take the wrench and go to loosening bolts, for fear of loosening the wrong one.

"The ginner came down to the engine room and said 'Mr. Bond, I think Charley Dilahunty jammed that engine.'"

"Why do you think so?" I asked.

"He replied, 'Because he said Saturday night that he did not expect that engine to turn any more until he got $2.00 per day for his services.'"

"Did Charley tell you this?"

"Yes he did!"

"Would you testify this in open court?"

Scene on Gray farm where Military Road crosses the St. Francis River.

"Yes sir, I certainly would."

"I was at a loss to know what to do. I walked off and sat down on a bench. The more I studied over it, the worse shape I found myself in. I called for my horse which was hitched to the fence, jumped into my saddle, with the desire to do the wrong thing. I went half a mile past Charley's house and a half mile further to my own house.

"I grabbed my shotgun and returned to Charley's house. I called. Mary, his wife came to the door. I said:

"Mary, where is Charley?"

"He is in here," she answered.

"Is he in the bed?"

"No sir."

"Tell him to come out here."

He came. I said to him, "Come here Charley." I opened the gate.

"Get on up the road to the gin house," I ordered.

He wanted to go back and get his hat.

I told him they did not bury men with their hats on.

"Up the road he went for about three hundred yards. He then stopped and said: 'I have not done anything to the engine.'"

"Get on up the road," I commanded. ["]There is no time here for apologies."

When we arrived at the gin, I said to him: "Walk up to the door and stop."

I dismounted, advanced on him with my shotgun in my hands and told him to get the wrench and unjam that engine. If he did not do it in ten minutes, I would kill him if he was the last man on earth.

He picked up the wrench; made two turns on a certain nut.

I asked him if the engine was ready for service.

He said, "Yes sir."

He opened the throttle and the engine moved off nicely.

I said to him, ["]I look for you to stay here and run this engine until night." It was about 12 o'clock. Charley said, "I have not had any dinner yet."

"That is all right," I replied. "I guess you will not need any dinner after today."

Charley weighed about 190 pounds. I, a little insignificant Negro, weighed about 108 pounds, so I thought it a wise plan to keep close company with my shotgun.

We ginned six bales of cotton after dinner. I weighed the cotton. At seven o'clock I sent a boy into the engine room to tell Charley to blow the whistle for quitting time.

I locked up the gin and got on my horse. Charley had cooled down and was standing at the door of the engine room. He said:

"Mr. Bond, I want you to forgive me for what I have done."

"What have you done wrong, Charley?"

"I jammed the engine and caused you to lose half of the day's work with all the crew."

"What prompted you to do that?"

"I thought I should have more wages—$1.75 a day anyhow."

"Why did you not walk up to me like a man and say so?"

"Well," he replied, "all I can say is I did wrong and I want you to forgive me."

I said to him, "This was your own contract—to help me set up the engine and run the gin for the season for a dollar and a half a day. Now Charley, I am going to give you $2.00 per day and I want steam at five o'clock every morning from now on."

We were good friends after that, and all went well."

THEOPHILUS BOND LEARNS TO FIRE.

Just before the close of the ginning season, Charley was chopping wood. His ax slipped and he cut his big toe nearly off.

There I was eighteen miles back in the sticks and had no one who knew anything about the boiler or the engine, and was really at a loss for some one to do this work. My son Theophilus, who was eleven years old at that time, had been around the boiler and engine rooms to help out, cried out, "Pa, I can handle that engine."

I would not hear to this. I did not even want him to attempt to do so.

He said to me, "Pa, I can put on and take off the inspirator. Charley has taught me that the only danger is allowing the water to get too low; and that it would always be safe if I kept plenty of water. I know how to handle the throttle to start and stop the engine."

"Let me see you put the water on," I said.

In a moment the inspirator was at work. I then told him to shut off the water and start the engine; to be careful and not turn on too much steam at once. He did so and the engine moved off nicely.

I said to him, "Shut it down and come with me. Now son, it appears that you know the most dangerous points about the engine and boiler. I know you are a child, and I cannot expect to put a man's work on the shoulders of a child. Here is what I want to pump into your head and mine; the lives of all who work about the gin as well as your own, are at stake; and if you should forget or go to sleep, your neglect would cause a serious disaster. I think you are a wonderful boy; your father's boy."

"I wish, son, that I had some way to show you how proud I would be if you should master the job and make a success of it.

"If you have a hundred and twenty pounds of steam and stop your engine, what would you do?"

"I would raise the flue doors and put on the water," he replied.

"That is exactly right," I said; "but I would like to know where you learned all this."

He replied that he had been watching Charley for the last six months, and he had learned by watching him do it.

I said to him, "Now son, there is one thing more I want to impress upon you. You are only a small boy and just eleven years old. You must not try to handle big sticks of wood. You must only handle small sticks of wood and trash, and call Henry when you want big sticks of wood put into the furnace. I will call you my little engineer and will pay you a salary for operating this plant. This will give your father a few hours to attend to other things pertaining to the farm."

We then went into the engine room and started up the cotton gin. I stuck close to the gin plant that I might be thoroughly convinced that he would not neglect his duty. I found he would use all necessary precautions and that I could trust the engine in his hands. This made me think that I was a great Negro. That I could have my own engine and make my own engineer.

We ginned equally as many bales as we had been ginning formerly.

I was never a healthy man, even to the present, and in those days I suffered a great deal with what was known as the sick headache.

On one occasion I was riding home with my little engineer behind me. I remarked to him that I was nearly dead with the sick head-ache.

He said to me, "Pa, that means that you will be in bed all day tomorrow. But I will be able to carry on the gin all right and you may lie in bed, as you will have to do with the sick headache."

"No son," said I, "I hope to be better in the morning and get up at four o'clock to get up steam."

He answered: "Pa, that will be unusual, for you generally have to lay in bed two or three days when you have these attacks."

We arrived at home, put up our horse, fed him, ate supper and retired. The pain in my head was so intense that I did not go to sleep until after two o'clock.

I was awakened by the noise of the whistle blowing. I turned over and found the little engineer was gone. It frightened me. I arose, dressed hurriedly, caught my horse, and at topmost speed rode for the gin. When I arrived the boy had up steam and they were ginning cotton to beat the band. I found everything in perfect trim. I had been so badly frightened that I forgot my headache and when I did think of it, it was gone.

Theo said, "Pa, what are you doing here? Why did you not stay in bed?"

Engineers surveying ocean to ocean highway that passes half dozen of
Scott Bond's farms in St. Francis County, Ark.

I answered him, "I was so frightened, and thought every minute
I would hear the boiler blow up."

The foregoing narrative is given the reader to show one of the
many trying times through which Scott Bond passed on the way
up. It is through such struggles as these that men are tried: and if
one passes unscathed, if he triumphs, then indeed is there added
another name to the truly great.

True greatness may be attained in one line of work as well as in
another. It is not the work, but the way it is done that counts. It is
the results obtained that make the sum total.

THE DIFFERENCE.

In this chapter we again write of one of Mr. Bond's experiences.
In his own words he says:

"I had at one time an acquaintance named John Harris. John and I are better acquainted now than we were some years ago.

Harris had been firing at the Box Factory, one of Madison's industries. He came to me and offered to fire my gin for me if I would give him $1.75 a day, which was twenty-five cents more than he was getting at the box factory. He guaranteed that he would give me first-class service.

"After some consideration I agreed to his proposition and he went to work.

Things went along nicely for some time. Then he asked for $2.00 per day.

I gave it to him.

The next season Harris insisted that I should give him $2.25 per day. I finally agreed to do so.

We had gotten pretty well along in the ginning season. I was rushing the work. Harris demanded a raise. At last I agreed to pay him $2.35 per day. I paid him regularly all the time, every Saturday night.

As I was passing from point to point about the gin plant and to my store, I met him one day, sixty-five or seventy yards from the gin, and asked him what he was doing so far from the engine. He informed me that the engine was running all right. I instructed him to keep close to his engine, so that should it become necessary to shut off the steam, he would be at hand.

Some time later I met him standing in front of my store, one hundred and fifty yards away from his engine rooms. I asked him what he was doing there.

He informed me that I could see what he was doing.

I then said to him, "You are out here away from your engine. If anything should happen—should some one get caught in the machinery, it would be impossible for you to get there in time to be of any service. You shall not fire any longer, I will do the work myself."

When I reached the boiler room, I looked around and Harris was right behind me. He said I should go back to my office; that he would attend to the engine and fire.

I said to him, "You are the man to go to the office and ask the bookkeeper to settle with you; then you can look for another job."

Duroc Red, registered hogs.

He said he would stay and do the work until I got another man; that I knew I was not able to handle the heavy wood.

I thought of the great danger to my crew and machinery by having so careless a man at the engine. I grabbed a shovel and ran him out of the boiler room. I replaced him the next morning with another man.

To show what many a colored man has to contend with when employing his own race in a place of this kind; Harris had never received more than $1.50 per day when firing for the white man, and gave him efficient service. I was paying him $2.35 per day for indifferent service and consequently much annoyance and poor results.

Harris went some thirty-five miles away and got another job firing for a white man at a saw mill for $2.00 per day. He worked twenty-five days and applied three times for a settlement. He would always be told that the man was not ready for settlement.

The last time he asked for a settlement, the white man said to him:

"Well, I am ready for a settlement now."

He opened a drawer and came up with a navy six.

Harris said to him: "That's all right. You don't owe me anything."

He came back to Madison, dragged around for a few days. I gave him his job back at the same salary and he gave me better service than he had ever done.

At the close of the season he came to me and said he wanted to go to farming; that he had made up his mind to show me what a man could do.

I owned a farm on the St. Francis River twelve miles below Madison. I rented Mr. Harris this farm, sold him twelve head of mules and horses and all the wagons and tools necessary to operate the farm. He paid for all this including his store account and had a bank account over and above all of $1,280.

THE MANNER IN WHICH I LEARNED
TO MAKE BRICK.

After buying the seven small farms and adding them to my main farm, I found that to make permanent improvement it would require worlds of brick for chimneys. Unfortunately for me I had never been about a brick kiln. I reasoned that I could learn to make, kiln and burn brick. I heard that a big kiln was to be burned in Forrest City, so when my crops were laid by I went to Forrest City, three miles from where I lived, on a Monday morning by sun up. I had to cross my sand pit on my way to the brick yard with my wagon and team; so I took my shovel and put on a load of sand, which was worth $2.00 a yard in the brick business at that time. I wanted to learn all I could about making brick. The yard was in charge of one of my old chums, Mr. J. H. Blount. When he arrived on the yard he said, "Hello, Bond, what are you doing here?"

"I came to work," I replied.

He said: "Well, I do not need you and I cannot use you."

I said: "I am going to work anyhow."

He asked who hired me. I told him, "Nobody."

"Well, how do you expect to get your wages?"

"Well, Mr. Blount," I replied, "that may come around by some hook or crook."

Mr. Blount laughed and said, "That is very cheeky in any man."

It was then about 7:30 o'clock. The man who had contracted to be there on time at 7 o'clock with his team to run the mud mill had not yet shown up with his team. I had a pair of fine mules with me at the time, on the yard, and I asked Mr. Blount to let me hitch my team to the mud mill and run it until his man got there. There will be no charge whatever, I told him. My object was to learn how to mix mud and mold brick; to learn how long they must lay on the yard before being set in the kiln. I kept this all to myself. The man who was to come with his team to run the mill did not show up. When we quit that night Mr. Blount said to me: "Mr. Bond, you need not come back tomorrow because I know the other man will be here."

I said: "Mr. Blount, that is all right, but this is a free country. I will surely be on time tomorrow morning."

The next morning I was on hand with a load of sand. I unloaded it and hitched my mules to the mud mill and waited the arrival of Mr. Blount, the manager. The hands began coming in. Mr. Blount was with them. He said: "Hello, Mr. Bond, you beat any man I ever saw. You just walk up and take a job."

We laughed over this. The whistles blew for work time. I said, "Mr. Blount, may I run this mud mill until your man comes?"

He laughingly replied: "Yes, if it suits you to do so, but I am sure he will be here in a few minutes."

"That is all right," I said. "I am ready to give him his job at any time he comes for it." I learned how to build a mud mill, how the clay was watered and prepared for the molds. I considered this in itself big pay. At 6 o'clock in the evening I hitched my team to my wagon and was ready to drive out, when Mr. Blount came up to the wagon and said, "Mr. Bond, it really won't be necessary for you to come back tomorrow, because I am going to write a note, put a boy on a mule and send after the man with whom I have contracted to do the work you are doing."

I looked at him, laughed in a jolly way and replied: "All right, Mr. Blount, I will surely be on hand on time in the morning." I was on hand before 7 o'clock the next morning with another load of sand, unloaded and had my mules hitched up to the mud mill. That day the proprietor of the brick works came out. He was a man who had several large business enterprises. He walked up to Mr. Blount, the manager, and held a lengthy conversation with him. While I was busy at work I could detect much of the conversation referred to me. In a little while Mr. Gray, the proprietor, came to the mud mill where I was at work and said: "Hello, Uncle Scott, what are you doing here?"

"I am sure, Mr. Gray, you are not a blind man, you can see what I am doing."

"But I mean: who hired you here?"

I replied: "No one."

"Well, from whom are you expecting your wages?"

"I am not looking for any wages. The Lord always makes things right."

"And you are depending on the Lord for your wages?"

"Yes, sir, certainly. Of course, all good things come from the Lord."

Mr. Gray and myself had, prior to that time, had quite a number of business transactions and they had all been as lovely as the month of May, so I continued to be on hand every day until Saturday 12 o'clock, when all the crew went to town to the office to be paid off. I hitched up my team and instead of going to the office I went straight home. I was on hand again Monday morning and by this time it had become a custom with me to hitch my mules to the mud mill. When the manager, Mr. Blount, got to the yard, he found my mules hitched up to the mud mill. I said to him, "Your mud mill man has not yet arrived."

Mr. Blount replied, "No, the boss had advanced him $15 on the work three weeks ago and for that reason I was sure he would be on hand."

"Well," I replied, "Mr. Blount, were I in your place I would have been sure he would not have been here, as there are two bad pay-masters—the one who pays in advance and the one who never pays."

The mud mill man never showed up and I continued to work. Everything moved along nicely. The following Saturday evening at 5 o'clock the crew knocked off and went to town to the office to be paid off. I again hitched my team to my wagon and drove home as usual. The next morning being Sunday, I went to the postoffice for my mail. I got a letter containing a check for $65, which I think was really more than I would have gotten had I attempted to make a bargain. Here is a lesson, especially to young men. It is always best to hunt the job, not the salary. Master the job and the salary will surely come and nine times out of ten the amount will be larger than expected. I remained on the job until the brick kiln was completed and wound up with one hundred and forty odd dollars in cash. I really know that I had gained more than a thousand dollars worth of information about making brick.

SCOTT BOND STARTS HOUSEKEEPING.

Scott Bond set a splendid example for young men, when in 1877 he was married to Miss Magnolia Nash, and went immediately to the Allen farm to make a share crop and began housekeeping in a little log house.

Let him tell the story:

"The first thing we did was to put up our little bed, then we looked around to see what was next. Just at this time in walked a white lady by the name of Mrs. Albert, she laughed and said:

"You children are fixing to go to housekeeping."

"I also laughed" and said, "Yes mam."

"She looked around a little and asked what we were going to do for something to cook in."

"I looked at wife, and wife looked at me, then we all laughed."

"I said: 'I don't know what we will do, Mrs. Albert.'

"She remarked, If you will come over to my house, I will see if I can find something for you."

"I went over and she gave me a skillet with a piece broken out of it and a lid without a rim, and a tea kettle with no top."

"One may think this a small wedding present, but it was a God send to us."

"We used the tea kettle as a pot, to boil our dinner in and the skillet with the lid on to bake our bread. When the bread was cooked, wife would take it out and put it up beside the jamb to keep warm, while she would fry the meat in the same skillet."

"We were so happy together that all this was real fun for us."

"We had as yet no broom to sweep the floor, nor had we a wash tub, or rub board."

"We had to borrow these things from my aunt who was my nearest neighbor."

"My wife usually went to borrow the broom and the wash tubs. This after a time became worrisome to our neighbors and ourselves."

"One bright day just as I was starting to the field my wife looked me in the face and said:

"Will you please go and borrow the tub and rub board for me this morning?"

"When I looked into her eyes, I saw her feelings were against continual borrowing."

I said, "certainly, I will go and get the broom and rub board." I got them for her and remarked:

"Wife, this looks tough, just hold your light up a few days and if the Lord will let me, I will show you a sight."

"These were the brightest days of my life, I could never tell when I had finished a day's work.

"Time rolled on that year, and wife and I made and gathered a bountiful crop. Then we had some money. We discussed the situation and decided we would only buy the necessaries of life. We had a crib full of corn. I swapped my wedding suit for a milk cow. When winter had passed and spring come, my wife's auntie made her a present of a kitten. A Mr. McCutcheon made me present of a bitch and by that time we had two cows, two sows and I had bought a beautiful little filly, named her Mattie and gave her to my wife."

"By that time, Biddie the kitten was grown and here it was, Biddie brought kittens, Queen brought puppies, both of the sows brought pigs, the cows were both fresh with young calves. I was ploughing for another crop. I ploughed the little filly up until Friday night. There came a big rain that night, so Saturday morning I turned the mare into the field where there was a large cane brake, as I knew I could not use her again before Monday morning.

"I told my wife I would go and get Mattie to have her ready to plough Monday morning. The cane was very rank and one would have to look very closely to find an animal in that thicket. I finally espied her and called her to come to me. When I called her, the little mare started and up jumped a fine colt. I said, 'Ain't this luck, turn loose one and find two?"

"I took them home. Wife and I looked the colt over and talked about our new horse. This stopped ploughing for a few days.

Corn planted in new ground.

The chimney of the old house in which we lived was constructed of dirt and sticks. It had caught fire and had to be thrown down. My wife had asked me several time if it was not time we had it rebuilt. This put me to looking and thinking. Rebuilt it and finished Monday evening and that night our first son Waverly T. was born. I had my hands full. The kittens, the puppies, the pigs, the calves, the colt and the wonderful boy. About the third day after the baby was born, the granny woman came to dress the baby. I had been up, off and on practically all night; this made me a little late getting up as it was about daylight. I was making up the fire and had not dressed. The boy needed dressing and was quite fretful. The granny woman came, and old folks like, did not knock, but shoved the door open and walked in. I was later that morning than usual. The kittens in the box were crying, the puppies under the house were whinning, the pigs had not been fed and as a matter of course, the sows and the pigs were squealing. I generally milked early, but being late that morning, I had not milked and the cows were lowing and the calves bleating and my big son was in the bed squaling.

When the granny woman shoved the door open she exclaimed, "My God! Aint this a sight?" This reminded me of the remark I had made to wife: "Hold me a light for a few days and I will show you a sight."

"I found myself standing in the middle of the floor, patting my hands and said to wife, 'Listen to what Aunt Eliza says, My God! aint this a sight? I told you a few days ago to hold me a light and I would show you a sight.'"

Wife and I made up our minds that we would lean together and march boldly up the path of progress, with the hope of being able to buy a farm and educate our children. My wife furnished me with another boy every eighteen months or thereabouts until she had borne me eleven boys in succession and nary girl. When my wife had given me seven boys I then made a contract with her that if she would give me three more boys I would set her free. The morning the tenth boy was born, with my arms around her neck, she exclaimed, 'Thank God I am free!' My wife was such a good woman she did not stop there, but gave me another great boy, which made eleven sons in succession."

"Here it was, boys, hogs, cows, mules, cotton and corn, peas and potatoes, chickens, eggs, milk, butter and pumpkins. We have been able from that time to the present practically to live on what we raised at home. I was growing financially stronger. I took charge of the whole Allen farm, and was raising the meat and bread that was consumed by all the hands on the place. We would kill and put up every year between ten and twelve thousand pounds of meat and barrels after barrels of lard. We grew cane for molasses and in fact produced every thing along these lines, needed on the farm. I made it a rule to fill every row of corn full of peas at lay by time. This alone almost made my meat every year. We grew as much cotton as our neighbors or more. Every time I sent my wagons to town I was able to send either a load of peas, potatoes or a country ham. Now even with 5 cent cotton I was able to put my oldest boys in college and keep them there for six years without losing a day. I only gave them home made clothing and underwear.

"The method of diversification and all the year sales of my products put me in position to make a payment on a farm or buy a farm every year.

"I would to God that it were possible for me to pump into my

Scott Bond and wife discussing new Hereford arrival.

colored friends all over the land, how easy it is for any man who wants to march boldly up the hill of success. I did not only serve God and make money, but I also made it a rule to make friends with all with whom I came in contact. I now value the friendships I have with all the people both white and black, far more than I do the money I have made."

"I not only grew cattle and hogs, but also three or four mule colts every year. This enabled me to replace the old mules as they would wear out or die.

"It was in those days that I learned to experiment in farming, as I had so much land to work, it was necessary to have crops that would come off at different seasons. Besides I soon saw that I could not furnish all that land with $250 mules and I bought only small ones. When breaking the land two would be used hitched to a large one horse plow. While this was slow work the land was broken good and deep. After this they would be singled out and each little mule was able to cultivate a full crop. It was impossible for my hands to cultivate deep. The result was they had to cultivate shallow. That was the reason I could make more cotton and corn than any of my neighbors. Necessity not knowledge compelled me to do that which years of experience has shown to be the best way to cultivate corn, cotton and everything else.

"That was long before the government started its work coach-along these lines, and today with the impediment of poverty removed, I am still doing what the government experiment stations prove to be the proper thing."

Scott Bond maintains that with fifty years experience in farming, the science of agriculture is at the very beginning of its development. He says that if he were a twenty year old boy, by the time he was fifty years old he would learn something about farming and that the mysteries of agriculture like the mysteries of the Bible will never all be unfolded to man.

He is of the belief that he can now take fifty acres and make more money with less expense than he used to make on five hundred acres.

PATTERSON, THE BEAR HUNTER.

At a certain time there came another overflow. This again aroused my ambition for the timber business. I remarked to Capt. Stearns [Stern], to whom I had been selling my timber, that I was going to buy the north half of section 12 and then I would not pay any one 15 cents to insure me $15,000. That there was over 2,000,000 feet of the finest cypress I ever saw in that brake.

Captain Stearns asked me who owned the land. I felt that it was no secret, so I told him, thoughtlessly the very things that Mr. Patterson the great bear hunter, asked me to reveal to no one. Mr. Patterson, being well acquainted with the swamp and the overflows and knowing the drift of the currents, when the entire bottoms were flooded, said to me: "Come and go with me and I will show you just where and how to cut your float roads. I have been here for forty years. I have never given to any living man the information I am giving you, and would not like to have you reveal it to any one." I thoughtlessly told Capt. Stearns where I intended to cut my float roads. He asked me to let him go in partnership with me. I looked and thought at once, now it is worth something to be in partnership with Captain Stearns and I told him all O. K. I told Capt.

Stearns who owned the land and what it could be bought for. The next summer, after my crop was laid by, I was very busy molding and setting brick to burn a brick kiln. A young man, I do not now recall his name, came to me and asked to hire my wagon and team," I told him I would like to accommodate him but I was using my wagons and team every day hauling wood to burn a brick kiln. He said he had to have a wagon and team somewhere, he wanted to move his camping outfit up on section 12, that he had contracted with Captain Stearns to cut out a float road through the south half of section 12 and through the north half of the same section. Then and there I remarked to the young man: "Sir I own the south half of section 12 and told Captain Stearns that I was going to buy the north half of section 12. Now I want to know who sent you to me for a team." He pleasantly replied: "Captain Stearns told me to come to you."

I asked him how he knew that Captain Stearns had bought the north half of section 12. He replied: "Because he told me he had."

Then I thought of what Mr. Patterson, the great bear hunter had told me. Then it occurred to me that Captain Stearns wanted me to know that he had bought this property. The next day, something, I do not remember what, caused me to be at Madison. I was standing on the front porch of a store house. It was a bright beautiful day. It happened that Captain Stearns walked right up to where I was standing. He seemed to have on his face as usual, one of his pleasing smiles.

I looked him in the face and tried to return about the same pleasant smile, and said: "Good morning Captain Stearns."

"Why good morning Uncle Scott."

I looked him straight in the face giving him about the best smile I knew how.

He said: "Well I saw that you had gone into the brick kiln business and had also agreed to go into the gin business, I came to the conclusion that you would not need the north half of section 12, so I went the other day and bought it and have the deed for it."

"I said: "You did? Captain Stearns you are one of those smooth slick Yankees. Now I don't believe there is a southern born Democrat in all of Eastern Arkansas that would stoop so low as to take advantage of a Negro's ignorance as you have mine."

He saw that I was pretty well keyed up, and remarked: "That is all right. We will still be partners, you own the south half and I own the north half and we will both work together as partners."

This of course pacified me. I had up to that time never known anything of Captain Stearns but a perfect gentleman and he had run for County Clerk on the Republican ticket and being a Negro of course I was a Republican, supported him during the campaign, worked and voted for him and had always thought that he and I were all O. K., as we had gone hand in hand through the campaign, so I felt good over the matter at last.

A few years later came another overflow. I prepared my logging and camping outfit. About the time I was ready to start, I met Captain Stearns.

He said: "Well, I see you are going to cut more timber."

I said, "Yes, sir, my aim is to make a killing this time."

He said, "Now when you get through cutting the timber on the south half of section 12 before you begin cutting on the north half, let me know."

I said: "All right."

This put me to thinking. I finally figured it out that that was only a matter of business and everything would work out O. K. So I called up my timber crew and lit out for the brake and went to work cutting and floating out timber. I cut and floated out about 145,000 feet which was about all the first class timber I had left on that section. After giving my boys instruction what to do I got into my boat and had to go about 18 miles before getting to Capt. Stearns. I landed at my home about 10 o'clock in the night.

Capt. Stearns lived about 300 yards from where I lived. I remained all night with my family. My wife had me a warm breakfast on the table by 4 o'clock. Then it looked like it was raining down pitchforks and it was as dark as dark could be. That did not deter me from my journey. I was at Capt. Stearns' house about three hours before daylight aroused him up, struck a match and said: "Captain Stearns I have cut all the timber that had been left on the south half of section 12 and I came to bring you the information you required of me."

He said: "Did you ever see it rain as hard as it is now."

"Yes, sir, this is a pretty good rain. But Captain I am after results.

Scott Bond's registered bull, weighing 850 pounds at twelve months.

It never gets too dark nor rains too hard when I am after that. What information can you give me?"

"Well I will have to go with you."

I said: "It is a long ways to the camp and we will have to go up stream so we had better start now." I finally got him to agree to turn out; and off we went. We arrived at the camp about 10 o'clock. Upon our arrival I said to Captain Stearns, "As you have not had any breakfast, I will have the cook prepare you something to eat."

He said: "No, I am very much obliged. I will run up to Hull and White's camp," which was about one-half mile from my camp. I had never been to that camp, but I heard them felling trees ever since my camp had been located on the south half of 12. My boys had finished all the work I had left for them to do and were sitting on the raft laughing and talking, waiting for Captain Stearns to return from the other camp. In a little while he made his appearance.

He said: "Uncle Scott, Hull and White refuse to let you cut any timber on 12, so get your boats, crews and camping outfit and I will carry you over here on lost swamp and there I will let you cut all the timber you want to cut."

I dropped my head and began thinking within myself. What a

nice thing I once had and had revealed all my business to Captain Stearns regarding the timber, and saw how nicely and pleasantly he had wound me up in his little web, as the spider did the fly. I realized the fact that I knew nothing at all about lost swamp, and there had been no float roads cut through it. I decided that was a lame job. I realized the fact that Capt. Stearns had done me a great injustice, not only taking advantage of my ignorance in buying the north half of section 12, but had even trespassed on my property without my consent by cutting the float road through it. It appeared to me that if Captains Hull and White were cutting timber above me for Capt. Stearns, they were compelled to come through my premises to get to the river, which was the only way to get out with the timber. I still had my head hung down and I saw pretty clearly that I could master the situation. So I raised my head and looked at Capt. Stearns and said: "Captain Stearns, lost swamp the devil. I know nothing about lost swamp and I am not going anywhere [and] you will never run a log through my float road unless I am dead.'

This aroused all the boys at my camp. They were up instantly and ready for a big row.

I said to them: "Quiet boys I will master the situation. You are out of your place."

This seemed to somewhat shock Capt. Stearns. He finally raised his head and said, "Uncle Scott wait until I come back."

"All right, sir,."

In about an hour, he returned with Capt. White, and Mr. Hull. Both of these men were perfect gentlemen and both were neighbors of mine.

They came up and said: "Hello Uncle Scott,"

"I am not doing much Captain." They both had on their faces the smile of southern born, aristocratic gentlemen. They said to me: "We learn from Capt. Stearns that you are going to prevent us running our timber through this float road."

"Gentlemen, that is true. I suppose that is Captain Stearns' timber you are cutting?"

He said: "In part that is right. But Uncle Scott we have a contract with Captain Stearns as long as this paddle I hold in my hand, and we are in the hole about $1500 with Capt. Stearns. We have about 250,000 feet of timber already cut and ready to float out, and

Unloading second cutting of alfalfa, June 15, 1917.

in case we can't pass through your float road it will be a total loss. If you will allow us to go through and run our timber this will put us something like $2,000 to the good."

"Capt. Hull, you and Mr. White are my friends and I have the highest regard for you both, but in this case I am compelled to shoot through you both in order to get to Capt. Stearns. He has taken advantage of my ignorance, by me telling who owned the land and what it could be bought for and also explained to him about the float road. In my absence, he went and bought the land and later I met him and he agreed with me that we would still be partners. Now here it is, I have my entire crew here and had let him cut timber on my brake for two years. Now he winds up by telling me I can go in lost swamp, and I told him lost swamp the devil, I was not going anywhere. So you can see I certainly regret very much that I have to punish you gentlemen to get to Capt. Stearns.

They and Capt. Stearns had a hearty laugh. Capt. Hull said: "We see Uncle Scott that you are in a position to master the situation.["] He being an old aristocratic gentleman, said: "Let's all be friends and make money. There is more timber here in this swamp than we can get out on this rise, so you can take your men and go to cutting and when we put our timber in the float road we will not allow it to stop until we get to the river. And when you start to running your timber do likewise."

This gave me great relief. When I could see that my neighbors were making money and I was making some myself. This gave me great comfort. So in a few minutes the axes were ringing and the saws were singing.

In the next few days we had another 140,000 feet of timber cut, cribbed and toggled ready for floating. Sometimes our crib of timber would be in front and sometimes Captain Hull and White's timber would be in front. This was rather a new line of work for myself and my boys and when we could get the white in front of us we would watch the skill with which they handled their timber. We were benefited by their skill and art in floating timber in the float road. So Messrs. Hull, White and myself worked together, hand in hand and we all came out well and made nice money.

BRICK.

On July 26th, the next year I finished laying by my crop and drove my team on the brick yard. By working with Mr. Blount the year before that I had learned just what to do.

I cleaned off my brick yard, planned my mud pits, had me a mud wheel built like the one I had run the year before for Mr. Blount.

My brother-in-law, Pat [Patrick] Banks and myself had been together from time to time, thought we would go in partners and burn a kiln of brick, after I had the yard cleaned off. The next day he came around to where I was at work, and said: "I have decided not to go in partners in the brick business, but you can use me anywhere you see fit and I will do all I can to advance you in the brick business, and you can pay me whatever you think is right."

I agreed to that and said: "I am going to make and burn the brick." So I moved off with my brick business.

I hired my molders and offbearers and after I had made brick two or three days, I went to see Mr. Blount, who was teaching school in Forrest City, to get him to show me how to set my kiln.

I effected the following arrangement: "I was to furnish him a

Hogs grazing on alfalfa.

horse, bridle and saddle, and every evening at the close of school he was to come down to the kiln. I was to board him at my house and we were to work from 4:30 to 7:30 or 8, and we would start in the morning as soon as it was light enough and we could set brick until 8 o'clock then he could have breakfast, get in his saddle and be at school on time.

This worked all O. K. After Mr. Blount would close over the eyes of the brick kiln, I had learned to set brick all right, and in five weeks time after I had got started we had made and burned 130,000 brick.

I had a partner, a white man by the name of Mr. Crawford. He and I had decided to put up a steam gin. I put my brother-in-law, Pat Banks to hauling the material to build the gin while I was burning the brick kiln. So I was ready to build my furnace at the gin plant by the time the brick was cool enough to handle.

By the 15th of October, I had my brick ready for the market and had completed my gin plant. I ginned a bale of cotton on that date. I had not as yet sold any brick, but happened to be in Forrest City the next day after I had ginned a bale of cotton. Capt. Wynne, who at that time was president of the Bank of Eastern Arkansas, came into T. O. Fitzpatrick's office and said: Mr. Fitzpatrick I have a subscription list here. We are going to build a church here in town and I want to see how much you will subscribe.

Mr. Fitzpatrick was a scholarly gentleman, yet he had a gruff way of meeting his friends.

He said: "No, Capt. Wynne, I have spent the most of my days building churches and school houses for the white people and Negroes of this county."

Captain Wynne was a very modest Christian gentleman and I noticed his face when Mr. Fitzpatrick made that expression. It appeared that he had thrown cold water over his face.

I remarked: "Captain Wynne, he is mistaken. The Negroes and a large per cent of the white people of this county have kept his hands in the government corn crib for years and years. Mr. Fitzpatrick has never paid a dollar in the way of building churches for either the Negroes or white people, and the Lord has simply loaned him this money, in order that he might help to build churches and school houses. Captain Wynne I wish I was a white man in order that I would have a chance to help build this church."

"Uncle Scott we would be glad to have you help us with this church."

"All right sir, here is ten dollars."

He handed me the list to sign my name, we were both standing at Mr. Fitzpatrick's desk.

As I went to pass the list back to Capt. Wynne, Mr. Fitzpatrick, who had not in all this time said a word, grabbed the list and struck it for $50.00. He said, the conversation between Scott Bond and yourself has changed my decision."

Capt. Wynne, as I have before stated was a modest Christian gentleman; and as he turned to go out, said, "I am so much obliged to you gentlemen for your generosity."

I did not know at that time what kind of a church they were going to build, frame or brick, but about three days later, the building committee came to my house to see me, they said:

"Uncle Scott, we learn that you have finished burning a brick kiln."

"Yes, Sirs, I have one that just blowed out a few days ago."

"We would like to know if your bricks have smooth faces and are well burned."

"Gentlemen, come to the kiln with me, I will let you be your own judge."

When we arrived at the kiln I said, "now gentlemen I will open the kiln at any place you want me to." They picked the place on the top of the kiln. I went to work like a June bug made the opening until they said that is deep enough.

"How did you manage to get such smooth faces on your brick."

I worked with Mr. Blount, who worked for Mr. Gray in Forrest City, in order to learn how to make brick, and I noticed that the coarser the sand they used, the rougher the brick were. So I found a real smooth white sand bed and used it so that my brick would be smooth.

"Well these brick are all right. What are they worth?"

"I am asking $9.50 per M."

"Well we will take $450.00 worth at that price."

"All right gentlemen. What are you going to build with these brick?"

"We are going to build a church at Forrest City, and will use these bricks for the front."

"Gentlemen is this the same church for which Capt. Wynne was soliciting?"

"Yes, this is the same church and we notice that you have given us $10.00 on it."

"Gentlemen, let me say right here, as this is the Lord's house, I will only charge you $9.00 and leave the half off."

"Uncle Scott this is very nice in you and we thank you for your kindness."

This was the first sale of brick I made at the kiln. Within the next day or two, I met Mrs. Graham,[15] who was a large land owner and a Christian lady. I said to her, "I see you are making extensive improvements on your farms. I see you are hauling brick from Forrest City to build your chimneys. Now as we are neighbors and own large farms adjoining, I would be glad for you to have your agents examine my brick kiln and if the brick and prices meet your approval, I would like to supply you with them."

"Why Uncle Scott, have you a brick kiln and what do you ask for your brick?"

"$9.50 per M."

"All right, I will instruct my agent to get the balance of the brick I need from you."

A day or so later, there were seven wagons from Mrs. Graham's at the kiln for brick. The wagons continued to haul until they had hauled off the last brick I had to spare. I did not get a chance to build but one chimney for myself, after making my brother-in-law a present of brick enough to build a chimney for himself, I said to my brother-in-law, "I begged you a long time to go in partnership with me in this kiln. If you had been a partner, you could not have worked harder than you did work, and you would have made wages, as you did make and would have been $350 to the good clear of all expenses." You see I only made two sales and sold out the entire kiln. Now Mr. Banks, we could have sold 500,000 brick just as easy as we sold what we did."

This encouraged me to burn another kiln the next year.

Mr. Blount, by this time had gone off to school. I wrote to Gray's Station, Ark., for Mr. Carey Brown, who was an all round good brick man. By this time I had gathered experience about the brick business by which I could economize in various ways. I went to work, doubled my capacity and burned twice as many as I did the year before. It did not cost me as much to burn these brick as it did to burn the others. I do not remember now the exact date when I got rid of these bricks, but it was a short time and a more handsome profit than on the other kiln.

Mr. Bond's example in this particular could be profitably followed every year by farmers during what is called the "lay-by time." There is hardly a community in the south where clay suitable for brick can be found but would be benefited financially and otherwise if those who have the time training and energy would get busy making brick.

THE SLAVES' METHOD OF SECRET COMMUNICATION.

In the time of slavery there were many methods of communication among the slaves. Some of these methods were unique. Information was conveyed in many apparently mysterious ways. Sometimes, the methods known as the clothes-line telegraph, sometimes the underground mail; at other times a code of signals would impart the desired news. All this remember in a way to keep the overseer in the dark as to what was going on.

Negroes used to steal something to eat sometimes, and if it was a hog, he would call it "Joe High." And if it was a beef, he would call it "Ben Low." In fact, they had a jargon name for everything. If by chance, the overseer should smell the meat and detect it in one's dinner basket, he would rarely expose the thief. In fact, few people conscientiously thought the Negro's stealing at that time a moral wrong; and today his conscience along these lines is in a measure eased as a reflex of the conditions of that time.

WHY SCOTT BOND HAS BEEN SUCCESSFUL.

As a rule when a white man employs a Negro to work for him he tells him to go ahead.

Mr. Bond has always made it a rule to say, "Come on boys, let's go."

Here again we repeat his words without quotations: I hired two men—Frank Rutherford and Richard Earwood. The contract was that they were to eat when I ate, get up when I got up, go to bed when I went to bed, drink when I drank, and rest when I rested.

I was to pay them one-half of their wages each month and settle in full when the crop was laid by. If they quit before the crop was laid by, except for sickness or death, they were not to be paid the balance. I did this to keep them until the season was over.

They went to work and did nicely until on the 15th of June. I noticed Earwood stopping and looking up at the sun. At last, about eleven o'clock, he stopped and said to me: "Mr. Bond, I have done the best I could. If I should stay to complete my contract, I would have $27.50 coming to me. I can't stand it any longer. I will have to quit."

I laughed and said to him, "All right. If you see a man along the road tell him to come to me and I will pay him a dollar and a half a day while your money lasts. Then I will give him a dollar a day and board the balance of the season."

Earwood left me and went his way. Rutherford stayed with me. One day as we were nearing the end of our work, I paused in the shade of a tree that stood in the middle of the field. The fresh turned soil in the rows in the shade looked cool and inviting. I stopped and sat down on my plow. As Rutherford came along, I said, "Whoa!"

He asked me what was the matter.

I said to him, "Sit down and rest."

He seemed astonished. He shouted, "Rest?"

"Yes," said I, "rest!"

He remarked that he had been with me from March until the 26th day of July and that was the first time he had ever heard me say rest. He was amused, and peal after peal of hearty laughter rang across the field.

It is this spirit of "get up and get" that has made Scott Bond the most remarkable man of his race. He never takes anything for granted, but must have evidence of effort by the results attained.

LATENT FORCES.

"I often think of the latent forces," says Mr. Bond, "of the Negro race, of its opportunities to do things and be somebody, that are passed by us unnoticed."

To illustrate:

"I was once engaged in tearing out an old fence row. It was covered with briars and vines. The fence was a post and board fence. I had a number of hands working. After we had cut all the vines, briars and bushes, one of the men put his hands on one of the posts and gave a push. Down came five or six panels of fence—the boards and posts were all rotten.

One of the men said, "Just look at that! If the cows had any sense, they could have had all the corn they wanted."

I said, "Stop, all of you, and listen to me for a minute. If we Negroes only knew our power, we could do a great deal to better our condition, financially. If we would only stop and look and think, fortune would be as easy for us to get as it would have been for the cows to get the corn."

Years after this I met a young man in Hot Springs, the great health resort, who knew me. He hailed me, saying, "Why, here is Mr. Bond! You don't know me, do you?"

I told him I did not.

Interior view of Scott Bond's gin plant.

He then said, "My name is Alvin Wofford. I used to work for you fifteen years ago. I owe all my success in life to you."

With tears of joy running from his eyes, he continued: "Your lectures made a man of me, but of all the talks none did me more good than the talk you gave us the day we were tearing out the old fence row. I want you to make my house your home as long as you are in the city, because I feel that I owe my success to you."

Mr. Wofford was married and had a nice family and home in Hot Springs.

Thus is shown in a beautiful way, that if the race used its latent power, it would forge ahead by leaps and bounds. And if individual efforts succeed so well, who can even estimate the advancement we could make if we work in union to attain a common end?

LEARNING THE MEANING OF
A "YANKEE TRICK."

One of the best things Mr. Bond tells us is how he learned what people meant by a "Yankee Trick." It is best told in his own words:

"When I was a small boy in the early years of the Civil War, one of my duties was to keep the flies off the table. My mistress and the overseer would sit at the table for hours and talk about Yankees and 'Yankee Tricks.' I wondered what they meant by "Yankees." I had heard people sing a song about "Yankee doodle dandy," and I thought a Yankee must be some kind of an animal.

After the war I asked a white man what a "Yankee Trick" was.

He said one day he was driving along a road in a wagon. Among other things he had a barrel of molasses. He met some Yankee soldiers and asked them to show him a "Yankee Trick."

They told him they would, and taking an auger he had in the wagon, bored a hole in one end of the molasses barrel and told him to stick his finger in to keep the molasses from running out. Then they bored a hole in the other end and told him to reach over and stick a finger in that hole. The soldiers then rode off. As they were leaving they said: "You asked us to show you a 'Yankee Trick.' That is one. Hold your molasses."

SCOTT BOND IN A JIM-CROW CAR.

Soon after the passage of the separate coach bill in Tennessee[16] some funny things happened. At one time I was returning from Nashville, where I had been to see one of my sons graduate. When I started to enter the train the conductor came to me and said, "That is not your car. Get in this car."

We obeyed the conductor as we had a right to do, and found ourselves in the car with white passengers. As I sat down I said to my son: "The conductor is mistaken. We will sit still and wait until the conductor comes back. We will then call his hand and have him let us go into our own car." This conversation attracted the attention of other passengers and they took in the situation. When the conductor came through and took up and punched our tickets, I remarked to him: "Colonel, I think you are mistaken. We are a little above riding in a car with white folks, as we are Negroes and I would like for you to show us into a Negro car if you have one hitched to this train."

The conductor looked a little strange but we had a hearty laugh and he had the porter show us into a car where the colored passengers rode, where I found the schoolmates of my boy on their way home from school. We chatted and discussed the exercises and the callings of the different boys and girls in after life. At another time I remember that soon after the separate coach bill had been passed in Arkansas, I boarded a train at Madison. This was what was known as a fast train. After I sat down the porter came to me and said: "This is not your car, captain, you should get up and go in the other car." I paid no attention to him. He went out and in a few minutes he came back and stuck his head in the door and said, "Cap', get up and go into the other car, you don't belong in here."

I still paid no attention to the porter. Shortly afterwards he came back with the conductor, who slapped me on the back and said: "Get up and go into the other car." I looked at him in a sarcastic manner and said: "What in the name of the Lord shall I do? The law says I shall not ride in the other car and you say I shall not ride in this car with niggers. What shall I do?"

The conductor smiled and said: "I guess we will have to have the legislature pass another separate coach bill." I said: "I have been made to feel very much embarrassed and as soon as I get to a county seat I am going to have papers made out and sue the railroad company for damages." The conductor said: "There is no use to do that, for this has happened unintentionally."

"All right, colonel, admit that what you say is true, I suffer from the effects of it just the same." This put me to thinking. I realized the fact that I was neither pig nor puppy and said to myself: "Somebody is responsible for this somewhere and at some time. Lord, is it I?"

SCOTT'S FRIEND GOES TO AFRICA.

Some very peculiar things can happen in life. Some years ago the Negroes in these parts caught what might be called the "African Fever" or a desire to move to Africa.

A man named Stanford[17] came through this part of the country and was persuading all the Negroes to go to Africa. He succeeded in getting quite a number to agree to go. They sold out their holdings, including real estate and personal property. He had night meetings among the colored citizens of this community. Dr. Stanford was a Negro, and was a man of note as a financier. He was a plausible fellow and would almost talk the horns off a frozen cow. He had a way of telling the people that, owing to the vast amount of tropical fruit found and the ease of getting gold and diamonds, all of which could be gathered by the handful, and even went so far as to say that there were pan cakes and molasses that the pancakes grew on trees, and that all one had to do was to shake the trees and feast. He was quite a historian and made a number of my people believe that what he said was true.

The day they were to leave, there were about three hundred of them. They met three hours ahead of time in a great body. I never saw nor heard such singing and shouting before.

Among the songs they sang were:

"Jesus my all, to heaven has gone,
He whom I fixed my hopes upon;
His track I see, and I'll pursue,
The narrow way 'til him I view.
I'll never turn back no more."

This and many other old Plantation Melodies were sung, and one of the emigrants preached a farewell sermon.

There were numbers of them who made prayers for the safety of the voyage.

There were two real old people—man and wife—named America and Hannah Shoulders, who were so old that any one could see that they were not strong enough for a journey of that character.

Numbers of people, white and colored, went to them and tried to persuade them not to start. They would reply to all alike, "I am heaven bound. There is more money to be made in Africa picking up mahogany switches than there is in growing corn and cotton here. Africa is my original home. There is no lynching and brutal treatment of its citizens. I am going home! If I fall by the wayside, I want my face to be towards Africa."

As old as they were, it was fortunate for them to reach the Promised Land. They only lived a few months after their arrival.

The people of this community of both races were very much excited over the "African Fever," white as well as black.

Home of Taylor Swift. Bought and paid for after his return from Africa.

A few days later I happened to be in Forrest City, the county seat. A number of the white people would say to me:

"Uncle Scott, do you think all the colored people are going to Africa?"

I replied, "No! There are ten million Negroes in the United States and it would hardly be possible to furnish them transportation in twenty-five years."

"Well," they would say, "I have no business in Africa, but I have been raised with them; they partly raised me. If they all go, I am going too. I can't live without them."

I said to them: "I am sorry to hear you say this, for as large as this world is, all broad-hearted people ought to be able to get a living out of this world."

Among the large number of blacks who went to Africa, some returned, some died for lack of knowledge of the laws of health, and others lived, thrived and did well. There was one named Harry Foster, a man from Georgia, whose transportation I had paid from his old home to Arkansas, who had a great deal of vim and "get up."

After he arrived in Africa he secured his two barrels of flour, one hundred pounds of meat, sugar and coffee and took possession of his twenty acres of land, cleared it, developed it and set it out in coffee trees, then bought twenty acres more from the government and planted that to coffee trees. The last I heard of him he was deriving an income of $1,500 a year from his coffee plantation.

There was another man named Taylor Swift, who lived on one of my farms for four or five years. I finally persuaded him to buy himself a home adjoining my farm. He had developed this place by clearing the land and building houses, and at that time had plenty of corn, mules and cattle and a nice little bank account. He too pulled out for Africa with about $1,800 in cash. Taylor was a good cotton grower. After he got to Africa and saw no cotton he was at a loss as to what to do. At the expiration of six months he decided to return to the United States. He took his family and pulled out for home via Liverpool. His funds were exhausted when he arrived at the English port and cabled back for transportation to Arkansas. He was glad to get back and to meet his old friends and we were all glad to see Taylor and talk with him about Africa and his adventures. Taylor was now in destitute circumstances; no home, no money and nothing to eat. But he had a host of warm-hearted friends. When he left he had sold his farm to a white man, a Mr. Newman Laughinghouse, but later I had bought it as it joined one of my farms. He sold a pair of mules with his farm. One of the mules he called old Nell. He met this mule in the road one day after his return, smacked her in the mouth and said: "Nell, I hope to buy you back and if I do you will live and die mine."

Taylor is more than an average man. He is really a good citizen, a good worker and always paid his obligations. He is well thought of by all who know him. When I met him after his return home he said to me: "Well, Bond, I am at home again. I got my start with you before I went to Africa and lost it and now I want you to sell me another mule on credit and rent me 15 acres of the best land you have. I made it here once and I can make it again."

I said: "All right, Swift, I will not sell you a mule but I will give you one."

"Bond, that sounds good."

Swift took the mule, made and gathered 14 bales of cotton and 180 bushels of corn that year. I had reduced his rent and practically gave him the corn and the hogs to make his meat another year.

Bird's eye view of Scott Bond's gravel beds.

There was a tract of 80 acres of land belonging to another party adjacent to the farm that he had formerly owned. I encouraged Swift to buy it, which he did, and now he has it in a high state of cultivation, all paid for with plenty of mules, cattle and hogs, an automobile and a fine bank account. This instance shows what a Negro can do in this country, if he will. Here is a man who came back home destitute and in debt. If he can do this, others can.

A RACE WITH THE STORK.

This story of another addition to the Bond family is intensely interesting and we let Mr. Bond tell it in his own way:

"I had always made it a point to be near home when there was an arrival expected. On one occasion the time approached when I felt it my duty to be at home as much as possible. Yet it was crop gathering time and my farming operations for that year were about 16 miles north of my home. My hands were gathering cotton and when ginned I would wait until I had a number of bales ready and would then get all my own wagons and the wagons of my neighbors and take in enough cotton to Forrest City to give the gin something to do. One Sunday afternoon as I sat talking with my wife I noticed that she was crying. I asked her what was the matter. She replied: 'You have always been near me, but this time you will not be able to be at home. You are in the midst of your picking and will have to be at the Allen farm.' I told her I had 18 mules and two horses and that I would be with her or my mules or horses would not have a leg left. I comforted her as best I could. I rode 32 miles a day, leaving home in the morning and returning at night. Some three weeks later as the time drew near I had been to the farm and was within three miles of home when I saw my son Theo., riding toward me. I knew what was the matter. I was driving one of the 38 wagons in the train. I called a boy who was riding my horse and gave him the team and mounting my horse turned and coursed my way through the woods, Theo following. I found on my arrival that I would still have time to go to Forrest City. I passed a few words with my wife and then went on to Forrest City. When I returned I found a bouncing boy awaiting me."

SCOTT BOND FINDS POT OF MONEY.

There are extant many stories of the finding of hidden gold in the fields and hills of this county. About three years prior to this writing there was a colored woman driving into Madison along the river road at the foot of Crowley's Ridge. She noticed an old pot that had been exposed at the root of a large tree by a heavy rain that had fallen the night before. She passed it by and at night as she was returning home she thought she would satisfy her curiosity by examining the old pot. A passer-by told her that a white man had found there that day a pot containing $8,000 in gold, all of which proved to be true.

As to myself, I was one time building a fence. I had a boy digging a hole for a gate post. He struck a hard substance that prevented him digging the hole. The boy's name was Willie Rucker. I said to him: "Willie, how long will it take you to finish digging that hole?" He replied: "Mr. Bond, I don't know. I have struck something hard like a piece of iron; I can't get through it."

I told him that was all right, to pull it out.

"Mr. Bond, you will have to start another hole [as] I can't get through this iron." I told him to get away. I got down and reached into the hole and put my hand through the handle of the lid of an oven. I had often heard that money had been buried somewhere about the place. It was in the month of February. It was very cold. I immediately found something else for Willie Rucker to do. The sun was about one and one-half hours high. I sent Willie to feed the horses. I covered the hole with a board and waited until night to remove the pot. It looked as if night would never come. When it was dark I got my spade and went to work. After digging for an hour and a half I pulled the pot up. It was dark. I could feel the seam around the edges but I could not remove the lid. As it was cold, I took it to my bed room and placed it on the hearth in front of the fire and got a hammer and tried to get the lid off. My wife and mother-in-law had retired by this time, and in tapping the rim with the hammer to loosen the lid it awakened my wife, who rose up in the bed and asked me what was the matter. I told her nothing; to lie down. She got up out of the bed and came to me and asked what I had there and what I was trying to do. I told her it was a pot of gold. Then and there wife got busy.

"Let me have the hammer," she said, "I will get the lid off."

By that time my mother-in-law had awakened and was up and at the fire asking what in the world was the matter. "Let me have the hammer," she said. "I will get it off." I was so worked up over my find I did not eat any supper. I thought that I had found a rich and unexpected treasure. By that time my two children were awake and at the fireside, and all were anxious to get the lid off the pot. There was a seam all around the edge where the lid appeared to be fastened on to the pot. But all the joys of earth have an end. To our chagrin the pot of gold proved to be a weight off the safety valve of an old-fashioned boiler. It weighed 29 pounds. It has often been said that Scott Bond found a pot of money. That is true; he did; he dug it dollar by dollar from the long rows of corn and cotton, working early and late or as he has often said: "From can't to can't. From can't see in the morning, to can't see at night." His pot of gold is the profits of his toil. There are thousands more like it buried in the fertile fields of Arkansas waiting for the energy and thrift of any who will dig.

SCOTT BOND'S WIFE FINDS CAN OF WEALTH.

He said: "When I bought my home place where I now live it was formerly owned by a man named McMurry. It appeared that Mr. McMurry and his wife did not always agree. They only had one child, a son. This young man always esteemed his mother very highly and gave her the greatest honor in his power. After he had grown to manhood he became a captain on the river and made quite a sum of money. Being so affectionate to his mother, it was said he had given her $500 in gold and that his mother had buried it somewhere about the place. When I bought the place mother, father and son were all dead and I bought the place from their estate. There was a jug cistern dug within ten feet of the north chimney of the house. It had always been said that colored people believed in dreams. One of my neighbors named Abe Davis met me one morning and said: 'I had a dream last night. I dreamed that you had found $500 in gold buried between the cistern and the chimney of the room where you and your wife sleep.'

"I had a hearty laugh with the old gentleman and passed it off. About three weeks later my brother-in-law's wife dreamed that a lot of money was found within three feet of the place where Mr. Davis dreamed that he found it. A few months later my brother-in-law came with another dream. He dreamed that he found it under the hearth in our bed room within five feet of the place where the others dreamed it was found. About a year after these dreams I was running a large farm about 15 miles away and always made it a rule to come home every Saturday evening to see my wife and children. Wife would always have our home in perfect order and she and the children would be eagerly awaiting my arrival. On this particular occasion I was a little early.

As I quietly rode up to the gate and looked over into the yard, and all the flowers were in bloom, my two little boys were out in the front yard playing. They had not yet detected my presence.

I sat there on my horse and noted the cows and hogs, chickens, boys and flowers, and I could hear my wife singing back in the kitchen, getting supper. All this appeared to me like home, sweet home.

I made my presence known and there was a hearty greeting. I

told my wife and children many little stories of what had happened during that week.

After supper was over and we had retired, the fire from the fire place made a brilliant light on the hearth. I said to my wife, "I admire the neatness with which you have painted your hearth." She remarked: "Yes, do you remember that sunken place in the hearth that was so hard to keep level?"

I said: "Yes, I remember it."

"What was the reason we could never keep that brick level?" she asked.

I replied: "I have no idea."

"Some crazy person," she said, "in laying the foundation for that hearth had put a tin can in with the dirt and one edge of the brick rested on the tin can."

"What was in the can?" I asked.

She replied: "Nothing but dirt."

I asked if the can was rusty.

She said: "No, it was bright. The top had been melted off and was pressed close together."

I asked how she knew there was nothing in the can but dirt.

"Because it was heavy," she replied.

I asked her what she did with the can.

She told me she had given it to Dora, the nurse girl. This girl was about grown. She said she told Dora to take it out and throw it away. I asked her where Dora threw the can. The next morning I asked Dora to come and show me where she threw the can. She walked over to the fence where I had a potato patch and said: "I threw it right over there in the potato patch."

I had only six rows of potatoes set out at that time and I took it row by row and searched diligently the entire potato patch for the can. This was on Sunday morning. I thought the matter over several times during the day, and remembered the dreams, all of which pointed to within eight feet of the place where the can was located. This confirmed in my own mind that by the can being bright and not rusty and the top edge being pressed close together and being heavy, as wife said; then taking into consideration the stories of the $500 in gold, I thought we had found the hidden treasure. On Monday morning I gave Dora another can and told her to go and throw it where she threw the other. She took the can, walked up to the fence and threw it over and said: "There is where I threw it." I got the garden rake and raked the ground thoroughly for ten feet around where she threw the can. I failed to locate it. I then hitched my mule to the harrow and literally tore my potato patch to pieces hunting the lost treasure. My brother-in-law came up as I was looking for the can and helped me hunt for it, but there was no can found. Some time after this, Dora became dissatisfied and moved back to Tennessee from whence she had come a year before. I then made myself satisfied, hoping she had availed herself of the hidden treasure.

BUILDS GIN AT MADISON.

In looking around Madison I began to think of what would be the best thing for our town and the community at large. It occurred to me that a first class steam gin outfit would be the next thing; handling as I was about 600 bales of cotton of my own, and seeing the surrounding country was increasing its cotton growing acreage.

I went to Mr. Ed Berry, who was a merchant and competitor of mine in the same town and made this proposition to him.

"You have a small one stand gin outfit in the town, now let me purchase one-half interest in your gin outfit then we will dispose of the outfit and put in a first class four stand continental outfit in partnership and you be president of the concern and you shall also have a say so, as to who shall manage the plant. I now own this court house square here in the town we will build our gin on the railroad switch and river bank, which will give us fine shipping facilities.

He said: "No, I will agree to nothing of the kind. In the first place there is not cotton enough in this community to support a gin of this class."

"I am surprised governor, you must be mistaken about this, because you handle upward of 250 bales from your own farm, and I handle something like 500 or 600 bales. This would of itself justify the plant, to say nothing of what might come from the country around.["]

His answer was "No, I will never agree to anything like that, and I shall not allow a building of that kind to be built where you say you are going to put it."

Farmers at Scott Bond's gin 1916.

"Do I understand you to say that I shall not build a gin on my own land?"

"That is exactly what I say and I mean every word I say."

"Well governor on what grounds are you going to prevent me from building?"

"On the ground that it will be obnoxious to my business interest. It will increase the insurance on my houses and stock."

"Now governor I don't have this to do but to show you how broad I am, I will agree to pay the difference between what you pay now and what you will pay for insurance."

"No, you don't have this to do, I am able to pay my own bills."

"All right governor we are going to put up a plant anyhow."

He said: "All right I will see you out."

My mind was thoroughly made up along these lines. I got my sons and consulted them about building a gin plant. They both disagreed with me on the ground that it would cost too much money, and that we were not in a position to put in that kind of a plant.

"Boys I think you are wrong. The man who sits down and waits is usually the man who is always behind. I can see our way clear, so come now, sit down and write these letters.

I wrote to three concerns that were putting out gin plants at that time, and got immediate replies from all the concerns, stating that their agents would wait on us in the next few days. Right here business picked up.

I had my mind already made up as to what kind of a gin I would put in. I had been to Forrest City and seen the continental outfit that had been put in by Mr. Fussell[18] and others, but I had no idea what an outfit like that would cost.

The first agent to call on us was Mr. Phillips, representing the Murray Gin people. The next was Mr. Dickerson, representing the Continental Gin Co. Both of these gentlemen explained the capacity, durability, etc., of their respective plants. Both claimed to have the best outfit, but I was unable to get either one to tell me the cost to us of his outfit f. o. b. our station. They were highly intelligent and were on to their job.

After I had explained to them the size of plant and the kind of buildings I wanted and the number of gins, they left and said they would return at a certain time, prepared to offer prices. I set the time for April 10. On that day I had a representative from three different concerns all anxious to sell to us. This gave me leverage and a chance to pull them all on prices.

After getting prices, f. o. b. our station from each of them, I managed that neither should know the other's proposition. We talked gin machinery from early afternoon until 6 o'clock.

Mr. Dickerson took me into a private office and said: "Uncle Scott, I am going to sell you this outfit regardless to what the price may be."

I told him all right, but he would have to lower the price away down from what he had quoted.

He asked what price the Murray people offered.

I told him I could not afford to tell him that, but the lowest price will get the order.

When Mr. Dickerson turned me loose the Murray man grabbed me and took me into the private office. He told me his factory had sent him to sell to me regardless of the price. I told him all right, but his figures were too high. That he must do more subtraction. He asked what price the Continental offered. I told him it would not be policy for me to say what their offer was.

Mr. Dickerson walked in and said: "Gentlemen, excuse me a minute. Uncle Scott, I have telephoned to Mr. [James F.] Wolfe, manager of the Forrest City Gin, he will be here in a few minutes."

Mr. Wolfe a fine stylish gentleman and an expert on Continental gin plants, because of his having purchased several of this make came in and said: "Uncle Scott may I see you privately for a minute?"

"Yes, sir."

"Now Uncle Scott, Mr. Dickerson phoned me to come over here and help him out with this sale. I certainly do know from past experience, what I have paid the company for two or three different outfits I have bought from them. From what Mr. Dickerson has told me, he has made you a very low price on this outfit. But I want you to know that I am not connected with either one of the factories. My trip over here is merely to help out Mr. Dickerson. I want you to feel personally that I am really your friend."

"That is all right Mr. Wolfe, I appreciate what you say, but Mr. Dickerson will have to get $375 under the price he has mentioned. This is a cash proposition and money makes the mare go."

"I don't blame you much Scott but I am afraid Mr. Dickerson will not be able to sell you. But it is all up to him and his factory."

Then we walked out and met Mr. Phillips and Mr. Dickerson.

Mr. Phillips says: "Let's have a fine cigar." The whole party had a hearty laugh.

"All right Mr. Phillips, I don't smoke, but I will enjoy seeing you all smoke."

"Well," he said, "Have a dry smoke."

"I don't know what that means." Then another laugh from all parties.

"Take the cigar and hold it in your mouth and don't light it."

"And this is what you call a dry smoke?"

Mr. Phillips said: "Uncle Scott I guess it is my time. Let me see you privately. Now if I just knew what price you wanted to pay. I have already cut this outfit down almost to the cost of manufacture and yet if I knew what you were aiming to pay for it, I would be able to sell you in ten minutes. I am willing to cut the price I mentioned you $100 less."

"Well that looks like you are getting down to the place and I think I will be able to let you know in a few minutes."

It was then about six o'clock in the evening. I stepped in the store and Mr. Dickerson said: "Uncle Scott it is all off. I will accept the proposition you made Mr. Wolfe."

Mr. Phillips said: "Uncle Scott I think I ought to have another chance."

Mr. Dickerson said: "Mr. Phillips, Uncle Scott does not talk but one time. I have accepted the proposition Uncle Scott made to Mr. Wolfe and it is all over."

"Yes, I meant precisely what I said to Mr. Wolfe. I am now ready for the contract, and I want the machinery delivered as quickly as possible."

Mr. Wolfe said: "I came over to help Mr. Dickerson make this deal, but it looks as though I have helped you out instead of Mr. Dickerson, for I do know that you have bought your outfit $1150 cheaper than I bought mine."

"I am much oblige to you Mr. Wolfe and also to Mr. Dickerson and his factory."

I soon saw that this was the Continental territory and they could better afford to give a gin away than to allow the Murray people to get a foothold.

The blue prints and their timber dimensions were soon forwarded us from the factory.

I then got a contractor from Little Rock by the name of G. L. Ball. Had the ground cleaned off and the foundation of the building laid. The building was completed by the time the machinery arrived. It was unloaded and put to place in the gin house in good shape. The engine and boiler were set at the proper place.

"Governor" [Ed] Berry, who was my competitor kept a keen eye on me all this time. He had decided within himself that he could not interfere with me in so far as the main building was concerned, but knowing I would have to have a large platform in front of my gin plant and seeing that I would have to extend it over an old street that had been condemned, because the town had lost its charter. I had learned from his actions that this was the ground on which he would object to me building a platform. I had a talk with my contractor and told him what was going to happen. I had all the timbers sawed and hauled and placed on the ground. Now I want you from time to time to have all the rubbish for 100 feet in front of the

View of one of Scott Bond's cotton fields in 1917

gin removed. But to remove it at different times in order to prevent suspicion. To have all the blocks sawed and timbers cut to build a platform 48 feet wide and 150 feet long. To be sure to have every piece cut and laid at the proper place, in order that the platform could be built in about 3 hours. Be sure to have everything ready. Because I was sure that Governor Berry was going to try to file an injunction to prohibit me from putting up the platform.

The contractor came in the store one morning and said he was ready to stretch his line.

I said: "I am afraid you are not ready. I am going to give you until 12 o'clock today to view the ground and be sure that you have every thing at the proper place, as I do not want to use any tools but hammer and nails."

At 12 o'clock I had my horse hitched to my buggy and gave orders to have the store closed and every salesman and all the balance of the crew that was working on the gin to get hammers and nails.

I said to the contractor: "Now when you stretch your tape line the 'governor' [Berry] will come and tell you to stop, but do not pay any attention whatever. You must not have a word to say to him under any circumstances. I will get in my buggy and drive full speed to the court house at Forrest City, because I know there is where he will have to go to get out papers to file an injunction and I want to be there sitting on the steps waiting to be made whole.

"Now boys each and every one of you; I want my orders carried out to the letter. Answer no questions and say nothing to any one, but listen to my contractor and do what he tells you. This is one of the times I want you to turn and turn fast. I want this job accomplished inside of three hours at the most."

I was at the court house door when the county judge walked to the door and called the constable. I raised up and said: "Judge, I suspect I am the man you want to see."

"Well yes. Here is Uncle Scott now. Uncle Scott, Mr. Berry has called me over the phone and told me you were building a platform over the county road."

"Now Judge you know Mr. Berry is a white man and I can't afford to dispute his word. Do you believe that being as I am a citizen of this county, I would have little enough sense to build an obstruction over the county road?"

"No, Uncle Scott that does not look reasonable. What are you building and where are you building it?"

"I am building a platform to my gin plant that I have just finished at the north end of one of the streets of the town that has been condemned."

"What kind of a plant are you putting up and what will it cost?"

"I am putting in a complete Continental outfit of the latest model. It will cost something like $9,000."

"Uncle Scott, that is all right. I wish the county was full of Scotts. But you know I am a white man and a democrat and have to try to favor my many neighbors and voters."

"There is my horse and buggy. Let Mr. Thad Sellers the constable, take him and drive down and see."

"How long will it take you to finish it?"

"Judge I guess it is about completed by this time. I had my arrangements made with my contractor to finish it in two or three hours as I was looking for just such steps as these."

"I will tell Mr. Berry by phone, that to comply with the law, he will have to come over here and get out the papers. I am sure by that time you will have it completed."

"I surely will judge and I am very much obliged to you for the manner in which you have explained things to me."

I got into my buggy and drove back home. When I arrived the platform 48 feet wide and 150 feet long was completed and the boys were unloading the machinery from the cars and putting it on the platform.

I stepped on the platform and said to the contractor, "I want to congratulate you for your shrewdness and swiftness."

"Did you have any trouble?"

"No, none of any consequence."

"When I ran my line out and drove my first stake, Mr. Berry came out and asked me what I was doing. I told him I was building a platform for cotton. He said I notify you to stop and don't drive another peg. I told him all right and kept on driving pegs and pushing the boys up."

"Later he came back with another white man and said, I now notify you in the presence of this man not to drive another peg."

["]I told him to go and see my boss. I am paid $5.00 per day to do this work and consider he is responsible."

"Where is your boss as you call him?"

"I suppose he is at the court house by this time. He said he was going there."

"All right, he is one of the slickest ducks I have run upon for some time, and I must give him credit for his shrewdness."

The next morning he brought the insurance papers and said: "Here are the papers you agreed to sign."

"All right governor let me see them. I called my son to read them over."

He read them over very hurriedly. Son read those papers again and read slowly and don't read so fast. When he had completed reading the insurance papers I said governor you have been in the mercantile business for 18 years, and your store has never burned. Now if I sign these papers the way you have them made out I see no reason why your store should not burn in 48 hours.

"You promised me you would sign them."

"Yes at the beginning I told you, if you would not interfere with me building the plant, in order to get along with you I would sign papers for the difference between what you had been paying and what you would have to pay now. But you told me you was a white man and could pay your own bills. For that reason I don't feel that I am under any obligation."

Along in those days I hustled all day and part of the night. I found out it was quite a job to install a plant like this and get it ready by ginning time. The thing that worried me most was that in handling the contractor, as he had been accustomed to working his men on the ten hour system, the sun was two hours high in the morning when they began work, and was two hours high in the evening when they knocked off. As a farmer I could not fit myself gracefully into this system, but I had to take my medicine and do the best I could. However I had my plant ready and was the first man to gin a bale in the county that fall.

This gin was largely advertised, by the different colored farmers all over the country. We had nothing to do but to go ahead ginning.

In a few weeks we were turning out from 25 to 40 bales a day and would often gin until 10 o'clock at night. I expected 800 bales of cotton for the season, but to my surprise we ginned 1,800 bales. This flooded the little town with worlds of money that fall. Mr. Berry, my competitor, did not gin a bale with me and did not allow any of the hands on his place to gin with me. Yet this gin had increased his mercantile business 100 per cent above any previous time.

I met him about the close of ginning season and said: "Governor how is your mercantile business? Is it not a fact that your business has increased 100 per cent as a result of the erection of this plant?"

"I could not say it has increased 100 per cent, but I must say I have done the best business this fall that I have done since I have been merchandising."

"I am sure you are right because I have paid out all the way from $350 to $500 a day on cotton seed and made the rebate checks in a way that all business men of the town could collect and share alike."

"Well you are right about that. I must compliment you for what you have done. I have kept you from ginning every bale this fall that I could. If I live to see another year I expect for you to gin every bale of cotton over which I have any influence. I see now that your gin plant is the making of our little town."

The next year Mr. Berry not only ginned his own cotton with me, but he actually went out and canvassed for the gin, and we ginned 2,260 bales of cotton.

This of course made me feel that I had accomplished a big thing in the manner in which I handled things at that time. I suppose any man white or black would have felt good over this.

I must admit here that Mr. Berry is away over an average man, for truthfulness and honesty as a citizen. He is fair and open in all of his decisions, as man to man, and has always shown that he was willing "to give to Caesar the things that are Caesar's."

BAD CROPS.

About 1911–12 it looked as though the climate or seasons were changing. The opportunities for progressive farming in these parts. Crops had begun to be almost flat failures.

August 1st that year I had an opportunity to take one of my neighboring farmers in the buggy with me for a drive over some of my farms. This gentleman got out of the buggy on different farms and examined the cotton and said: "All the cotton I have seen up to date and would average for 1 to 1 ½ bales to the acre." Prospects then were fine for a big crop.

It began raining on that day and rained every day in the month of August, and when the rain stopped cotton took the blight and millions of bolls dried up without maturing. All the crops that season were cut 75 per cent. I had never seen a failure in this country prior to this in all my forty years of farming. But I decided that while I had worlds of sweetness, I must also accept some of the bitter.

I started next season as usual to farming, thinking we would make a good crop. Just as we got well under way there came an overflow. The mighty Mississippi swelled out of her banks and inundated the whole of our part of the country. From Crowley's Ridge to Memphis, a distance of 40 miles was one vast sea of water, sweeping to the Gulf of Mexico, bearing on its muddy bosom wreckage and driftwood from the country above.

Farmers lost heavily in stock, produce, fences and houses. This caused me to build a boat which would carry 20 mules and several tons of other stuff, and with this I conveyed many people to high ground from the overflowed lands about me. It also required about four weeks of hustling night and day to manage such a vast quantity of produce and to help care for a large number of people and stock.

FINDING MONEY.

I remember one time my aunt found $47 on the river banks at the Allen farm. It was customary for the women on the place to do their laundry work on the bank of the river. My aunt had taken her wash tub and wash board down to the water's edge and had about completed her task and was returning to the house. About two-thirds of the way up the bank she espied at her feet an old-fashioned, wide-mouthed snuff bottle. She had her apron tucked up around her waist to make a pocket for small things. She stooped and picked up the bottle and dropped it into her apron. She had a bundle of clothes on her head and a wash board under her arm. The bottle dropped through the apron and rolled down the hill. She started after it and caught it just at the water's edge. When she opened it she found $47 all in dimes, black from age. She and her husband had a task every night sitting up rubbing the tarnish from the pieces that the inscription and figures could be read. This money was probably buried by some of the slaves on the farm before the civil war.

SCOTT BOND BUILDS A CONCRETE STORE.

The first store house of concrete in St. Francis County was built by Scott Bond on the old court house square. Mr. Bond says:

I had purchased this square at cost of $750.00. At that time there were only frame buildings in Madison and I concluded that this would be a beautiful site for a store. I made up my mind to erect a building of concrete, 30 feet by 120 feet long, three stories high; the lower story being a twelve foot basement running full length and breadth of the structure.

I had bids from contractors in Little Rock and elsewhere, who, on different occasions, came and submitted bids for the building. I finally closed with Mr. Delano of Forrest City, Ark., his bid being the lowest and best.

In talking with contractors I found that I had best be my own architect so I made my own plans. In my trips to St. Louis, Kansas City and elsewhere, I learned that cement and sand would hold for Yankees and I concluded it would hold for me. I used old sawdust chains, band saws and 2-inch pipe for reinforcing. This material I had picked up at different saw mills about the country. A building of this kind was new to numbers of people in this locality. There was a gentleman, Mr. James Fussell, of Forrest City, considered the "bull dog of the boneyard," who came over and after inspecting the entire structure called me and said: "Don't you know that you are throwing away a good deal of money on this building?" I asked him why he thought so. He replied: "Don't you know this thing will crack and fall to the ground?" I remarked that I hoped it would not; that I had been over the northern states and had seen the Yankees erecting such structures and that if sand and cement would hold for them, with proper mixing it would hold for me.

He said: "I hope so, but I am very much afraid it will not. Our bank will let you have all the money you want, as you seem to be one of the fellows who always succeeds."

The contractor, Mr. Delano, after getting the first story up, attempted to carry up the mortar with a gasoline engine. He tried it for two days, but it proved a failure. I went to the building and saw he had ten Negroes to carry the mortar. The following colloquy occurred:

"Good morning, Mr. Delano."

"Good morning, Uncle Scott."

"I see your gasoline engine was a failure."

"Yes," I said, "gasoline sometimes fails, but we as Negro laborers have never yet failed. We have always been faithful and obedient. When you say go, we go. When you say come, we come. That is what it has taken to make the sunny south what she is; to clear her forests, build her railroads and cities and to make her fertile fields blossom as the rose."

As construction advanced, I found that the contractor had taken the work too low. Mr. Delano insisted on giving bond on the contract. He gave me a mortgage on his home. He saw he would lose, and like any other man began to worry over the matter. I told him he should not worry; to carry out his contract and give me the best results and I would make everything all right. I finished the building. It is substantial and elegant. It is the only building of its kind in the county. I have lately installed an electric plant for lighting throughout. The cost of the building was several thousand dollars less than it would have been had I employed an architect.

OTTO B. ROLLWAGE.

In speaking of some of the notable people among whom he lived, Mr. Bond says:"One of the greatest men of the country hereabouts is Mr. Otto B. Rollwage.[19] To convince you that my saying is true, on one occasion this man was elected mayor of Forrest City at a time when he was 500 miles away. His election was unanimous.

"He is not only great in some things but proved himself, great in every way. He pays more taxes on city property in his town than any other individual living there. He was in the mercantile business about twenty years and was well thought of by all who came in contact with him in a business way, both white people and black people. He was the bull dog of the bone yard. During those many years my entire business was done with his firm, and while they handled thousands of bales of cotton that was grown by me, and hundreds of car loads of potatoes, which made my business with them amount to $8,000 or $10,000 per year, I can conscientiously say that they kept the best set of books ever kept in Forrest City. Their books were so perfect, regardless to the amount of business that we could settle with them in 20 minutes. I was never able in all the years I dealt with them to detect a single mistake in their accounting.

"At the time I was married, which was the second year I did business with them, as you will note, I have already stated I was financially weak. When I went to buy my wedding suit, Mr. Otto Rollwage waited on me himself, and at that time he was quite small, weighing only about 115 pounds. Being unable to find a suit in their stock to fit me, he went with me to every store in town; when we could find a coat we could not find a suit in town. We were at last compelled to buy coat at one place and trousers and vest at another place. One of the things that struck me most forcibly at the wind up, was trying to buy a white bow suitable for the occasion, we could not find one in the town. To my surprise Mr. Rollwage said: "By the way, I think I have the very thing you need up in my room. Come and go with me." He opened his trunk and took out a white bow and said: here is one that I bought for a similar occasion, but did not get to use it, and it will really be a pleasure to me to make you a present of it."

I said: "I certainly thank you Mr. Rollwage, this is very kind in you."

He said: "You are more than welcome. I only wish I could do more for you. Now wait, I think it will really be nice for you to have a white vest to go with that black suit. I have a beautiful white silk vest that has never been worn by anyone. I bought it at the same time I bought the bow, and I am sure the vest and tie will look well with your black suit."

"Mr. Rollwage that would be very nice, but I could not afford to have you do this, as I am a colored man and you a white man, I feel this would really be too much."

"No indeed Uncle Scott, I am willing to do anything I can do for you. I will also put my gold watch and chain in the vest."

"I wish I could show you, Mr. Rollwage, how much I appreciate your kindness."

I can say that I was married with a gold watch and chain that belonged to the greatest man in town.

We were about the same size.

The following night I was married to one of the greatest girls St. Francis County has ever produced. I had often heard the saying that it was lucky to marry in borrowed clothes. I have oft times attributed my success in my undertakings to the fact that I was married in a suit of clothes belonging to a great man.

Mr. Rollwage is today one of the leading lawyers of Eastern Arkansas.

HANDLING COTTONSEED WITH DIFFERENT OIL MILLS.

The cottonseed business has had one of the most remarkable careers of any southern industry. At one time cotton seeds were a drudgery and a nuisance. Today it is one of our greatest sources of revenue. The value of cottonseed has in a few years grown from less than nothing to hundreds of millions of dollars annually. One year I was doing business with the Richmond Cotton Oil Co. of which Mr. Sloane was manager. At that time I was operating three gin plants of my own and was also leasing one large plant at Widener, Ark., from the Richmond Cotton Oil Co. I was an extensive cotton grower, therefore always boosted the price of cottonseed. That season we handled something like $250,000 worth of cottonseed for the Richmond Cotton Oil Co. At the close of the season Mr. Sloane acknowledged that we had handled more seed for him than any other customer on his books. Mr. Sloane was pleased with the amount of seed we handled, but he did not like to see us boost the prices of seed to farmers. The seed market has always seemed to me to be a complicated affair. I have never been able to understand why the market for cottonseed was not quoted as are other products of the farm. Most of the original producers of cottonseed are Negroes, so it may be that the seed buyer does not think it necessary for the Negro to know the daily prices for which seed is selling. But as I have always inquired into the price of seed and have kept myself posted on the prices to the farmer and for that reason have been called a cottonseed booster.

The second season of my connection with the Richmond Cotton Oil Co., the local market opened at $13.50 per ton. I was advised by Mr. Sloane and other oil mill men that was the price to pay for seed. I loaded two cars and shipped them to Mr. Sloane at Memphis. The invoice when returned showed that I was receiving just $13.50, precisely the same I had paid for the seed. I had paid for the cost of handling and loading. All this fell on me, which showed I had lost $1.50 per ton on the deal. I called Mr. Sloane over the telephone and asked him what was the matter. If one bought seed for $13.50 and sold for the same, how long did he think a man could stay in the market. He replied: "Well, Uncle Scott, I have always told you that you were too much of a booster on cottonseed; that you needed a lesson and I think there is no better time than now."

I said to him: "Do I understand that you will not pay any more for the two cars of seed you have on hand?"

He said: "I will make the next cars $1.50 per ton more."

Scott Bond's store—looking north.

At this time I had five cars more ready for shipment. I had an idea that the world was pretty large, so I started out to hunt another market. I spent $7.50 the next few days looking for better prices. The last mill with which I spoke was the Buckeye Cotton Oil Co. I had a long telephone talk with them and noticed in the conversation that Mr. Sloane had had quite a talk with them in regard to the price of cottonseed. I was turned down cold so far as any advance in price was concerned, and held down to $13.50 per ton. By this time it occurred to me that I had been blackballed as to prices at all the mills. We were paying from six hundred to eight hundred dollars a day for cottonseed and had ten or eleven thousand dollars tied up in cottonseed at this time. I knew I could not stand this forever; that something must be done. I took the train for Memphis to visit some of the oil mills. I first went to Messrs. Cook, Gray & Co., who were my commission men and who were handling a large amount of cotton for me each year. I found Mr. Gray in his office.

I said to him: "I have fifteen to seventeen carloads of cotton seed and I would like to know what is the price per ton, and what could they be sold for?"

He replied, "I know I can get you $16 and I may be able to get

$17 per ton." Fortunately for me he called up the Richmond Cotton Oil Co., and sold the seed to them for $16.50. I said to Mr. Gray:"That price is all right.You go and close the deal with a written contract and I will pay you $50 for your trouble."

Mr. Gray said: "That would be useless, as the sale will be all O. K."

"No, Mr. Gray," I said,"I have been blackballed by all the mills in the country and Mr. Sloane is the author of the blackball game. If he finds that these are my seed he will be sure to turn the deal down. If he asks you where the seed came from, you tell him it makes no difference he will have to give you $16.50 f. o. b. station, where they are loaded and I will guarantee that the loading point will be within the $2 freight limit."

Mr. Gray got in his car, went down and closed the deal. I told him it was all right, I would go home and ship the seed to his account, and when the seed were all in to tell Mr. Sloane to make the invoice to Scott Bond, Madison, Ark. When the last car was in and Mr. Sloane was instructed to whom to make the check and invoice, he said to Mr. Gray: "Why that nigger has put me in the ditch I dug for him, I had him turned down cold by every oil mill in the country."

Mr. Sloane came over to Madison to see me. He found me at my gin plant. Mr. Sloane said to me: "Uncle Scott, you are a dandy. I must congratulate you.You put me in the same ditch I dug for you." He enjoyed the incident and laughed good naturedly over my play. He said he would be glad to handle my seed for the rest of the season and was willing to allow me a nice fancy profit. From that time on our business relations were very pleasant and the Richmond Cotton Oil Co., handled about 225 tons of seed for us at a nice profit.

A TRIP TO KANSAS CITY.

I had a cancerous growth on my cheek and learning of a specialist in ailments of this nature in Kansas City, I decided to visit him for treatment, as it was claimed he could eradicate the growth without the use of the knife.

I was in Kansas City some 15 days and was out practically every day, taking in the city and surroundings. I had long heard it talked in the south, by numbers of colored people who had lived in the north, and from white people who had lived up there about the social difference between the races north and south. I had not been in the city many days until I had realized that the condition was just what I had long made up my mind that it was; i. e., that a Negro in the eyes of the majority of the white people was the same north and south and soon found out that the colored man's financial opportunity was far greater South, than north. I visited all the factories, and the Swift and Armour packing plants, which were the greatest I had seen up to that time. I saw miles and miles of viaducts over which thousands and thousands of head of stock were driven daily to the slaughter pens. In going through all the stockyards and slaughter pens, I saw hundreds of white people of apparently every nationality at work and was very much surprised to see no Negroes at work in all these vast places except two colored women and their job was to examine the tinware as it was made to see if it would leak. I had heard so much of the opportunity of colored people in these places that I was very much surprised to find the two women were the only colored employees.

During my stay in Kansas City, I stopped with a very nice family, named Smith. After taking in a large part of the city I remarked to Mr. Smith that I was somewhat surprised.

He asked me how.

"I had always been informed by northern people visiting in the south that the colored people had better chances in the north than in the south."

Mr. Smith said: "Why Mr. Bond, the rumors going south along these lines are wrongly represented. Right after the war I left the state of Mississippi with my wife on a wild goose chase to this place, in order to better my condition along all lines, and the only advantage I have found for colored people, is the better facilities for educating their children. I obtained a job in the post office as helper when I first arrived here and I have held the same position for years; have not lost a day, have never been late to my work, I have apparently given satisfaction year in and year out. White men of all nationalities have been employed here in places beneath mine and every one of these men has been promoted from time to time over me until they fill some of the best positions in this building. Despite my faithfulness and proven ability, I have never been promoted above the position in which I started. I am sure that if I had remained in the state of Mississippi on the farm and been as faithful there as here, I could by this time have accumulated thousands of dollars.

"My brothers and friends have frequently written me of their success along financial lines in Mississippi. Today I have not saved a dollar above what it his taken to keep my family up. Mr. Bond, in my estimation the south is the only place for the Negro."

I then visited Leavenworth, Kans., where the soldiers were stationed. This was one of the greatest events of my visit to Kansas. I found the post one of the most beautiful sights I had ever witnessed. I was accompanied to this place by Mr. Will Rhoten, a brother-in-law to my oldest son. He was very dark but handsome, well built and nicely dressed. My son had written him and asked him to meet me at the train, chaperon me while in Leavenworth. He accompanied me to the beautiful spot where the soldiers were encamped. He showed me the ground and buildings and finally stopped at the barracks of the colored soldiers. Mr. Rhoten introduced me to the officers in charge. It was 12 o'clock and about eating time. We had dinner and I enjoyed the dinner immensely. The hospitality was all that could be desired. Every thing was as neat and clean as a pocket in a shirt.

When dinner was over the Sergeant in charge said to me: "Well Mr. Bond you are from the south."

"Yes sir."

"I want you for my benefit to relate to the boys something of the conditions of the south."

I said: "Gentlemen the south is still on the map and is moving up along all lines morally, socially and financially."

The Sergeant said: "Mr. Bond, I want to ask that you do us a favor. I see that you are going to say the things that will be of benefit to this barracks and I want the officers of the post to come down here, I want the officers to be present."

The note was handed to an orderly with instruction that he must report for duty when the officer arrived.

In a few moments 10 or 12 of the white officers appeared. The Sergeant said: "Mr. Bond, in order to save time I will introduce you

Scott Bond's herd of registered Herefords.

to some of the leading officers of this barracks by saying to them gentlemen I want to introduce you to Mr. Bond a farmer from the extreme south. I want him to tell us about the south and the north.["]

They saluted saying: "Mr. Bond."

I said gentlemen, I want to congratulate you on your splendid barracks, your beautiful flowers, on the neatness of your grounds as one of the most beautiful I have ever seen, and last but not least I want to further congratulate you on this regiment of colored soldiers. I must say in your behalf that you deserve great credit for training these soldiers. Your success has been wonderful. The only way one can tell they are colored soldiers is by their black skins. Their neatness and their politeness, their carriage place them as leaders in all the south.

I want to say in behalf of our colored soldiers that the position they now hold is one of the grandest positions ever occupied by an American citizen. Your faithfulness and obedience to your commanding officers will I am sure bring you out more than conquerors. When you have filled your contract with your government and the officers before whom you now stand not only the Negroes of the south but all of the citizens of America will be proud to lift their hats to you, and will point with pride to the glory of your achievements. I want to say further that, we the Negroes of the south are looking upwards and onward to greater efforts and successes along all lines.

Hundreds and hundreds of the race are doing their duty serving God and striving each day to be better citizens. And for myself let me say here, I am leaving no chip unturned. I have educated all my boys who are old enough to receive it in the college in the city of Nashville. They have returned home with their sheepskins and are now taking hold of the wonderful opportunities offered in the south. And Sergt. Rhoten of your regiment who is a brother-in-law to my oldest son, who has paid us several visits is in a position to substantiate all that I have said. Now when you have finished your term of enlistment with the government I beg and plead with you to return to the south, which is in one sense of the word, our father-land, which is the greatest and only place that nature has prepared for us to dwell. We, the Negroes of the south despite our mishaps are letting down our buckets where we are.

We live in a part of the country where we can master one of the greatest commodities of the American continent, the fleecy cotton that is grown by southern Negroes.

It seems to me that providence has prepared the south for us. We are the only nationality on the globe that can master the situation properly. The cotton plant can stand more brutal treatment than any other plant on earth. For this cause and many others I believe the south to be the natural home of our race. I can say for myself that I started in 1875 with nothing and now pay taxes on $250,000 worth of property, and can say that I am really proud of the reputation I have made among all races and especially among the better class of white people. The bonds of friendship between the white man and the Negro grows stronger every day. We have more banks, more money, and the lands are increasing in prices."

Upon my return to Kansas City I was shown one of the stations of the underground railroad over which so many slaves travelled to freedom. The building was peculiar from all other buildings. The manner and plan of its erection caused me to inquire about it. It was situated on the bank of the Missouri river, and was very attractive because of its color. It is the only building I ever saw that was painted black. In conversation with one of the old white residents of that city, the whole story of the U. G. R. R. was related to me. I was told among other slave escapes the story of Henry Box Brown. The gentleman who told me these stories was anxious to have me meet Bishop [Abraham] Grant,[20] of the African Methodist Church, who at that time lived in Kansas City, and after my return to my room, I had a telephone call from Bishop Grant asking for Mr. Bond from Arkansas. I replied: "Yes sir, this is he."

"Well Mr. Bond I would like to have a man of your reputation come out and have dinner with me tomorrow at 2 o'clock."

"Thank you Bishop but I have an appointment at that hour, but as I will be in the city for a week more I shall be glad to accept your invitation at any other time you may appoint."

"Then Mr. Bond, the next day at the same hour, if it meets your convenience."

"Thank you Bishop, I shall be glad to avail myself of the opportunity."

Promptly at the appointed time I met Bishop Grant at his home and introduced myself as the little man from Arkansas.

"Walk in Mr. Bond. I am really glad to meet you."

I was very favorably impressed with Bishop Grant. He was a man of large stature, fine appearance and a head full of brains. He immediately began to ask me questions pertaining to the customs of the south and the relations between the Negro and the white man. The answering of these questions seemed to impress the Bishop very much.

When dinner was ready, we repaired to the dining room. A delicious meal was elegantly served. The dinner seemed to strengthen the Bishop's questioning powers, as to the south and its customs.

He said: "Mr. Bond, from the way you answer my questions, about the relations between the races in the south, conditions are far better than I had been led to believe. I should be glad to take you around and show you our different enterprises."

He showed me a beautiful building that had been taken by the white and colored people as a hospital for colored people. It was nicely arranged and the appointments were of the latest and best. It was neat and clean, and seemed to have everything demanded in sanitation. We next visited ———— school, where I was introduced to the faculty, and was requested by them to address the school in my own way, which I did and it seemed to please every one.

This school was well equipped and had several shops for the manufacture of farm implements.

When we returned to Bishop Grant's home he asked me how I was impressed with the advantages of his northern town.

I replied to him that so far as his hospital and schools were concerned, it was grand and then asked him if he did not believe the south was the real home of the black people.

He said that he really did, but would like for me to state my reason for so believing.

I said to him: "We have our bitters in the south, and I have always heard that where there was no bitter there was no sweet, and the sweet of the south, is so much greater than the bitter, for the colored man, it makes me believe the south is really our home. The races are rapidly beginning to understand each other along financial lines. I note all the legislation of the south has tended to broaden the channel between the two races along the lines of so-called social equality. All this betters our condition because it drives us closer together and helps us in many different ways."

He then asked me what I thought of the influence of Christianity on the southern Negro.

I told him they were making wonderful progress among the race.

He asked me why I thought so and what was bringing about this condition.

I told him that since we had learned to discard the two by four preacher, and were following such men as himself and others of great character and ability, there was gradually developing a higher, a holier and more spiritual conception and practice of Christianity by colored people.

He then asked me of the economic or financial growth of the Southern Negro.

I told him they were making great strides in the acquisition of material wealth. They were buying land, building houses and rearing better families than they had heretofore. The white man of the south was improving the Negro every day, by offering better chances for financial development. And I thought that the southern Negro had spent more money for hymn books and Bibles than any other race in the world, for their means.

Mr. Rhoten had often spoken to me of the advantages of living in the north, that a colored man could go to places of public entertainment any where and would be treated the same as a white man.

I had my doubts about this, so on one sultry August afternoon we were passing a fine cafe, where they dispensed soda water and ice cream. I said to Mr. Rhoten: "Let's have some soda water and ice cream."

"All right Mr. Bond, there is a nice place down here where we can be served."

I said: "No I don't want a nicer place than this cafe."

I remembered what Mr. Rhoten had said and thought this would be a good time to put the thing to a test. He still insisted that we should go to another place. I turned suddenly and said here is the place let[']s go in. This was one of the most up-to-date places of the kind I had ever seen.

When I walked in I could readily see that it was exclusively for white people.

But as I had made up my mind to convince Mr. Rhoten, I ventured to carry the thing through. When we walked in, the tables were so arranged that they seated four persons. I walked up to a table where two white men were seated. I gave Mr. Rhoten a chair and invited him to take a seat and sat down myself. We had not been seated very long, when another table was vacated. The two white men got up and moved over to it. This showed me conclusively that Mr. Rhoten was mistaken in his way of looking at things in the north. We sat there for at least 30 minutes. No one had yet come to take our order. I raised up out of my seat, looked at Mr. Rhoten, who was very dark, and exclaimed in a very loud tone: "Now Mr. Rhoten, don't ever come south any more and tell me and my people that there is no discrimination in public houses in the north. I am a southern Negro and am proud of the financial opportunities offered us in the south.["] This conversation attracted the attention of all who were in the cafe and all stopped talking to listen to our conversation. The proprietor finally spoke and said: "Take your seat and I will have you served."

I have always felt above pushing myself in places where I was not welcome, both north and south.

Mr. Rhoten and I walked out. We had a hearty laugh. I told him I would not put him to another such test while I was in the city.

HIGH COST OF LIVING.

Food and feed became exceedingly scarce in the later years of the war. The Union and Confederate soldiers had taken turns in ridding the country of these things. There were no meat, no salt, no tea, no coffee, no bread except a little corn bread and that had to be sparingly used. For salt the dirt from the smoke house floor was dug and put up ash hopper fashion. This was leached out, and the perfectly clear water that dripped from the hoppers was used to salt the food. At one time, when cleaning the barrels and trash from the smoke house, there was thrown out with the other rubbish, a piece of old dried beef that had fallen from its hangings. It lay in the heap for some time until it rained on it and softened it. Scott's mother noticed that the dogs had been gnawing at it. She picked it up and found upon examination that it was perfectly sound. She took in to the wood pile, got the ax and chopped away the part the dogs had been gnawing, washed it and then chipped some of it off and cooked it. She prepared some for her mistress and gave some to Scott. He says it was the best dried beef he had ever tasted. Think what this must have meant to people who had not tasted meat for six or eight months.

One night, Mr. Bond's step-father went some eight miles away on a foraging expedition. He secured a yearling that was really fat and brought it home. He cut it up and Scott's mother cooked some of it. Just about daybreak they awakened little Scott and asked him if he did not want some meat. He said yes, he arose, got a hunk of corn bread and went to the pot with a flesh fork and took out a piece. Again the superlative applies. At breakfast time Scott's mother wanted the mistress to have a bite of the delicious beef. She took some on a plate and when the madam, who had been used to break-fasting on a corn doger and such wild stuff as could be gathered in the fields, came into her dining room, she inquired where the meat came from. Fearing trouble if the truth were known, she was informed that Scott's step-father had killed a bear. The almost fam-ished woman ate the meat and wanted more but was persuaded to

Hogs following oats harvest.

wait until dinner time as too much might be injurious, since meat had been so long absent from her table.

She said: "No Ann, bear meat never makes one sick, no matter how much they eat." She finally consented to wait until dinner time.

The ensuing year showed very forcibly what hard times really were. There was no corn, no hay, no meat, no salt; the only corn we saw was the seed corn we planted. Mrs. Bond had 80 bushels of wheat in the garret of the great house. That would be sacked up and taken some distance to be ground on an old fashioned corn mill. On the way to the mill travel would be by night and hide in the daytime from "Jay-hawkers."

We would have batter cakes and butter milk for breakfast, peas and greens for dinner and sweet milk and mush for supper, all cooked without other seasoning than salt water from the hoppers. The mush was black because it was made from the wheat ground on the corn mill and not bolted.

Mr. Bond says that the crop that year was the best he had ever seen and there was not a sick person on the place that year.

At one time the rebel soldiers hauled 240 bales of cotton out on the lawn and cut the hoops loose. One of the officers told Scott's step-father that he could have all the cotton he could steal that night and put where he could not see it, for the next morning he was going to set fire to it and burn it, to keep it out of the hands of the Yankees.

Mr. Bond says: "My step-father took me from the feather bed and removed the under tick, emptied the straw from it and with the assistance of another old man removed and hid two bales of cotton, which later was smuggled into Memphis and sold for $1.10 per pound. From this it can be seen how much 240 bales that went up in flames would have brought.

Mr. Bond says: "I stood and looked at the burning cotton and wondered to myself if those men knew how many drops of sweat it took to produce it."

When the Cotton was sold in Memphis, certain purchases were made: one pint of salt, $5.00; $2.50 a yard for check goods. About that time Mrs. Bond, the mistress was showing signs of mental derangement and had asked Scott's step-father to bring her a gallon of peach brandy which he did at a cost of $25.00.

SCOTT BOND'S MOTHER.

I have said little about my mother. She was a slave and as such was house maid. This brought her in close contact with the white people and gave her training not common to the masses of colored women of her day. Her duties were such however, that she could give but little attention to me. Still her sympathy and love for me was as great as any woman ever bore in her bosom for a son. I can remember on one occasion when I was quite small my heels were chapped. In those days, Negro boys were not allowed to wear shoes until 12 or 14 years of age. When I would walk early in the morning or late in the evening, blood that would ooze from the cracks in my feet, would mark my tracks.

On one occasion when my mother had finished her task as maid in the house she came to me late at night and took me from my bed to look at my feet. In those days, tallow was the cure all. One of my heels was so chapped and cracked open that one could almost lay his finger in the opening. She got some tallow and warmed it in a spoon and having no idea how hot it was poured it into the crack in my heel. As I held my heel up and my toe on the floor, the hot tallow filled the crack and ran down over my foot to my toes. I cried because of the intense pain the hot grease caused. My mother quieted me as best she could and put me to bed. When she got up next morning she examined my foot and to her amazement the hot tallow had raised a blister full length of my foot as large as one's finger. When she saw this she cried as if her heart would break and said as the tears streamed down her cheeks: "I did not mean to burn my child. I did not dream the tallow was so hot."

As mentioned before, slave boys rarely wore shoes until they were 12 or 14 years of age. It was great fun to go 'possum and coon hunting in those days or rather nights. Young Scott would take long trips through the woods and swamps with the other slaves and would risk all the dangers of briers and of being bitten by poisonous reptiles because of his bare feet.

On one occasion when the dogs had treed a 'possum little Scott was the one to climb the tree and shake him out. The 'possum was away out on the end of a limb. The boys and men on the ground assured him the limb would not break. He let go the body of the tree and started out on the limb, which broke under the added weight and there was a squirming mixture of limb[,] boy, 'possum and snapping dogs on the ground. Fortunately he was not bitten. Scott came out of the scrimmage victorious with a fall and a 'possum.

On these trips the hunt would continue until all were loaded down with game, then they would return home.

On another occasion his mother had secured a pair of old boot tops and had a pair of shoes made for him. The first time he went out his mother insisted that he wear the shoes. He put them on and started out. When he reached the wood pile he pulled off the shoes and hid them in the wood pile because their unfamiliar weight [en]cumbered his progress.

It was on one of these hunting excursions that he so sprained his ankle that the next morning his foot was as large as two feet. An old slave woman advised him to hold his foot in cold water. He accordingly crawled to the well where the mules were watered and put his foot in the tub of water standing there. One of the hands rode up to water his mules and compelled the boy to take his foot out of the tub. The mules drank all the water and left the tub empty.

Scott put his foot back into the tub and shortly another man came along, drew water for his mules and then filled the tub for Scott's benefit. About this time the overseer came along and asked him what he was doing. Scott withdrew his foot from the water and showed him his swollen ankle. When asked about it he explained the cause of the accident. The overseer called one of the hands and had him empty the tub and fill it with fresh water for Scott and told him that was the best thing he could do.

Mr. Bond says that after all these years as he looks back upon that time, he wonders whether it was kindness in the overseer or the saving of a valuable Negro boy that prompted the action.

His mother was away above the average slave woman, in her training being a housemaid and seamstress in the days before the sewing machine. She came in daily contact with the most cultured and refined white women and was thereby immensely benefited. She had no time to give to her boy except late at night when her daily work was through and most other people were in bed. For this reason, Scott missed his mother's kindly ministrations in the years when most needed.

Poultry wire was unknown, the poultry yards were fenced with rails to keep the hogs from devouring the young fowls. Imagine if you can, a rail fence built tight enough to keep the hogs out and little goslings, turkeys and chickens in. It was one of little Scott's principal duties to march around the poultry yard and look after the young fowls. In cold weather the frost would bite his bare feet. In rainy weather he acted as a brooder. Boys in those days wore single garments, a long sacklike slip with holes cut for head and arms. When it rains, goslings will stand with their heads up and drown in a short time if left to themselves. Little Scott would gather little goslings under his slip as the hen hovers her brood and thus protect them from the falling rain. It must have been a ticklish task to have a half hundred little geese under one's single garment scrounging and crowding for warmth.

After the war when his step father started out on his own hook, Scott's mother continued in the same line that she had been trained. It was Scott's duty to see after the fowls and at times to look out for the welfare of the sitting hens. His mother would mark the eggs which she would put under the hen ready to set. Scott would have to keep

Another view from Military Road at old St. Francis ferry.

the nests in repair and keep fresh eggs from the sitters' nests. Upon one occasion, Scott in his round, found a nest out of repair. He removed the hen, took the eggs from the nest and put them on the ground. He repaired the nest, put the hen back on the nest and left the eggs on the ground. The next morning his mother discovered the eggs on the ground and took the boy to task for his absent mindedness. Drawing him across her lap, she took her slipper and was applying the treatment in the most approved way. That the operation was painful to Scott, goes without the saying. His mother told him she was not punishing him for the value of the eggs, but because of his forgetfulness; and seeing far into the future she told him further that his absent mindedness was the only thing that would ever "misput" him in life. Scott noticing the tone of her voice looked up and found her crying. He says, that from that moment, he felt no further pain from the slipper as his mother continued for some little time to wield it.

SCOTT BOND FORGETS HIS WIFE.

The writer has known Mr. Bond quite intimately for a number of years. He is in many ways remarkable. His mind is as alert and logical as the mind of any one that has come under his observation. One most unusual thing is that Mr. Bond's mind is always clear, yet he is at times the most forgetful mortal alive.

Many years back he drove with his wife to Forrest City. He left her in a store while he went to transact some other business. When he got through he drove home. Upon his arrival one of his children said: "Pa where is ma?"

Mr. Bond said: "There now, I left her in Forrest City."

He turned his horse around and drove back to town for his wife.

THE GRAVEL BEDS.

One time when I was down in the swamps hauling logs, about 4 o'clock in the afternoon I saw a double rig. I said to myself, "It means something to see a double rig come away down in the swamps like this."

There sprang from the conveyance a well dressed noble looking gentleman. He came to me and said: "I suppose this is Mr. Bond."

I said: "Yes sir, this is Bond."

"Mr. Bond, this is Mr. Saul, but not the Saul that we read about in the Bible. I am here representing Memphis parties who want to make a deal with you for your gravel in Crow Creek."

"What do you want to pay me for it?"

"What do you want for it?"

"I don't know."

"Why is it you don't know?"

"I reckon it is because I haven't got sense enough."

"What am I to do? The company has sent me here to buy it and we want to know what you want for it."

"Go back and tell the company you have found the gravel and the Negro that owns it but he did not have sense enough to make a price for it."

"That would be no advantage to the company."

"Suppose you name me a price for it."

"I can't do that," he replied.

"That looks strange to me. You must be a smart man or the company would not have sent you out here. You want the gravel and you can't say what you will give for it. Then give me an approximate price, about what you will give for it."

"How would $2.00 per car catch you, and we load it?"

"I dropped my head and began thinking. It looked as if I could see piles of money way up ahead of me. I thought of the thousands of car loads of gravel in the creek. His proposition looked so good that I was afraid to say yes. I finally looked up and said are you in a position to close the deal with me this evening?"

"No, but I can within the next ten days."

"Go back and tell your company that you have found the gravel and the price. If I charge you any more than that you can't tell the difference."

"You will hear from me in the next few days."

Mr. Saul went back to see the committee and upon inquiring found that they would have to pay $5.00 per car for crossing the bridge at Memphis.

In a few days I had a letter from Mr. Saul stating these facts and that they would not be able to take the gravel.

At that time I did not own more than 20 feet of the said gravel pit which extended lengthways through a 160 acre farm. I saw that I had to get busy and make some arrangements by which I could buy the farm.

At this time the farm was owned by another party who had bought it from the New England Mortgage Co., and had five years to pay for it in. I was so deeply interested in this deal that I did not sleep any that night. I had breakfast and was in my saddle bright and early to see the other party. There had been a severe storm a few weeks before which blew down his house and barn. I had heard that the party said he was going to pay the rent on the farm and was going to turn it back. When I arrived on the farm the man was gone, but I did not stop until I found him. He was three miles away plowing in another man's field.

I said: "Hello Mr. Walker, what are you doing here plowing? You have a good farm and good land. How is it you are working with this man?"

"I needed a little cash and I thought this was the best way to get it."

"I heard some time ago that you were going to pay the rent on that place and turn it back. Is there anything of it?"

"Yes, Mr. Bond, the storm came and blew down the house and barn and the company wants $1,500 for it so I decided to pay the rent on it and turn it back."

"That is a number one good farm Mr. Walker and as you have a wife and children I think you are making a mistake."

"Maybe I am, but the way times are now and at the present low price of cotton, I feel that I will never be able to support my family and dig $1,500 out of that farm."

"Suppose you let me have an option on that farm?"

"What do you mean by an option?"

"I will pay you $5.00 in money and when you pay the rent and get ready to turn it back, I will be in your shoes. I will have charge of the farm."

"Do you aim to pay the cash right now?"

"Yes, just as soon as you get to the court house and have the proper contract drawn up."

"That is just like stooping down and picking up $5.00."

"Yes, you are right about that. I am ready now. We will go right now."

He got his wife, we all went to the court house, the writings were drawn and the money was paid.

In a few weeks after that the R.[ock] I.[sland] Ry. which had bought my brother-in-law's gravel which lay south of me and exhausted his pit, and came to me to buy my gravel.

The Road Master said, "I understand that you own all the gravel above here, is, this gravel for sale?"

"Yes sir."

"The company instructed me to find out if it could be bought."

In a few days, the superintendent of the road sent his attorney to make the deal with me for the gravel.

He asked me what money would buy it.

"I have been offered a royalty of $2.00 per car."

"I am sure my company will not pay that for it."

"Well, that's my price on it."

"That settles it. We will not pay that for it."

"All right my friend there is no harm done."

View on Klondyke Farm.

The next week the bull-dog of the bone yard, the superintendent of the road came down in his palace car, and brought with him the attorney and some other officials.

He sent me word to my store to come at once and meet him out at the gravel pit. When I arrived the gentlemen were all out of the car and walking up and down the gravel beds. I met them and said, "Good morning gentlemen."

Mr. Cahill, the superintendent said: "I suppose this is Mr. Bond."

"No, Mr. Cahill, this is not Mr. Bond, this is Uncle Scott Bond. I have my doubts as to whether you mean the word Mr. or not, and if you do you can not afford it here in the south. So you will please call me Uncle Scott."

There was a hearty laugh between the superintendent and his officials.

"All right Uncle Scott we came down here to buy your gravel and want to know what you will take for it."

"My price is $2.00 per car royalty."

"You will never sell your gravel at that lick. We would not think of paying that for it."

"All right gentlemen there is no harm done."

"About how many cars of gravel have you here?"

"I could not really say. Somewhere about 20,000 cars."

"About how long have you owned this gravel pit?"

"O, I can't remember the exact date. I think about three weeks."

"What was your object in buying this gravel pit?"

"My object was speculation and profit."

"Is this man that lives right below you here whose gravel we bought, your brother-in-law?"

"Yes, that is correct sir."

"We bought his gravel for ½ cent a yard."

"That is true sir, but he was not nine days old and did not have his eyes open. Your company nor no other company will ever remember buying this for ½ cent a yard. That man made you a present of his gravel, but there is no reason on earth why I should do the same thing."

"How far does your line go above here?"

"About half a mile."

"Let's walk up to your line."

"Here we go."

We walked up to within about 200 yards of the line and sat down on a log.

Mr. Cahill said: "Bond you have a nice gravel bed here."

"Yes sir."

"Our company will never consent to pay you $2.00 per car royalty. I will go back to Little Rock and report to headquarters stating to them we will have to make other arrangements as there is no possible chance of buying your gravel."

"All right, Mr. Cahill there is no harm done. This gravel will not burn up. It will be here the balance of my days and if I don't get the value of it my wife and children will when I am gone."

I had several of my white friends after that, who said: "Uncle Scott you have made a wide mistake. You could have made thousands of dollars selling your gravel to the railroad company at their price."

"Gentlemen, this may be true but I can't see it that way."

Ten days later I got a letter from the officials of the road at Little Rock enclosing transportation there and back saying they wanted to close the deal with me for the gravel.

I had my son answer the letter telling them I begged to be

excused. I was very busy at the time arranging my farming affairs and it was a matter of impossibility for me to get off. I was returning the transportation with many thanks.

The next week Mr. Cahill ran his palace car to my town where I lived and sent the porter over to my store to tell me to come over to the depot, that he wanted to see me.

I told him to go back and tell Mr. Cahill he must really excuse me as I had some very important business to attend to at the bank of Forrest City. I was just getting into my buggy. If he really wished to see me I would see him after I got through with my business at the bank.

By the time I got to Forrest City in my buggy, Mr. Cahill had gone to Forrest City with his car and had his porter standing at the bank waiting for me. He remarked that: ["]Mr. Cahill is at the depot on his car waiting to see you at once."

"All right." We walked on side by side together until we got opposite the bank, and as I attempted to step in he grabbed me, and I tried to get loose, he said:

"Mr. Cahill wants to see you and he is the superintendent of the railroad."

I looked the young man in the face and smiled and said to him: "Yes and I am superintendent of all my own business. I will see him as soon as I am through with my business in the bank."

This attracted the attention of the bankers. I walked in and the young man came in behind me. We all had a little laugh and when I was through with my business in the bank I said, "All right young man we will go."

When we arrived at the car the porter opened the door and invited me into the car. I lifted my hat and spoke to Mr. Cahill.

He greeted me and said: "Bond I came to see if there was any possible chance to make a deal with you for the gravel."

"Yes sir, certainly. Of course the gravel is for sale."

"We will never be able to give you $2.00 per car for it. At that price you would make millions of dollars off that gravel pit."

"That may be true, but at that price if the gravel answers your purpose for ballast it will be cheap to the company."

"Why to think of it. The idea of me buying your brother-in-laws gravel for ½ cent a yard and here you want me to pay you $2.00 a car."

"Mr. Cahill that is no argument whatever. My brother-in-law is a good old modest Christian and he left the price entirely to you, believing and thinking your conscience would make you treat him right about it, and I suppose you did, but that day you left your conscience at home. You could not have given the old Negro less than ½ cent a yard. I am going to make you a proposition Mr. Cahill. I am going to see what is in you. I am going to cut the price down to $1.25 per car."

"Now Uncle Scott that looks as if you are using some judgment."

"Yes, that is judgment in favor of the Company and disastrous to myself."

"Now," said Mr. Cahill, "I will make you a price, I will pay you 35 cents a car."

This price raised me from my chair. I grabbed my hat and said, "Good evening Mr. Cahill."

"Hold on Bond wait. We want to get together in this gravel business."

"No, we will never get together. I see we are too far apart."

I bade the gentleman good evening and pulled out for home.

About two days after this interview, a man walked into my store and said: "Good morning is this Uncle Scott Bond?"

"Yes, this is Bond."

He was very commonly dressed with a slouch hat, rough looking shoes and overalls.

He said: "You have a very nice store here."

"Yes, it does tolerably well for out in the country in the sticks."

He remarked: "I understand that you have two or three good farms."

"Yes sir the officials of this county make me pay taxes on 12 farms, and the truth is we Negroes should own all the farms. We have them all to work."

"I guess you are right."

I noticed the gentleman, from his conversation was cultured and very refined. He finally said: "I understand that the railroad company has been trying to buy your gravel."

"No, that is not true they have been asking me to give it to them and that I do not expect to do."

"What did they finally offer you?"

Scott Bond's overhead cable excavator.

"They offered to pay me 35 cents a car for it."

"Don't you really believe that you can make big money at that?"

"Yes sir, I can make a little money at 35 cents a car, but that is nothing like the value of it and I don't intend to sell to any one at that price."

"How would 40 cents a car catch you?"

"Do you mean to say you would give me 40 cents a car?"

"Yes, if I can close the deal with you I will give you 40 cents a car."

"You are a stranger to me. What bank or where could you give me reference that I might know as to your responsibility."

"I can give you reference to any bank in Little Rock, that you prefer and also the Rock Island railroad."

I dropped my head and thought a while and said to the gentleman. "When you see Mr. Cahill, tell him you are not half way."

The gentleman laughed and we jollied around and finally bade me good bye and left me.

The next week Mr. Cheney, the station agent of the railroad at Madison came into the store and handed me a telegram. It was from Mr. Cahill and stated that he would be down on a certain day to go over the gravel situation with me, and requested me to meet him at the spur.

On the day appointed I met him at the spur and climbed into his car and we went over the spur as far as it ran, got out and went up into the gravel pit. We walked up into the pit about half way and sat down on a log.

He said, "I understood you to say that you bought this gravel pit for speculation."

"That is correct."

"Well if you don't sell it to us it will be impossible for you to find a market for it."

["]Mr. Cahill, do you see that big hole up yonder?"

"Yes."

"Do you see all these holes up and down through here?"

"Yes."

"Well the Iron Mountain [Railroad] came in here with a crew and spent a whole day in here digging holes and inspecting this gravel and have made two surveys for a track to this gravel pit."

We all got up and walked over to one of the holes that had been dug.

"This gravel goes down quite a distance," he said.

"But the Iron Mountain people will never come in here."

He pointed down stream toward my brother-in-law's and said, "You know I have a contract with your brother-in-law for his gravel for as long as we want it. I will wait and let the flood rains wash the gravel down there and get it from him."

This stampeded me for a few minutes. I raised my head and looked him in the face. "If you have got the gall to look a poor old Negro in the face and tell him you are going to wait for Providence to rob him and then you get the washings for nothing, do you know what I am going to do?"

"No."

"You see that narrow place down the creek there?"

"Yes."

"I am going to get my log wagons and haul and sink piling and nail plank on them to prevent the gravel from going down."

"You can't do that."

"Yes sir, I saw a man drive some fence posts across this creek and nail the plank on three and four inches apart. When the creek got up the leaves and trash stopped the cracks and the gravel accumulated until it was as high as one's head on horse back."

"If you do that you will overflow the farm. Isn't this your farm?"

"Yes, this is a farm that I gave my wife. It is a very sorry farm. It rarely grows anything except a little hay and peas. This farm hardly amounts to anything. I have 16 farms on St. Francis river which is the most fertile land in Eastern Arkansas, and before I would give my gravel away, if I could I would set fire to it and burn it up."

We had a hearty laugh with Mr. Cahill and his brother officials.

"It looks as though you don't aim to let us have the gravel at all."

"Well yes, I am really anxious to sell the gravel, but I have a great wife and if I would give the gravel away my wife would leave me."

"I now offer you 40 cents a car for your gravel."

"Mr. Cahill that is no inducement. You offered me 40 cents last week."

"I never met you last week."

"No you did not but a man came to my store and offered me 40 cents and I was sure you sent him."

"Did he tell you I sent him to you?"

"No sir, he did not, but when I asked him for reference he gave me every bank in Little Rock and the Rock Island Railroad and that made me know that you had sent him to offer 40 cents."

"We need the gravel it is convenient here to us and I would like to handle it for you."

"All right sir, I am very anxious to make a deal with you for the gravel. I will make you a price of 45 cents. How does that catch you. Come let's close the deal."

"Mr. Cahill you are coming by degrees. It is slow but I guess it is sure. I had my mind made up at the start not to take less than $2.00 as I had been offered $2.00, but as the Lord says to, the sinners to make one step toward me and I will make two toward you. I am going to make two steps toward you by falling down to an even dollar."

"Uncle Scott there is no chance for us to trade the company never will stand for me to pay you a dollar royalty on this gravel."

"Well I am too broad minded Mr. Cahill to ask you to do something that the company would not approve of."

He replied: "I am sure at that price you would be able to get as much as $40 a day royalty and you would get $40 a day royalty when we get in here with our steam shovel."

"That is true Mr. Cahill but $100 a day would be better."

"You will never be able to get that for your gravel." So good bye."

"Good bye Mr. Cahill, call again when it is convenient."

He laughed and said: "All right."

The next day Mr. Pierson who was at that time attorney for the Rock Island came down. Mr. Pierson, born and reared in the south, was a cultured hightone gentleman. He came into the store and I invited him into my office. We sat down. He said:

"Uncle Scott I came over to see if there was any possible chance for me to make a trade with you for your gravel, for the Rock Island Railroad."

"The gravel is for sale, Mr. Pierson, and I would certainly be glad to make a deal to sell it to the Rock Island Railroad."

"The price that I have been offered Mr. Pierson will never buy it."

"I now make you a proposition of 50 cents a car for the gravel."

"Mr. Pierson, that is not enough money. How long will it take you to get what gravel you need for your road?"

"I could not answer that question. It would require thousands of car loads of gravel to ballast our road, and we expect to put in a steam shovel so we can load something like 100 cars per day."

"And we will be using gravel from time to time, as long as the Rock Island Railroad is in existence; and as you know this pit is inexhaustible. There will be gravel here for ages and ages. I am sure fifty cents per car is a top price and more than we have ever paid anyone from whom we have taken this amount of gravel."

"All right, Mr. Pierson, I will take fifty cents a car for it, for a few thousand cars, anyhow."

"You have a nice price, Uncle Scott, I am sure."

"Now Mr. Pierson, the next thing is a contract."

"He agreed to write a contract and send it to me for inspection by my lawyer.

"In a few days the contract arrived, and with several modifications was agreed to. In the contract was a clause, making payments due and payable the 15th of each calendar month; the company to furnish me at the close of each day a report of each car loaded; and also a clause requiring either party to give thirty days notice before the contract could be terminated.

"At the expiration of the first month, the Company owed me $380.00 for gravel loaded, and I received a check for $80.00 only. When I added up my daily reports I found the amount paid $300 short.

"My son said, 'Pa, let's write them at once, and show them their mistake.'

"I told him no; the Company would make it all right next month.

"The next month our daily reports showed that the Company owed us over $500.00. We received a voucher for only $300, which was $200.00 short of the amount for that month. Then my son got wild and said:

"'Papa, I told you that!'

"This manner of payment continued for six months. By this time the daily reports showed that the Company owed us a balance of over $900.00.

"Then I told my son to get his typewriter and we would have to go after the Rock Island people good and hard.

"He was ready and eager. I told him to address Mr. Cahill, Superintendent of the Rock Island Railway:

"'Mr. Cahill, this will, according to the terms of our contract, notify you to stop loading gravel at my pit at the expiration of thirty days.'"

"What else, pa?"

"That is all. I signed it and had him register it that I might be sure of its delivery.

"A few days later the road master called at my office to know why I had notified them to stop loading gravel.

"I told him the reason was because they had not complied with the contract. I was asked in what way?

"You are not paying me the money as you agreed to pay me."

"I have been told that your voucher was forwarded you each calendar month."

"That is true, but the vouchers were not large enough—Son, turn to your gravel account and let me see. Get your reports for each month, and explain to the gentleman the difference."

"This was a very nice gentleman. After checking the report for the first month and comparing the voucher, he said:

"That will do; I suppose the remainder are as you say they are. And you say the Company owes you a balance of $900.00?"

"Yes sir, that is correct."

"I will go to the office this evening and explain the matter, and have them remit you at once."

"In due time the voucher for the $900 came and enclosed with it was a blank withdrawal notice for me to sign and return to Little Rock. I acknowledged receipt of the $900.00 but did not mention the notice.

"I was shortly afterward requested by the road master to withdraw my notice that they might not be stopped from loading gravel.

"I declined to do it on the ground that I had been mistreated in other ways.

"He asked what I meant by other ways.

"Well, sir, I had rather explain that to Mr. Cahill, the superintendent."

The gentleman bade me goodbye, and said, "We can get together, and shall try to do so at once."

"The next morning the Station Agent at Madison came to my office and notified me that Mr. Cahill had authorized him to furnish me a pass to Little Rock; that he wanted to see me.

"I managed to get all my plows in good running order, and the next morning, took the train for Little Rock.

"I called at Mr. Cahill's office. After the usual greetings were exchanged, Mr. Cahill said:

"What is the trouble you want to stop us from loading gravel?"

"Mr. Cahill, the Company is in debt to me. It is good honest money and I think I ought to have it."

"We sent you the balance of the money we owed you on the gravel."

"Yes sir, you did; but you owe me outside of that $580."

"How's that?"

"You owed me for some mules and cattle that you killed—over

$500; also a loss of $1,180 on account of the negligence of your road."

"What was the negligence?"

"I gave your agent at Madison a written notice for three cars to load potatoes in with the understanding that I would begin loading potatoes on Monday morning. On that day I put my hands and teams to work digging and drove to the station with seven loads of potatoes. I found no cars and no ware room, and the agent refused to let me unload them on the platform. There was no shed where I could store my potatoes and I unloaded them on the switch; and as I had the hands employed I was compelled to continue digging. There lay three cars of potatoes in sacks and they were severely damaged by the hogs and sun."

"My potatoes were delayed several days from the market. I had telegrams in my pocket from Pittsburgh and Chicago, offering me a certain price for potatoes, but when the potatoes arrived there was a loss in weight and they were badly damaged by the sun. The price received made a difference of over $1,100. I came to the conclusion that that was too much money for any old one-gallused farmer to lose after toiling through the hot sun and bad weather."

"Have you not sued the Company for this amount?"

"Yes sir, I have."

"It seems as if you have no confidence in your law suit.'

"I have but little confidence in the law suit."

"Why did you sue us?"

"Mr. Pierson, your attorney who sits here, some years ago when an old colored man got killed by your train at my town, and his wife made me administrator of his estate and had me sue the Company for $10,000. I employed two of the best lawyers in my county, and they and others with myself, thought we had a good case. When the case was called and we had gotten about half of our witnesses introduced, Mr. Pierson, who was sitting in the Court room with his book open in his lap; when we reached a certain point in the case, stepped to the Judge and handed him that part of the law. When the Judge read the law, he said to our lawyers, "Gentlemen, you have no case here." My two lawyers looked at each other and sat down. Since that time I have had no confidence in any case where Mr. Pierson was opposing counsel."

Mr. Pierson, Mr. Cahill and myself all joined in a hearty laugh.

Then Mr. Cahill said, "Uncle Scott, this is no place to settle a claim. There is the claim department over yonder and there is a gentleman there who will satisfy you about the claim."

"No sir; I can't go to see him any more. I was there to see him once and he asked me why I tied the mules on the railroad to have them killed. He then offered me less than half what my mules and cattle were worth. I told him that it was not fair; that I could not take that amount. I was a hard working old one-gallused farmer, and it was hard to be treated that way."

"He told me that was all he would pay me. I got my hat and left him and said some day the Lord will fix it so I will get my rights. So then Mr. Cahill, I believe you can handle the Claim Agent better than I can and you must either proceed or stop loading gravel."

Mr. Cahill then told me he would turn me over to Mr. Pierson, who would make a settlement with me some way or another.

Mr. Pierson said, "Come, Uncle Scott, and go with me to my office."

When we arrived at his office he said to me, "The Company will look for me to get something off of this account."

"Mr. Pierson, you can't look to me to reduce the account very much as I have to pay my lawyers' fees and the cost of the court as far as the case has gone. But to show you how broad I try to be in my dealings, I say write me a check for $1500 and I will withdraw the notice; and that will be allowing you $160.00."

He handed me a check for $1,500 and I signed a withdrawal of notice, got my hat and coat and was going down in the elevator. I said, "The Lord did fix it."

This gave them a second start in loading gravel. The reports and vouchers balanced for the next three or four months. Then in the clerical changes in the railroad offices there began to appear discrepancies of $50.00 to $100.00 monthly. This continued for six or eight months. I again gave the Company thirty days notice to stop loading.

When the Company received the notice they sent me a check for what they owed me to balance the daily reports and also wrote me a very nice letter to show the cause of the mistake, and asked me to withdraw the notice in order that they might continue. I failed to answer the letter and in a few days the Road Master called to see me. After the usual greetings and complimenting the store and business, said:

"What is the trouble this time, Uncle Scott?"

"No trouble at all. The Company has paid all the balance due and there is no trouble whatever."

"The trouble then is with us. You failed to withdraw your notice."

"Yes sir. I came to the conclusion that you were not paying me enough. You must add fifteen cents, thus making sixty-five cents a car."

"You will have to see the Superintendent about that. That is out of my power."

"I am not worried about the matter. The Superintendent will have to see me," I said.

We shook hands and bade each other good-bye.

The next morning the agent at Madison told me that the Superintendent had wired him to give me a ticket, and for me to come to Little Rock, and he would pay the expense and pay me for the time I lost in coming up there.

I told him to write the Superintendent and tell him it is just three days till Christmas and I had to settle with hands. And that I really could not go to Little Rock. But I had promised my wife and boy that I would spend the holidays in Little Rock, and I had arranged to leave here on Christmas eve.

I received a letter from the Superintendent telling me he would furnish transportation to my wife and me and would pay my expenses there and back.

On Christmas eve I got a notice from the agent that a special car was on the track near my store, to take me to Little Rock.

This train took us to Forrest City and then we took the fast train for Little Rock. When the train left Forrest City the conductor came around and asked for tickets.

I told him I had no tickets.

He then asked me for the money.

I informed him that I had been informed by the Company Superintendent that my fare was paid from my place to Little Rock.

He wanted to know how he was to know that.

I said to him, "The only way for you to know now is by me telling you."

"You must either pay or get off."

After the conductor left, my wife said to me, "They are going to put us off. You have the money—pay him."

"Wife, you need not worry. There is no danger of them putting us off[.]"

By this time we had passed two or three stations.

The conductor came again to collect fare. I told him I would pay the fare of my wife and boy, and he could put me off.

My wife said: "I have the money—I will pay your fare."

I told the conductor that if he would walk back to the rear end of the train he would find the Road Master; and he had our fare.

The conductor and Road Master came back into our car laughing. The Road Master remarked, "Well, Uncle Scott, you are having more trouble."

"No; no trouble, just a little misunderstanding."

When the train arrived in Little Rock I was invited into the Superintendent's office.

"Well, Uncle Scott, I see we are in trouble again."

"No sir, there is no "we" in this. The party who broke the contract is the one that is in trouble."

(There was a hearty laugh.) "What do you want to do about it, Uncle Scott?"

"I just want you to add fifteen cents more to the car and make it sixty-five cents a car."

"You made a contract with me for 50 cents a car."

"Yes sir, but I am now making a contract for 65 cents a car."

"That is more money than we can pay."

"All right; if you can't use it, there is no harm done."

"You agreed to let us have a few thousand cars at 50 cents."

"Thought that three thousand cars was a few, and you have loaded out something over three thousand cars."

"All right, we will draw up another contract at 65 cents per car; and I want to say right here that 65 cents is all we shall ever pay.

"We will take the track out of the pit before we will pay any more."

I accepted the contract at 65 cents.

By this time I had collected enough money from the gravel pit to pay for the farm three times over. Thus it will be seen that the gravel pit, farm and all had really only cost me $5.00.

This contract continued in force for about twenty-four months, after which time I took the contract for loading the cars myself at 25 cents per yard additional.

The railroad company would build traps or bridges in the gravel pit over which we would drive mules hitched to slips or road scrapers and dump the load into the cars below.

SCOTT BOND CHANGES HIS METHOD OF LOADING GRAVEL.

I had at that time a man named D. A. Rudd who was superintending the loading, and who came to me and said, "I believe we can try an arrangement of cables and blocks that will be more efficient than the method we now follow in loading this gravel.'

He made a rough sketch of what he proposed. It looked to me as if the plan would work, so I instructed him to find where the material for such a plant could be bought and the price of the same.

By this method we got in touch with firms in different parts of the country and learned of the development made in this style of excavating. Among the firms who replied was the Cable Excavator Company of Philadelphia, whose drawings were nearest to our ideas of what would give the desired results in our gravel beds. I had an outline sketch of our pit made and forwarded to this Company by our supervising engineer, Mr. Dan A. Rudd, and asked them what it would cost to put in a plant such as we were designing to place.

They replied that if we had the gravel and the quantity was great enough to warrant the outlay, and had a market, they could put in a plant that they would guarantee to load 800 yards per day.

I asked that they send one of their engineers to go over the situation, and if he would say that the gravel bed did not warrant the outlay, I would pay all his expenses and $10.00 per day for his trouble.

They accepted the proposal and wired the date when their representative would arrive in Madison.

In the meantime I took the catalogues showing the pictures of the plant I proposed to put in and went to the superintendent of the Rock Island Railway and said, "Mr. Copely, I have come to save the Company money in the way of loading out gravel. You have lost thousands of dollars in the way of tracks and traps, because every big rain takes out your tracks laid in the bottom of the creek and carries away your traps.

"If you will give me a contract for $20,000 worth of gravel and take your track up out of the channel of the creek and put it upon the bank, you will have no more traps to build and lose no more track. Go back over your record and see how much money your company has lost by these big flood rains. If you will split this amount half in two and add it to my future loading, I will be in position to load gravel for you rain or shine, hot or cold, and as many cars as you may want. Here is a catalogue showing the picture of the plant that I propose to put in. It will cost in machinery, erecting, etc., $15,000.

"This company agrees to put the machinery in and that it will load a car every ten minutes, with the understanding that I pay them $2,000 as soon as the plant is all up and tested."

Upon his arrival we went over the gravel pit. He said that he thought that we had as fine gravel as he had ever seen, and the quantity was apparently inexhaustible; and proposed to put in a plant that would load a car in ten minutes, at a cost of $12,000 for the machinery.

I told him his proposition was all right, but his price was too large. That I had been figuring with other companies, and was sure I could get a plant for less money.

He claimed it was their purpose to put the best material into the job.

I told him that was just what I was expecting, and that was just what the other fellow had promised to do.

We discussed the matter for four or five hours, and I finally agreed to pay him $8,500 f. o. b. Philadelphia. There were five car loads and the freight on same was over $900. I had my attorney to draw a contract. It was signed and witnessed. I now felt that I was all right.

In a few days I got a letter from the Cable Excavator Company saying that their engineer had made a mistake; that the price he had given me was too low—they could not give us the plant agreed upon with a two and one half yard bucket, and for that reason, they would have to cancel the contract.

Scott Bond's store—looking south.

I answered this letter by saying: "I have your letter of recent date and contents noticed in which you say you will have to cancel your contract with me. I have always been of this opinion, that it takes more than one to make a contract and that it takes more than one to cancel a contract. From the reference I have of your firm, I know you are responsible, and the terms of this contract will be carried out to the letter."

A few days later I was up the St. Francis River rafting logs. My oldest son had brought a gentleman up to me in my gasoline launch and introduced him as the head of the Cable Excavator Co., of Philadelphia.

I told him I was glad to see him as the president of his Company, as his visit would no doubt save us a law suit.

He replied, "Mr. Bond, the man sent here had no right whatever to make the price he did on this plant. I am sure we can't come out on a plant of that size at that price. We will absolutely lose money. But I will say that we can put in a plant with a yard and a half bucket for that money, and that is all I will do."

I said, "All right Mr. Hadsel, you know best. But I have your telegram stating that your agent would be here on a certain day to see me and showed me documentary evidence that assured me that he had the power to make a deal with me. I will say there is no doubt about me putting in a plant from another concern; and as I have your contract signed by your agent and witnessed, I will proceed at once to have a plant put up and will see that the Cable Excavator Company pays for it."

Mr. Hadsel said, "Mr. Bond, that wont do. As there is no machinery of this kind in the south, and as it will be a big advertisement for our company, as you have agreed to pay us $1,000 cash as soon as the plant was finished and tested—If you will pay us $2,000 instead of $1,000, and as I see you have a contract with the Railroad Company for $20,000 worth of gravel, I will go ahead and carry out this contract."

"That is all right. Your $2,000 will be ready. Mr. Hadsel, we must have an extra specimen of writing covering this additional $1,000, as you know the least you add to a contract or the least you take from it renders the same null and void."

He smiled and said, "All right."

I turned to my boy and asked for paper. I instructed him to write that I would pay Mr. Hadsel $1,000 additional the first payment. The paper was signed and witnessed. Mr. Hadsel left me saying that he would forward me the blue prints at once, that I might get out the timbers by the time the machinery got here, which would be in sixty days.

When we received the blue prints we found that many of the timbers would have to be forty and fifty feet long, and that it would require twenty thousand feet to erect the plant.

We wrote to all the mills in the state that we could think of, and were turned down cold, as none of them sawed timber of that length. I was then puzzled as to what to do. I was running a saw mill of my own at that time, and after consulting my forces I found that, although our mill was only erected to cut at most sixteen and eighteen feet, we could, by a little manipulating and shifting ahead on the carriage, cut the desired length.

Mr. Rudd, our supervising engineer, then went up the river and cut cypress trees the desired length and rolled them into the water. By the time we got the logs all into the river, the water was so low that we would have to break up the rafts and roll the logs over the sand bars for some times a quarter of a mile. This led me to believe that I had quite a job on my hands. But I had always succeeded in my undertakings. The difficulty only fired my ambition.

When we at last got the logs to the mill we made the necessary changes and finally got a fairly good lot of long timbers—36 to 50 feet.

By this time all the machinery had arrived and we at once started the erection of the plant, which required about six weeks.

The blue prints required two pieces 12x14 inches by 75 feet, and two pieces 12x14 inches by 80 feet long. Having learned of the creosote plant about eighty miles away, I went to that plant and explained my wants. The manager informed me that owing to their contract with the Railroad Company, he could not make a deal on the outside for timber.

I informed the manager that my work was for the R. I. Railway, and I would call up the superintendent and have the timbers come to me through the R. I. Ry.

I called up the superintendent on the long distance and explained the matter to him.

He phoned the manager that it would be all right to let the timbers come on through the R. I. Railway Company, with the understanding that Uncle Scott Bond would settle for them immediately upon delivery at the gravel pit.

I then wired the Overhead Cable Company to send their constructing engineer, as we were ready to begin the erection of the plant.

This engineer cost me $7.00 per day.

When he arrived, I gave him a force of carpenters and helpers, and at once started to build a seventy-foot tower for the machinery.

In six weeks from the start the plant was completed and ready for the test.

The plant stood the test of eighty cubic yards an hour which meant a capacity of 800 cubic yards a day. With this great plant, with seventy-five horse power, I found I was able to load a car every seven minutes.

Neighbors far and near were anxious to see the overhead cable way, and crowds of people came each day to the gravel pit to see the show.

We were now in position to load all the cars the railroad people would furnish us.

With our inexhaustible deposits of gravel and our splendid excavating plant, we were often urged to add a plant for the manufacture of concrete bricks, blocks, tiles and other objects. Thousands of dollars in contracts were offered until at last we have decided to put in a plant to cost about $75,000 for this purpose.

We have a very great advantage in doing this because the railroad has placed more than a mile of track and a $2,300 bridge in our gravel beds.

Crow Creek gravel is positively unsurpassed for concrete purposes. Our beds are the first west of Memphis and are located right at the base of Crowley's ridge.

There are three periods known geologically as the Mississippi embayment periods, when the Gulf of Mexico swept as far north as Cairo, Ill. At these periods when the salt water covered all this part of Arkansas, great beds of oysters flourished, and today their history is written in the immense deposits of oyster shells to be found along Crow Creek. This calcereous deposit would furnish an unequaled base for fertilizer, and tests are being made to determine the value thereof.

It might be well to state here that there are many valuable mineral deposits in this part of Arkansas, among them are iron, lignite and salt—whether in paying quantities or not, remains to be determined.

On the same farm through which the gravel beds run is one of the finest orchards in this part of the state. There are five varieties: wine sap, Arkansas black, Ben Davis and Early Harvest apples, and Elberta peaches. This is especially a commercial orchard for shipping. The trees are still young. We have marketed three crops of Elberta peaches, shipping to Memphis and selling in nearby towns. The apples have been in bearing for two years and the 1917 crop promises to be fine.

Mr. Bond says that this part of Arkansas is excellent for fruit, and that in addition to supplying the home table with a delicacy and a necessity, can be made a source of revenue to the farmer, large or small.

The orchard is so close to the railroad track in the gravel pit that the cars are loaded right at the orchard.

Just opposite the orchard Mr. Bond has a fine field of alfalfa that is one of the most promising pieces of this legume in this part of Arkansas.

The three farms joining the home place are being seeded entirely to pasture and feed crops, and are being made convenient for the breeding and growing of stock.

An industry that Mr. Bond contemplates installing in his orchard is an apiary. He is of the opinion that not only will the honey pay, but the bees will be of much benefit in fertilizing the blooms on the fruit trees. He also is arranging to utilize the extra spots on his fruit farm for the growing of truck and melons for the market.

SCOTT BOND AT RAVENDEN SPRINGS.

In the overflow of 1889 I had gone through much exposure, trying to save my property, my neighbors and their belongings. One who has never seen the mighty Mississippi on a rampage, can form no conception of the devastation and ruin wrought by the muddy, angry flood as it sweeps on in its irresistible rush to the sea, bearing on its murky bosom the wrecks of home and forest. From this exposure I had contracted a severe, deep seated attack of malaria. I had been treated by the best doctors in my county but none of them seemed able to master my ailment. I had taken so much medicine that it looked as if none would now take the slightest effect. I dragged along in this condition for twelve months. At times they would put a spring mattress in a wagon and haul me to town that I might make settlements with people on my different farms. I would sometimes lose the use of myself. I would be walking along and would fall to the ground and could no more rise up than a baby. Some one would pick me up. I would feel fine and would toddle along until I made another misstep and down I would go again. I only weighed 96 pounds and had almost given up hope of recovery.

One day I was sitting on a log and attempted to diagnose my own case. I first asked myself: "What in the world can be the matter with me." I looked back to the time when my complaint first started, and thought of the manner in which I had taken ill and the hundreds of bottles of medicine I had used. I then sent for Dr. Van Paten [Patten],[21] one of the best physicians in the state of Arkansas, who had been treating me.

When he came I told him that it seemed that my case was beyond the reach of medicine. I said, "you and all the other doctors in the county have failed to effect a cure of my complaint. I would like for you to try to think of some way by which I might get well."

Dr. Van Paten looked into the fire for a few moments as if in deep study. He finally raised his head and said: "Well, Uncle Scott, if you can stand the trip I would have you get ready and go to Ravenden Springs[22] in Randolph County, Ark.["]

At that time I could hardly put one foot before the other. I went home and told my wife to pack my trunk as I was going to Ravenden Springs. I made arrangements that night with my brother-in-law, Pat Banks to go with me to the Springs. The next day we started out and while at Forrest City waiting for the train, Capt. Wynne, who was at that time one of the leading merchants of Forrest City and withal a Christian gentleman, walked up to us and said to me, "Good morning Uncle Scott. How do you feel?"

"I feel quite well but I am very weak."

He called Pat Banks aside and said to him, "Pat that man is your brother-in-law, he can't get well. If you take him away you will have to send a box for him. Were I in your place I would persuade him not to go."

Pat said: "He has full confidence in his physician. He advised him to go and I can't advise him not to go."

When the train arrived, we boarded it for Ravenden Springs. We got off at a little station called Ravenden Junction, distant seven miles from the Springs. Conveyance hence was by stage coach. The driver came to me and asked me if I was going to the Springs.

I told him yes but I could not walk.

He said: "All right I will take you in the stage coach."

Suiting his actions to his words he and my brother-in-law lifted me into the coach. It was seven and one-half miles of the roughest riding I had ever seen. Just before I got to the Springs the driver asked me where I wanted to stop.

I told him I wanted to stop wherever I could get the best attention.

He said: "The Southern Hotel is the best place but that would cost me $60 per month."

I told him money was no object. I wanted to try to regain my health. I was sure at that time the driver knew that I was a Negro.

FROM SLAVERY TO WEALTH

Mr. Bond pointing to the grove where Dr. Washington addressed the
assembled thousands near Madison, in 1911.

He never asked me and as I had always been a Negro and I was satisfied that he knew that I was. My brother-in-law, who was with
me, was a bright mulatto and one who did not know the difference
would readily take him for a white man.

By this time the coach had reached the little town and had driven
up to the Southern Hotel. He pulled a cord and the landlord came
out. He informed the landlord that he had a sick man who was
unable to walk.

The landlord summoned two fine looking white men, porters
and told them to take me up to room 82.

When we got to the room there was a lady dusting the room, and
a white man making a fire. The room was soon in readiness and I was
put to bed. I was by this time quite exhausted. I slept from six o'clock
until 9 o'clock that evening. When I awoke my brother[-in-law] Pat
asked me how I felt. I told him very good after my nice nap, for it
was the best sleep I had had for a long time. I was asked by the porter
what I wanted for supper. I told him I only wanted a drink of water.
He insisted that I should eat a little something.

I told him he might bring me a few spoonfuls of oatmeal with cream and sugar. After eating the porter removed the dishes, and left us to ourselves.

Pat said: "Look here bud, these people are mistaken. They take us for white folks."

I said: "Well Pat you are right. They have made the mistake. We did not intend it. We will put the best foot foremost and will do the best we know how. We will not put ourselves on them, and will not entertain any more than we have to. I trust the Lord it will all work out for the best."

When we first arrived at the Springs my stomach was so badly deranged that the water would not stay with me long enough to reach blood heat. I do not believe any man could get nearer the end than I was and not die. Pat and I talked the matter over that night. I awoke the next morning somewhat refreshed.

Pat rose and dressed. His hair was very black. After combing it he turned and asked me how I liked his appearance.

I told him he looked all right, but I must have him to change his hair. Instead of roaching it to just brush it down his forehead. The darkness of your hair will by contrast make your face look fairer. He did so and asked how that caught me.

"That looks all right Pat. I think you will make it through." His hair was perfectly straight and he was neatly dressed.

I told him when he went to breakfast they would ask him where he was from, and I said to him that he must say he was from the St. Francis basin; as they knew that part of the country was full of malaria and that would account for his dark complexion.

The last bell was ringing for breakfast in the dining room and the porter came to my room for my order for breakfast.

I ordered two soft boiled eggs, a cup of coffee and some bread or crackers.

I relished my breakfast very much. I then had a good drink of that wonderful water. When Pat returned to my room after eating, I asked him how he enjoyed his breakfast.

He said: "Fine. Everything is up-to-date."

"Did you have a full table?"

"More than a dozen full tables."

"They must have a large dining room."

"They have. This is a wonderful building."

Let us here explain to the reader, the reason why we were able to carry ourselves among these white people in the manner in which we did, was that Pat was the carriage driver for his white people before the war, and I was the house boy for my mistress; hence from being in constant contact with our owners and their guests we were the better prepared for this occasion.

I said, "Now Pat, there is one thing left undone. You cannot read and write, so you go to the clerk and call for the register and in registering my name I will register yours."

That scheme worked. The clerk took up the register and said, "Come on and let's go."

He came into my room very politely and brought the book to the bed. I took the pencil, registered and said to Pat, "As you have no glasses I will register for you."

When the clerk was gone, Pat turned to me and said: "That worked like a charm."

"That is all right. My only object is to try to get well and I hope the Lord will be with us."

I then told Pat to go out and find the best doctor in town and have him come to my room.

When Pat returned with the doctor, I said: "Good morning Doctor. This is Bond from St. Francis County, Arkansas."

"Dr. Williams, Mr. Bond."

"Doctor, I sent for you for advise as to how I should treat myself in drinking this water."

"How long have you been here?"

"Just came last night."

He told me the water was all right to drink all I could hold. He said that after I had been there a few days, I would have a ravenous appetite, and that I should be careful not to overeat myself, especially at the start. He advised me to take a weak toddy in the morning before breakfast.

I told him that I had not drunk whisky in years and years. That I was tee-totaler.

"Mr. Bond I do not mean that you should use it as a beverage but for sickness."

By this time I was sitting on the side of the bed.

He said: "I see your feet are swelling."

"Yes, sir."

"Now, if you had some real good whiskey to bathe your feet in, it would help a great deal."

"All right doctor, we will get the whiskey, I suppose you have plenty of it in your town here?"

"No, there is no whiskey in our town. The only place where you can get good whiskey, is to send to Memphis for it."

"Pat look in my pocket book and give the doctor $10.00. He being a physician knows where to send to get the article he recommends."

"Mr. Bond shall I have it expressed to you?"

This suited Pat. I think at this time he had a half pint flask in his valise. He had learned of his master in the dark days of slavery to drink, and continued in a moderate way. One could never tell he had taken a drop.

The whiskey arrived in a few days, and for Pat's benefit I sent out in town and bought 2 pounds of loaf sugar that he might have his toddy every morning.

The next day Dr. Williams called.

"Hello Bond, how are you feeling?"

"I am O. K. doctor. I feel that I am improving."

"You look better. Has your package come?"

"Yes sir. It was brought in this morning."

"Here is your change. It cost $6.00 per gallon."

"Well doctor," Pat says, "it is all right. There is sugar and a glass on the dresser and if you indulge you can sample it and see what kind of goods it is."

"I am a fine judge said the doctor, I will see what quality of goods you have."

He made his toddy, drank it and said: "That is fine."

"He told me to take a half pint and put it in the foot tub and have Mr. Banks bathe my feet good every morning and to bottle it up again and use it several times.

I noticed after the doctor had drunk his toddy he seemed to brighten in his conversation. I caught the hint. I said: "Pat will go home in a few days. It will be several days or a week before I can get out. Whenever you feel like you want a toddy you know where my room is, it will be here for you."

"All right Mr. Bond, I will come in once in a while to see how you get along."

I was improving rapidly so I told my brother [in-law] Pat he had better go home and look after his family and mine. Tell wife I am doing fine and have improved each day since I came to the Springs. Fill your little flask before you start.

He said he had enough to last him until he got home.

I told him to take the money from my purse to settle his hotel bill.

I must say that I had never seen anything in all my days that improved one as the water at

Theophilus Bond.

Ravenden improved me. My appetite was ravenous.

The proprietor came to my room one morning and said: "Mr. Bond, it is no trouble for me to send your meals to your room, but I think that if you would walk to the dining room for them you would gain much more rapidly."

"Now Mr. Blackshire,[23] I would be more than glad to do this, but it is impossible for me to sit on anything hard. I am as raw as a piece of beef."

"You don't say so. I notice that when I come to your room you are either sitting on a pillow or on the side of the bed."

"I will have my wife fasten a pillow in a chair so that you can sit at the table."

"All right, Mr. Blackshire I will certainly appreciate that."

I was dressed for dinner and when the bell rang I walked into the dining room. Mrs. Blackshire was standing at the table with a chair and pillow and invited me to have a seat. All this was strange to me as I did not see any colored servants either in the dining room or around the building. I had always been used to colored servants and this seemed very strange to me. However I braced up, ate my dinner and spoke but little with any one.

In a few days I was able to go out and walk around town. The customs and habits of the people there were very different from what I had been used to. It was not a farming country because of the mountains and rocks. One could only see gardens and truck patches. The people all seemed nice and pleasant. All lived at home and lived principally on their butter, eggs, mutton and cattle. It was the greatest place for eggs I had ever seen. Plymouth Rock was the chicken mostly found there and they were full blooded. There were five little stores in the town and the market was chiefly of poultry and dairy products. The merchants there, paid 5 cents per dozen for eggs, in trade and 4 ½ in cash. Frequently I would notice that some of the people would have to carry them back home. In this I saw a chance to make some money. I went to all five of the stores and told them to buy all the eggs they could, and I would take them off their hands at 5 and 5 ½¢ per dozen. This raised the egg market and eggs continued to come in. I ordered twelve empty cases. As soon as these arrived, I had them packed and shipped out. I then ordered fifteen cases, but only got nine. I was at a loss for want of cases to ship eggs in.

I went to Dr. Lambert, the leading merchant and asked him to help me get cases to ship eggs in.

"Mr. Bond, egg cases are very scarce and I would advise you to use barrels. There are many empty barrels in town and I will show the man how to pack them in barrels."

I told him we would try the barrels. He had a load of wheat straw cut to half inch lengths. A layer of this to the depth of three inches was first put in the barrel, then a layer of eggs with the big end down, then a layer of straw and a layer of eggs until the barrel was full.

I shipped the second week nine barrels and twenty-four cases of eggs. I made enough profit on eggs while there to more than pay my hotel bill which was $60 a month.

The customs of the people of Ravenden Springs were very different from the customs of the people among whom I had been reared. They were apparently very good natured and were friendly among themselves. They were fairly good workers. It was very strange to hear the old gentleman who discovered the springs, tell the story of his discovery. He said he had been sick for many years

Dr. Booker T. Washington addressing 5,000 people
in grove at Madison in 1911.

with indigestion. He finally got to the point where he could only
eat wheat bran and water. His wife had been dead many years. He
had a son and daughter living. The daughter kept house and cared
for him. He said that he owned the whole town of Ravenden
Springs, which was built on a part of 160 acres that he had donated
from the state many years before. Only a few acres here and there
were suitable for cultivation because of mountainous topography.
His health was so bad that he could not walk. The best he could do
was to crawl about in the middle of the day. He said he had a dream
one night. He dreamed that there was a spring which if he would
use the water thereof, it would cure his complaint. He tried the next
day to get his daughter to get him down to where the spring flowed
from under the mountain. There was only one way to get there at
that time and that was very difficult.

His children laughed at him and told him that was only a dream
and there was nothing to dreams. He thought of a way to get there.
He walked as far as he could then slid down on his stomach until
he reached a bush he had seen in his dream. He tied a rope to it and
let himself down to the bottom. He then crawled about 100 yards

to the spring and lying on his stomach, drank all the water he could hold. Then looked about for a place to lay down. He went to sleep and when he awoke it was 11 o'clock at night. He then said, thank God I am better. He said when his daughter came home that evening between sun down and dark, she looked everywhere for him, but could not find him anywhere. She called but no answer. The next morning he heard a searching party coming down the path cut on the face of the hill. He hallooed and the girl said, that is pa. He said, yes this is pa. She walked to the edge of the cliff and said, pa, what in the world are you doing down there. He told her he was resting and sleeping and that he had had more sleep last night than he had in the last five weeks.

She asked how in the world he got down there.

He told her the only way to get to him was to go back 250 yards and she would see how he slid down to a bush and the rope was still tied to it where he let himself down.

This is the dream of which I have been telling you.

The searching party was composed of three ladies, his son and another man. The party went back as directed. They found the place and after some time the men risked the descent to him.

He said good morning to them and said he believed he had found the spring of Holy water. His daughter asked him if he thought the water was doing him any good. He told her yes he was feeling better already.

How to get him home was the next thing. We would have to go two and a half miles to get around the foot of the mountain.

The old man said: "Thank God I am at home. I want my bed. This is my home. I am going to stay here until I get well."

A tent, bedding and other things were secured and a camp made for him. He remained there for two weeks. His meals were let down to him on a rope. In six weeks from the time he began drinking the water he could eat almost anything. From this the rumor spread abroad about the healing waters. People from every direction came and were benefited. Finally a party from St. Louis came to buy the 160 acres. They offered him $300 for the land. He said: "No money won't buy the place."

In three weeks more they offered him $1,500. He finally sold the place to them for $2,000, reserving a homestead of 5 acres during

Farm bought for Theophilus Bond by his father.

his life. I am sure his view of the healing properties of the water was correct, for I gained 28 pounds in 6 weeks.

The springs derived the name from the number of ravens that nest there every year.

I remember while at Ravenden Springs of discussing different topics with others, among the subjects discussed was inevitably the Negro. One remarked that the Negro was no good at all. Another remarked that it was natural for the Negro to steal. Still another said he had no use for a Negro in any circumstances.

In as much as I was in the conversation I felt it was my time to say something. I could not afford to give myself away, so I told them I thought the Negro was all right in his place, and that I had several large farms and I considered the Negro the best labor on earth to handle cotton.

Dr. Lambert said: "I think Mr. Bond, you are about right. The Negro is just the thing to handle cotton."

Another gentleman asked how in the world I got along with them.

I told him that one must learn to handle them. To always be positive and frank and one could always make good laborers of them.

I met a young man at the springs, whose father, Dr. Sparkman lived at Haynes, Ark. He was very nice and courteous to me. Whenever I would meet him on the street he would always bow and say good morning, and on the day I left for home I met this young man, Mr. Sparkman, at the depot. He came up to me and said: "Hello Uncle Scott." This was the first time I had heard the name Scott, while at the springs. We were seven miles from the hotel at the springs.

We boarded the train and occupied the same seat all the way home as there was no Jim Crow law at that time. It was then I learned that every Negro in the south had a white friend and that every white man had a Negro friend.

When I arrived home and met my friends they were pleasantly surprised at my improvement in both health and looks. I met Capt. Wynne on the street in Forrest City. He stopped and smiled. He looked and then said: "Uncle Scott you look really fine. You have fooled us all. I never expected to see you come back here alive." He called other men and told them to look at me. "I never would have thought that he could possibly be made to look as fine as he does. At the time Scott left, I went to his brother-in-law and asked him to try to persuade him not to go, that if he did he would have to be brought back in a box. He went to the springs as a dead man, and went at once to buying eggs. He shipped nine barrels and several cases of eggs to Forrest City. This glutted the market. He shipped a large number to Memphis. Look he has two dozen of the prettiest Plymouth Rock hens I ever looked at."

My wife and children were delighted at my improvement. I met Dr. Van Patten and told him I was certainly surprised at him.

He asked me how. I told him he had sent me to Ravenden Springs and he knew there was not a Negro on the place.

He said that he had never given that a thought that there were no colored people there; but "I see the water has saved your life. You look sound as a dollar."

I told him that I thanked God that my health was good again and that I did not go to the springs to deceive any one. My only thought was to get well.

He asked me how I got along and how was I treated.

I told him I was treated royally.

He asked me where I stopped. I told him the Southern Hotel, the best place there was there.

He said: "I am sure you were treated right for that is the best hotel in that part of the country."

He asked me if I was ever challenged there as to my race identity.

I told him no, not in the least.

THE MADISON CEMETERY.

On one occasion I was at church and heard a fine sermon. At the close I noticed a Mr. Barnett, a citizen of this county. He said: "My business here is to see the colored people of this community. The grave yard in which your forbears and mine have been buried for many years belongs to the railroad. The entire tract of 80 acres in which the cemetery is located, will eventually be used to make dumps and fills for the R. R. and as we have no deed to the land they can dig up the bodies and put them in the fill for cars to run over. The officials of the R. say that if we will have the land surveyed and pay the cost of it, the company will deed us seven or eight acres."

I replied: "Mr. Barnett you are right, we should do something. You are the right man in the right place. We will now take a collection." The collection amounted to $9.00. Sixteen dollars was collected by the colored people of this community and not a dollar by the whites.

About three months later Mr. Barnett came to my brick kiln where I was burning brick. He was accompanied by the county surveyor. He said: "Uncle Scott, I have been all over town and could get no one to help me survey the grave yard."

I told him he could see my position, that my crew needed my attention and that I was busy as I could be. It certainly looked as if he could get some one to carry the chain.

He said he had done his best and there was nothing to do but for the surveyor to go back.

I said: "That will not do. I will stop and take my son and we will go and do the work as that is a very important job."

We both stopped and in a half a day had surveyed the cemetery.

White and colored for 50 years had buried promiscuously in that grave yard.

After the survey, the railroad made a deed. Mr. Barnett had three white men appointed as trustees for the cemetery and bought net wire, and fenced in all that part of the lands that was of any service for burying and prohibited any colored people from burying in it.

I then gave the matter serious thought. It looked very hard, as we colored people had furnished all the money and done all the work.

I went to the trustees and asked them if they thought it fair, after we had furnished all the money and done all the work, to cut us off from burying in the same grave yard in which for over a half century our relatives had been buried.

I was told that they were handling the business to suit themselves and no Negroes will be allowed to bury there.

I asked what would be done about those already buried there. If we would be allowed to go in and beautify the graves of our relatives.

They said, "No this is a white grave yard and we will allow no tresspassing."

I told them all right. I believed the Lord would provide for us. He always had.

"I own three acres of land, a beautiful spot lying north of and adjacent to the old grave yard and I am going to make my people a present of this spot for a grave yard. That will only leave a hair's breadth between the white and the Negro grave yard.["]

I said: "Gentlemen, you have brought us from Africa here against our will, our transportation was paid by you. We had handcuffs on our hands, and through the magnificent power of God, he has taken irons off our hands, and placed into those same hands the ballot the greatest boon to the American citizen. As we have to live here in this wicked world today working side by side and mingling our forces in the cotton fields and factories, in the stores, the woods, we buy goods from the same counter, it looks as if it would be no harm in being laid in the bosom of mother earth as we had worked together in life.

A few days later I walked into a grocery store and met two of these trustees. They said they had thought over what I had said, about the piece of land I was going to give the colored people, and they had decided that the better way to do would be for me to deed

Colored cemetery—Madison, Ark.

that piece of land to the white people and they would give the old grave yard to the colored people. That if I gave the colored people the piece of land I spoke of the white people would have to always drive past the colored grave yard to get to the white people's grave yard.

I told them I could not agree with them, because if it would be a disgrace to be buried with those now living it would be disgracing those that are already dead, and that it was not my object to disgrace anyone. I always thought that it was better to elevate than to degrade.

I then immediately deeded this piece of land to my people free of charge. Posts were hauled, a net wire fence put around the land, a house was built for tools for the cemetery and to this day our people are glad to accommodate their white neighbors with the necessary tools when they wish to dig graves for white people.

This incident is a real picture of conditions as they exist. The class of white people, who take the stand these people took, are like myself in many ways. They are none too well educated and have felt the heavy hand of misfortune. They rarely take the same view of things that the cultured and wealthy white people take.

SCOTT BOND BUILDS GIN AT EDMONDSON.

From the success that I had in buying my first gin plant, I made up my mind that as the making of the cotton was done principally by the southern colored man and that in as much as there was success in one gin plant, I went into another county—to Edmondson, a town owned and controlled exclusively by colored people, about twenty-five miles from my home at Madison and started to build another gin. I made a few trips about the country around Edmondson over the many hundreds of acres of land owned by those people. They had at thime [the time] two little cotton gins, modeled on the old style, where cotton was handled in baskets to the gin and the seed taken in the same way to the railroad. These gins were practically worn out and it required twice the number of hands to operate them as would have been required to run one up-to-date plant. After seeing how this community could be benefited by putting in a first class modern plant, I drew a plan for this gin plant and went to two or three of the leading citizens and explained same to them. I said to them: "A plant of this kind put right here at your station would be the making of your little town."

The farmers' deeds and titles to the land in the town and its immediate surroundings, had been made and put on record, by a noted lawyer named Edmondson, a scion of the old Edmondson family who prior to the civil war owned all the land in and about Edmondson. He had made these deeds so as to prevent any white man ever being able to get a deed to any of said land. This being a very important point in law, to protect the Negro and to prevent any white man from ever getting a deed to any of these lands. The Negroes of the town then formed the Edmondson Home and Improvement Co., with the object of buying all the land in the vicinity and cut it up into small farms. It was inserted in all deeds given by this club that these lands could not be bought by white people. This club did an extensive business. They bought and sold thousands of acres of land. There were only two little stores and the post office in the little town. I saw this was a fine locality for an up-to-date gin plant. The citizens called a mass meeting of all the neighbors. The time was set and I was asked to come down, explain all about the erection and operation of an up-to-date gin plant.

Enjoying life after forty years' toil.

I met them and said to them: "Friends and fellow citizens, the object of this meeting is to find out whether or not you want a first class gin plant in Edmondson. I have the plan by which I can make the machinery take the cotton from your wagon, put it in the gin stand, roll the cotton on the platform and put the seed in the cars on the track, and every farmer will get to a half a pound, the amount of seed he had in his bale. This can be done with one-fourth of the labor you now use on these two little plants, and will gin twice the amount of cotton per day that you now gin. I will furthermore guarantee that your little town will grow more in one year than it has in the last ten years. In other words it will be the making of this town.

It will require about $10,000 to equip a plant like this. It is left to you to say how you want this plan laid. I will give you the opportunity to come in as stock holders and raise the money and build this plant or I will furnish the money and put it up at my own risk. All I ask is the patronage of the entire community. I will gin a bale of cotton as well and as cheaply as can be done in the country, give as good turn out as can be secured anywhere, will pay as much for cotton seed as the market will afford.

One of the leading men of the community said: "I move that Mr. Bond be allowed to come into our town and put up and operate a plant along such lines as he has offered."

The motion was carried unanimously.

I ordered the machinery for a complete outfit consisting of four gin stands and double hydraulic press. Put in concrete foundations for all the machinery. This being the fourth plant I had built, experience told me to leave no chip unturned. All the machinery, including belts, pulleys, pipes and tank were bought from the Continental Gin Co., Birmingham, Ala.

I thought then and think now that they handle the best and most complete gin outfit made.

The day the plant was completed there was a bale of cotton standing at the gin waiting. We got up steam in the morning trained up the belts and was in fine running order by 12 o'clock. When we started to ginning this bale, the machinery worked perfectly. At the blowing of the whistle all the neighborhood gathered to see the new gin work. The seed were rattling to a car 150 feet away. This was a real treat to all the people of that vicinity.

I owned and operated this plant successfully along mechanical and financial lines for two years. During these two years you could almost see the little town grow. The gin turned out from 45 to 60 bales per day. It was a source of revenue to Edmondson. We paid out monthly from three hundred to five hundred dollars in wages. Mr. Pat Ward of Edmondson, was secretary and manager at a salary of $75.00 per month. The engineer and ginner drew salaries in proportion. Seeing the gin business was a success the second year after I built this plant I was offered an opportunity to lease the Richmond Cotton Oil Co's Gin at Widener, Ark. I took advantage of the offer and leased this gin and supplied myself with wood and coal sufficient to handle the plant that fall. I had a strong competitor at this place, and soon saw that it would take some financial hustling to succeed.

I had been accustomed to this and had learned how to change gloves in handling different classes of people. I made up my mind to go after the business and get results.

When the season opened we were on hand ready for ginning, and I succeeded in handling my competitor like a pocket in a shirt.

This Widener gin gave me control of four different gins for that year. The fourth being a gin I owned on one of my farms 12 miles up the St. Francis river. You can readily see that this would be a big job for an educated man to handle. For an uneducated man this must have been a double load.

SCOTT BOND OVERCOMES OBJECTION.

I was at this time equipped with two grown boys who had finished college and were material of my own shaping, we were well able to meet the emergency. I made one of my sons, Theophilus general manager of all the gin plants. The older one, Waverly T. Bond was secretary and treasurer. The only worry to us during this ginning season was car shortage. By the time we got our plants in full operation we found it a hard matter to get cars to ship our seed. The seed houses at Edmonson, Widener, Madison and 12 miles up the river were all full to overflowing, all from the lack of cars in which to ship seed. This right in the middle of the ginning season.

I phoned and sent night messages to the officials of the Rock Island Ry., asking and begging for cars to relieve our seed bins. Sometimes we would get one car a day and sometimes would get none. By this time the ginning proposition began to get serious. We were paying out four and five thousand dollars a day. Still the seed houses were packed full and the seed had begun to deteriorate. Right at this juncture my Widener competitor who was one of the leading citizens of this county, and was called the "bulldog of the bone yard," by many, refused to allow me to load my seed on cars on the siding at Widener.

I laid my complaint before the agent at the Widener station. He told me that gentleman had no right, ground or authority to prevent me loading on the siding. He said he would both wire and write the company that night in reference to the matter. I paid no attention to this obstruction, I was only worried about the car shortage. I went to Little Rock next morning to see the R. R. officials. I was invited in and given a seat and told that I could see the superintendent in a few minutes.

When my turn came I was invited into the superintendent's office.

"Good morning Uncle Scott."

"Good morning Mr. Cahill."

"I see that you are being interfered with down there about loading your seed."

"Yes sir, to some extent I am."

"I will attend to that at once." He called his stenographer and started to dictate a letter to Capt. Fussell at Forrest City, Ark., as follows:

"Sir: I have been informed by Uncle Scott here in my office that you had forbade him loading cotton seed on the industrial track at Widener, Ark., and I would like to know what authority you have to stop any one from loading seed on this industrial track."

I said: "Mr. Cahill, sir, with all honor and respect to you as a gentleman if you can't dictate a better letter than this I would prefer you would not dictate any at all. I beg to say I have not complained to you about any difficulty about loading seed since I have been here in your office. I think the better way would be for you to say you had been advised by your agent at Widener that he had prevented Uncle Scott from loading seed in the industrial track at Widener."

"I would be more than glad to have you know that I am a Negro and a Republican. Mr. Fussell of Forrest City, Ark., is a white man and a democrat. And this Negro and the white man will be down there face to face. He would likely want to know why I had gone to Little Rock to see about this industrial track and had not been to see him. For this reason I would prefer you would not write any letter, as the Negro and the white man would be involved in a difficulty and you will be sitting here revolving around in your high chair. When I get home I will go and see Mr. Fussell and take care of the situation. My business here is to look after another matter entirely."

"Every seed house I have between Memphis and Madison is rammed full of seed. I have up to date about $25,000 tied up in cotton seed, and these seed are heating and damaging. I understand the R. R. Commissioners have made it very plain that where people are handling perishable goods, they must have first choice of cars for shipping purposes. You will please note that I am paying out over $5,000 a day for cotton seed. I note cars up and down the line are being loaded with lumber which does not appear to me to be perishable goods. I am a country man, living away back out in the sticks and uneducated. I also have large obligations to meet. Unless you furnish me cars and relieve my condition at once I will be forced to enter suit against the company for damages. I had rather do anything else in the world than to resort to these means."

"Well Uncle Scott how many cars will it take to relieve you?"

"If you can furnish me eight cars a day for the next ten days, as all my gin plants are running at full capacity, I think that will finally relieve the situation."

Ulysses S. Bond.

"I will guarantee you six cars tomorrow."

"Please say you will have four cars placed for me today. You can see it is taking worlds of money per day to handle these seed. For an uneducated Negro living in the country in the sticks to have to carry a burden of this kind is pretty tough."

"I will do my best. I will instruct our car distributor to set one car at each of your different plants this evening."

["]All right Mr. Cahill. Shall I go home, lie down and sleep sound, knowing that I am going to get six cars a day for the next eight or ten days? You can readily see that if I don't get at least six cars a day for the next ten days it will be impossible for me to sleep."

On my way back from Little Rock, I stopped at Forrest City to see Mr. Fussell in regard to loading cotton seed on the industrial track at Widener, Ark. I found him on the platform of his gin plant at Forrest City.

It must be noted that Mr. Fussell has been for many years one of the strongest factors, financially, socially and morally in Eastern Arkansas. His power and influence were felt and exercised in everything that meant upward and forward in the development of the county and state, and it required on the part of an humble Negro like myself much care in approaching a man of his standing.

I had to change gloves to handle a matter like this.

I said, "Good evening, Mr. Fussell."

"Good evening Uncle Scott."

"I am on my way from Little Rock home. I have just left the office of the officials of the R. I. Ry., and they claim that they have been notified by the agent at Widener that you have prohibited me from loading cotton seed on the industrial track there and they attempted to take the matter up by writing you through the mail. I told them to please not write as Mr. Fussell and myself were citizens of St. Francis County and taxpayers and that we could settle the matter between ourselves. I am now here in your presence ready to go over the matter with you."

"I would be pleased to have you know that I did not rent the Richmond Cotton Oil Gin at Widener to prevent you as my competitor from making money. This gin had been run for years by different people and it never had occurred to me that you would object to me renting and operating this plant. As all of our business along financial lines has been pleasant for twenty or more years. You being the president of the Bank of Eastern Arkansas and all of our business has been pleasant with thousands and thousands of dollars dealing every year, I was at a loss to know what had been the cause of his difficulty. I decided within myself that I must have made a mistake somewhere at some time, and I am very eager to know, Mr. Fussell where this mistake was made."

"Uncle Scott, you have made two mistakes in your life."

"All right, Mr. Fussell, if I have they were unintentional. I would be glad to have you show me the ground upon which I made them."

"When you went that Negro's bond for shooting that white man you made the mistake of your life."

"Let's see. The man whose bond I went had an old gray-headed decrepit father. This old man came to my office and said, 'Uncle Scott, I came to you this morning with tears in my eyes to ask you what to do?'"

View on Jack Davis farm.

"Well Brother Whitfield, what will you have me to do?"

"The officers of this county have arrested my son for shooting at that white man, and put him in jail. I have been informed that the ropes have been prepared and they are going to lynch him tonight. I am here to ask you to advise me what I can do to save him?"

"Who do you trade with?"

"I trade with Mr. Fussell."

"Have you any land or property of any kind?"

"No, I have no property except some mules, cows, cotton and corn, and Mr. Fussell has a mortgage on the best part of that."

"Who does your son trade with?"

"Pettus and Buford."

"Has he any property?"

"Yes, he has five or six mules, some cows and plenty of cotton and corn."

"You go to Mr. Fussell and tell him that I sent you. Tell him that you came to ask him to help you save the life of your son, whom you are expecting to be lynched tonight. Tell him that you will give him a mortgage on your mules, cows, cotton and corn and that you will get your son to give him a second mortgage on all of his mules, cows, cotton and corn if he will go on his bond and turn him loose. Whitfield the chances are that he will not do this, but he may call me up and tell me to go the bond and then I will be justified in going the entire bond myself. Now old man, brace up and quit crying and go along. I am sure that this will work like a charm.

"The old man went and tearfully laid his case before Mr. Fussell, who said, 'No, Whitfield, I cannot afford to do that. This was a white man that you shot at, and I can't afford to go a colored man's bond for shooting at a white man.'"

"The old man was at a loss. Whitfield was well acquainted with Mr. Otto Rollwage, a prominent lawyer and he knew that Mr. Rollwage was also friendly with me. Mr. O. B. Rollwage called up at my office in Madison but I had gone to Edmondson. He then called me over long distance at Edmondson. He said to me, "Uncle Scott, old man Whitfield is in a lot of trouble. He is here in my office and wants you and me to make bond to let his son out of jail in order that he may escape death tonight.

"I told him when he had made the bond and had signed it that I would give him the power of attorney to sign my name to the same. This was done at once. Mr. Rollwage found the sheriff and had Whitfield turned out. We both knew that he would run away and never return. This has been years and the man has never returned. Mr. Rollwage and I handled the case and settled the bond.

"Now Mr. Fussell you can see at a glance that it was policy for me to do this as it was for the welfare of the entire community. The white man at whom Whitfield shot, you see Mr. Fussell, had allowed himself to be too familiar with that class of Negroes. They had been associated in some kind of game and there was quite a crowd, both white and colored present and it was said that this Negro was a winner. It was said that after he won the money in sight that he also won a mule and the white man refused to deliver the mule and that this brought on the shooting."

Just at this time a well known citizen, Mr. Bud Horton, came up. Mr. Fussell called Mr. Horton and related the conversation that had just passed between us.

Mr. Horton said, "Mr. Fussell, that white man was a desperate character and you and I cannot afford to countenance that kind of a white man associating with that class of Negroes."

Mr. Fussell being a true hearted gentleman said, "Bud, I guess you are right. If that was the condition of affairs it should be tolerated by nobody."

I said, "Now Mr. Fussell, that is my first mistake, please tell me the second."

"When you went that white man's bond that Mr. Sweet had arrested for hiring the hand from his farm out of the crops to dig shells, then and there you made a mistake."

"I think that it was policy for me to go this man's bond because he owed me an account of $69.40 in the store, and when he walked into my store with the sheriff Saturday evening and told me that he was under arrest and that he wanted me to go his bond until Monday morning at 9 o'clock, Mr. Fussell if I had said no that debt would have been paid, don't you think so?"

"I guess that you are right."

He met the court on Monday morning and that was the end of my responsibility on his bond and Mr. Nimoos, one of the biggest merchants in Eastern Arkansas, went his bond for the Circuit Court.

Mr. Fussell said, "Uncle Scott, you were all right. You did what I or any other man would have done under the circumstances, and I will say right here after looking over our dealing I think that we understand each other. Go ahead and load all the seed that you want to and anything else that you want to do in this county let me know and I am with you."

When I got home I met my son, Theo. He said: "Pa it looks as if your trip away brought us some comfort. We got four cars today."

"Son that may be true. Christ went away in order that the Comforter might come. We have the promise of six cars a day for ten days beginning tomorrow. I am sure this will give ease."

It was the duty of Theo the manager of all the gins to visit all these plants, pay off the labor and check up the bookkeeper at each plant. This he was well prepared to do, and he kept everything in good shape.

At that time our pay roll at the gin plants alone amounted to about $1,800. I am proud to say that we were very successful that year with the gin business and closed up in fine shape and made some money.

A FROG FARM.

While clearing a piece of land on one of my farms last spring I found a low place some 15 acres in extent, the greater part of it covered with water. I could easily have drained it into a nearby bayou or slough, but thought I would try another way to make it profitable. I could see enormous frogs on the chunks and logs. This gave me an idea. I had often read and heard of bull frogs as a delight for the table, so I came to the conclusion to investigate this line of activity. It was not long before I found out that frogs were more valuable than chickens and cost infinitely less to feed. Without going into detail I have the frog industry under way and unless I am very much mistaken I shall make it return a handsome profit.

SCOTT BOND BUILDS SAW MILL.

When the great flood of 1912 reached its crest, I found the entire community was financially embarrassed. I wondered what would be the best thing for me to do to better my condition. I concluded to put in a saw mill, as I had vast quantities of timber about 12 miles up the St. Francis river.

When the waters receded there was no time to hesitate so I put in a saw mill and had the timber cut and rafted down to the mill, and made arrangements with Messrs. Rudd and Stewart two colored men from Mississippi to operate the mill. These men were experienced in this class of work. I soon found I was threatened with an injunction. This came from a class of men that had never done anything themselves and had always objected seeing any one, white or black succeed in a business way. It consisted of three-fourths of all the white men in the town in which I lived. I felt that I was right and went about the matter in a business way. I tried to explain to those people in a way that I was harming no one by putting in this mill; that it would give employment to a number of people and cause hundreds of dollars to be spent in the town, that would otherwise not be spent. They said I should put in no saw mill here. "This is a white man's country, and white men are going to rule."

I said, "Well gentlemen I think in part you are right, but you must realize the class of white men who object to me putting in this mill

Scott Bond and son Theophilus planning the bull frog farm.

are carpet baggers from the north and do not represent the sentiments of aristocratic southern born democrats. I have been in the
state of Arkansas since 1861, some 50 odd years and consider that I
am a tax payer and a citizen of this state. I would prefer not to be
molested and to go along with this enterprise."

I went to the officials and taxpayers of the community and laid
the situation before them. They told me to go ahead and they would
see that I was not molested. Yet the injunction was brought.

I hope the reader will see my condition with a vast amount of
property, farms and people and stock to be fed from my hands to
be handicapped like this.

Feeling proud as I have always felt as a citizen of this community,
I would not permit myself to yield to this narrowness.

I was compelled to answer the charges of the injunction and went
to the court house the morning the injunction was filed and the
attorney they had in charge, being a reputable, broad-hearted southern born gentleman who had won numbers of cases for me, said to
me: "Uncle Scott I am getting out papers to file an injunction to
prevent you from putting up that saw mill. I thought I would call
you and let you know what I was doing."

"All right judge I have always tried to be obedient to the laws of my land. Now what will you have me to do?"

He said the object of his client was to have me stop.

"You mean to stop building up the mill?"

"Yes, that is the object of this injunction."

"All right, I shall stop now. Now what else judge?"

"That is all that is the end of it. That is all my client Mr. Edwards is asking for."

This was on Monday morning. I hope the reader will note, that Mr. Edwards' attorney just asked me to stop and did not tell me not to commence any more. So I stopped all that day, went home and went to bed and realized that I would not be in contempt of court if I should start on Tuesday morning. Knowing my opponent was a hired man, and compelled to go about 75 miles to his work, in order to hold his job, that I could double my forces and go to work until Saturday night, before he could get back. His associates in the town, who were opposing me, began at once to telephone and wire Mr. Edwards that I had begun work again. But by me knowing that he was financially tied to his boss, I felt no uneasiness. I doubled my crew and finished all the lower part of my mill by the last of the week and was putting all my machinery upstairs when the next Monday came. Mr. Edwards was on hand. I was at the court house and met Mr. Edwards and his attorney in the office. The attorney said to me: "Uncle Scott what in the world is the matter with you?"

"What do you refer to judge?"

"Why the filing of that injunction."

"Judge I did just what your client asked me to do. He asked me to stop and I stopped all that day and judge you did not tell me not to start any more, so I did not think I was showing contempt when I started again Tuesday morning."

There was a hearty laugh between the lawyer, his client and myself.

"I will fix you this time so you will stop and not start again."

"All right judge, but I don't see how you are going to do that, because I have completed the lower building and do not need another inch of space on the ground. I am now working up stairs up in space. It don't look like anybody could object to one working up stairs."

"You seem to have some idea of what law is but when I get through with you this time you will be tied and the chances are, you will have to pay a large sum of money for contempt of court."

"All right judge, what you say, I suppose is true. You are a good lawyer and know your business."

The next morning the deputy sheriff came to Madison and served his papers on me. After reading the papers, I thought I had detected a mistake in them. I asked him please to read them again slowly. I had detected the mistake and said to the sheriff, "As you go back to the court house will you please leave these papers with Mr. Walter Gorman who is my attorney?"

Waverly T. Bond.

He replied: "Yes, Uncle Scott, I will."

It was about six o'clock in the evening and we all stopped. I went to my office at 7 o'clock that evening and called up my attorney and asked him if the deputy sheriff had left some papers with him, and if he had reviewed the contents of the same. As I expected, he laughed and said:

"Keep on at work, those papers can not harm you."

The case was set for fourteen days later. By that time I had finished my mill and had sawed something over a carload of lumber. All the white people of our little town who had induced Mr. Edwards to file the injunction in the face of all the laws of the community in which we live, were saying, some of them, he will be ruined forever; others that he thinks he is smart, but he will get left this time.

The case was to be tried before the Chancery Court and I found out the day before the trial that unfortunately for my opponent, there would be no trial on that day because of the illness of the Chancery judge. On the day set, however, Mr. Edwards and his witnesses dressed up and went to the court house for the trial, while I and my crew were cutting lumber to beat the band. About 11 o'clock, one of Mr. Edwards' friends, who was a great factor in the opposition to the mill, sauntered up to the mill and said: "What are you doing?"

I said: "I am cutting lumber to beat the band."

"Don't you know that this is the day for the trial?"

"That certainly is the fact. Why in the world didn't you notify me in advance?"

He laughed and said: "It was none of my business to remind you. I thought you were able to take care of yourself."

"That may be true but any one is liable to forget."

"You are surely into it because they will surely get judgment against you for all sorts of offences against the law today."

"Well, I guess you are right, but as I did not think of it this morning, I will just keep on sawing, as I may not get to saw any more after today."

By this time Mr. Edwards, my opponent and his witnesses began to arrive and to give out the news that the trial was postponed. The fellow who had just told me that this was the day for the trial said: "That nigger must have been aware that the trial would be put off because he was perfectly contented and was sawing lumber to beat the band."

The hearing was postponed another month. At the expiration of that time I had cut and shipped 10 car loads of lumber to the J. O. Nesser Lumber Co., Chicago, Ill.

When the day of the hearing of the injunction arrived, I was on hand with my attorney and defense. The case was called. When the other side had presented their case my attorney got up and explained to the judge where the other side had no case whatever. He explained to the judge the mistake that had been made in issuing the papers. The attorney on the other side rose and said:

"That is a mere technicality in law."

The judge ruled that a technicality was just as great as any other part of the law and that he would have to find some other point in law to offset this technicality. This could not be done by the other side and the court ruled that they had no case.

First, they sat down on their rights too long. The evidence shows this man Scott Bond had already put in the boom at his mill[,] something over $15,000 worth of timber[,] and had on the ground machinery and buildings which would amount to about $25,000. This within itself would demand a $40,000 bond. I find here your bond would not equal one one-hundredth part of this amount. On these grounds the court dissolves the injunction.

It was then I felt good over my case and was indeed sorry for the other side, for they did look pitiful.

Dan A. Rudd.

I am sure one can see along here what a great hill I had to climb, trying to feed about 800 colored people and about 475 head of mules, being handicapped by that kind of people.

I want to say right here to both white and black, that whenever any man in the south tries to serve God, do right and live a good citizen, God says, "He shall wax fat and grow strong." I would be glad to have the reader to note here that the sentiment of the class of white people who oppose me, was not the sentiment of cultured refined white people of the south.

I moved on with the mill, finished cutting out all my timber and made a success of the same, and got enough profit out of it to help feed all those people and to make crop that year.

FLOODS AND CUT WORMS.

Following the overflow of 1912 as the water went down, I fol-

lowed with my ploughs and seed as they do in the valley of the Nile.
I got a very early start as most of my land was bedded before the
water came. This gave me an unusually early start. Cotton and corn
came up to a fine stand. There was nothing to do but get scrapers
and hoes to work. When the hands on the different plantations went
to the field on Monday morning, behold, instead of scraping and
chopping, we had to go to planting as the cut worms had eaten off
the entire crop. This was the case with all the farmers of this part of
the country. This brought on heavier expenses and more hustling.

We got the second stand all O. K. By this time the weather had
grown warmer and the cut worms gave way to the heat. We succeeded in chopping over and saved about two-thirds of a stand. We
were plowing up and planting over corn and cotton the entire season. Finally after the whole year's labor, we were unable to grow
any corn whatever. We succeeded in gathering about a half a crop
of cotton, about 475 bales. The prices of cotton that year were normal.

This was my second crop failure. But I always made it a rule to
keep in good cheer, and said to my sons, who were at that time partners with me, in the mercantile business: "Boys this is the second
crop failure, but these failures seldom succeed each other, we are
going to make a crop. There is no feed in the barns for the mules
and no meat and bread for the hands. But we will grow a crop anyhow, so come on and let's go."

This encouraged my boys and we all started out in good cheer,
business picked up. About the time we got under headway plowing, came the 1913 overflow. Again as the waters receded we followed with the sowing. This unusual thing of one overflow
following an overflow, it seemed that the whole earth was alive with
cutworms. It seemed that it would be impossible to hold a stand of
corn or cotton. The 1912 overflow was the first in 15 years.

We would start to planting on a hundred acre piece. Before we
could get over we would go back and upon examining the seed in
the drills we could pick up a handful of seed and cut worms. These
pests had actually bitten off the sprouting plants before they could
get through the ground. I had always been a fellow with a good
nerve but this test certainly put me to thinking. I came by the saw
mill and called Messrs. Rudd and Stewart aside and held a consul-

tation with them. I said: "Look here boys this thing is coming to a test. I am practically at a loss what to do."

Mr. Rudd said, "what is the matter?"

I said: "The two overflows have filled the earth jamb full of worms. We have ploughed up and planted the second time. I have used all my teams to such an extent in ploughing up and planting the second time, my hands have become disheartened and discouraged. The better part of them were already in debt because of the short crop the year before. They all seemed to be dragging and doing no good. I am at a loss what to do."

Mr. Rudd said: "Let's shut the mill down [as] the logs won't rot in the river. Let's take the hands and go and make a crop. The farm is the foundation of the saw mill, the store and every thing else."

I said, "No Mr. Rudd, that will not do, for when you take hands from a saw mill and put them to work on the farm it looks as if the saw mill unfits them for farming. Don't believe we will ever get them to work on the farm."

Mr. Rudd said: "Yes I will go to them and tell them we are going to shut down the mill. Come and let's go to the farm."

I told him all right, he could go and try. This would give us some extra teams and the chances were that we would get planted the third time. It may be that we will have a late frost. If so we might make a pretty fair crop. This was done and we succeeded in planting over the third time.

By this time the weather was so hot that the cut worms could not do the damage they had done earlier. This required hustling almost night and day, trying to get a crop. The cotton looked for a while as though it might be prosperous, but we had an early frost and gathered very little corn, and only gathered 250 bales of cotton.

GLOOMY TIMES AHEAD.

By this time people far and near were alarmed over the condition of affairs. The question was with merchants and laborers. "What is to become of the country?" Levee and county taxes twice a year. No corn, meat nor bread in the entire country. All these things had to be shipped in from other points. By this time I could hear of my contemporary merchants all over the county, making assignments, throwing up their hands and walking out. This condition of affairs began to make me wonder. I was always one of the fellows to hold on and never give up under a burden, no matter how heavy, I said I have not failed in life. There is no excuse for complete failure and I will never allow myself to concede to one. So I got both my sons in the office and shut the door.

I said: "Boys times are looking very critical. These many failures have put our entire country to a loss. What can we do to succeed?"

One boy would say one thing and the other would say another. The subject was discussed pro and con. I had never up to this time given a mortgage. And the boys were unable to figure out any means by which we could make another crop. I looked at them and really felt sorry. I said to them: "Boys, I do not yield. This is nothing. Let's go and make another crop."

At that time I saw no way whatever. I went home and went to bed, but did not sleep any that night. We were already in debt and then had to make a crop; not a dollar to make it on, not a pound of meat and no feed for stock.

I met my boys at the store, braced up and scraped up the best look I could get on my face and said: "Boys we are all right. We are going to succeed."

This seemed to cheer them up wonderfully, as they were boys who always had confidence in their father's financial ability.

They said: "All right pa, whatever you say goes."

I took the train for Memphis and went to my commission man to whom I already owed a nice little sum of money. I found him to have a pretty long face on him. It looked something like a horse collar. All the commission men up and down Front Row, in Memphis seemed to wear the same kind of face.

I went into Wilkerson and Carrol Cotton Co.

"Good morning."

"Good morning Uncle Scott. Walk in and take a seat."

"Thank you sir." And I sat down.

"What are the people doing in Arkansas?"

"They seem to be doing the same things I see the merchants doing up and down Front Row."[24]

"How is that Uncle Scott?"

Sheep grazing in grove.

"All of us like the people of the entire south are wearing long faces looking like horse collars."

This created a little laugh.

"Well Uncle Scott what are we all going to do?"

"That is just what I am over here for now, to find out what are we going to do. As for myself I am going to succeed. I do not know what the balance of the people will do."

"You seem to be in good cheer."

"Yes, sir, I always have been and always will be as long as there is breath."

"I will admit that I am in debt and owe more than I can pay at this juncture. I only feel humble for one cause. That is if I can live and have health I know I am going to succeed."

I have a proposition to put to you. I admit that I owe you and others more money than I can pay and I have not the heart to ask you to furnish me any more money to make this crop with. I am willing to secure you, with a mortgage for $10.00 on every dollar I owe you and will owe you, at the close of this crop. In doing this I shall ask you for enough money to secure my outside obligations, with the different banks of my town and others, which will give me about $10,000 to operate on and meet my outside obligations. This was agreed to, when the papers were fixed up and signed, which took about five or six days. In the meantime seeing that I had the arrangement made, I asked him to write Ely, Walker and Co., St. Louis and say to them I have made arrangements to get the money to pay them. Also the Forrest City Grocery Co.

"All right Uncle Scott, we will do that."

"When I am gone you will forget this. Please dictate these letters in my presence."

I saw both letters written, grabbed my hat, caught the next train out for home feeling all O. K.

Met my boys, got them in my office and related to them my entire business trip. They were well pleased, but Theo dropped his head and said, "Pa that is something I never saw you do in your life."

"My boy, that is true your father has never experienced such times as these in all his many years. While it may look a little tough to you, you should look back on this and see that it is worth something to be able to furnish the collateral."

At the time this contract was made and agreed to, I failed to have Mr. Wilkerson to give me a copy of the agreement we had entered into, thinking his word was O. K.

In eight or ten days I drew on him for $500. In about fifteen days more I drew on him for $1,500. A few days later I drew on him for $975. This draft was not honored. I said to the party who returned the draft to me: "I will go at once and find out what is the matter." I went to Memphis next morning and called on Mr. Wilkerson. He bade me good morning and asked how was everything in Arkansas.

"My business over here is to find out why you did not honor my draft."

"I have already cashed several drafts for you."

"That is true but they were nothing like $10,000. At the time I gave you the mortgage you agreed to let me have that amount of money at once. I explained to you plainly that I was giving you as security $75,000 worth of property for what I already owed you, and also for the $10,000 to meet my outstanding obligations."

"Well money is very hard to get hold of. It is mighty scarce and I don't know about that."

["]You don't think Mr. Wilkerson that I would give you that

amount of security on all my property and leave all my other cred-
itors imperiled who had always befriended me?"

"The other fellows can wait as well as I can."

["]That is true, but you are secured $25.00 for every dollar that
I owe you and the other people have no security whatever, and they
are not going to wait. I am going to pay them and I am going to
sue you, if you are the last man alive."

"You have no written contract to show that I promised to let you
have $10,000."

"That is true but I have your word and I thought at that time
your word was worth $500,000. Mr. Wilkerson I am bound to sue
you. There is no way for me to get out of it."

"On what ground are you going to sue me?"

"On your signature in black and white." I am in a position to
produce two letters, one written to Ely Walker and Co., of St. Louis,
and one to the Forrest City Grocery Co., of Forrest City, Ark., telling
them you had made arrangements with me to let me have $10,000."

"I have never written any such letters."

"Just press the button and I will show you."

Mr. Wilkerson's son came in. I said to the young man: "Please
refer to your files and see if you don't find two letters written on
the 15th of March, one to Forrest City, Ark., and the other to St
Louis, Mo.["]

He did so and brought the letters in.

I said to him: "We will excuse you. You may go in the other
room."

Mr. Wilkerson read the letters carefully and then he got up and
said: "Uncle Scott I have done all that I can do."

"Mr. Wilkerson that is all a government mule can do. If you have
done all you can do, I am too broad to ask a man to do something
he cannot do, but I am going to make a crop and pay the other right
away. I will not bother you for any more money."

I took the train and came home. At that time my boys and myself
had about $30,000 life insurance and had been carrying the same
for a good many years. I had the boys write and ask the insurance
people if there was any chance of me drawing on my policies.

My letter was promptly answered. I was informed that the insurance people would be glad to furnish me with what money I needed

and the blanks for loans was sent me. These papers were defective on account of the lack of my wife's signature. She was in ill health and I had sent her to Harper's Ferry, in Virginia. When the papers were sent in they sent me a check for the money. This put us in position to meet our obligations and to go ahead with my farming.

After all these disasters, ups, and downs, the crop was finally made and gathered and it only amounted to 250 bales when there should have been 1,000 bales.

I paid Mr. Wilkerson all that I owed him and a part on the old debt that I had formerly owed him.

This crop followed the 1913 overflow and was up to that time the most disastrous of all. At this time the entire south was alarmed over the condition of affairs. There was no money in the country, no corn, no meat, no bread nor hay. It had got to the place where it was not a matter of collateral, it was a matter of finding the money. Everybody was looking one after the other, asking one another what could be done.

By this time I had put in operation what is known as the gravel pit. This plant cost about $15,000 to get it in operation. Half the proceeds from the gravel sales to the Ry. Co. had to be paid on the plant. After giving half of the proceeds each month and paying the labor and other operating expenses, there was left a net monthly balance of about $400. With the proceeds derived from the gravel pit I was able to buy one carload of oats in order to start to plowing. This only amounted to about one sack to the mule around. By the time we had gotten in a way of plowing the oats were all gone.

Now I want to say to you that you can imagine what must have been the condition of the country at this time. There were more merchants, more bankers and more farmers threw up their hands and made assignments and went out of business than I had seen at any time in all my life.

I had always thought that I could raise my bristles as high as any dog in the bone yard, but all this put me to looking and thinking. I thought of an old maxim that I had long heard of: "If you dread the bulls' heels you would never skin his eyes." So when I looked around and saw all these mules and about 800 Negroes to be fed the question uppermost with me was "Where in the world is the money coming from?"

I then began to get myself together. I saw that it would take some financiering to get through this condition. I called Theo in and said: "Son what in the world are we to do? It looks like one of the famines in the time of Abraham and Joseph. What do you think we can do son?"

'Pa I can't say, but I have always thought that if any one in the world could win you were the man that could win."

"Well son you are right and right here we are going to win."

"All right pa. It has always looked like you meant everything you said. I have always found it to come out that way."

"We must have $10,000 from somebody, somewhere at this time."

"It will take all that to do us any good in this crop, but I don't see where in the world you will get it from."

"Neither do I, but it must come."

I had been farming for myself for forty years and never known what a crop failure was in all these many years. Then to have to take three in succession, this being the third, I must admit that at this juncture things looked dark.

I finally made up my mind to start out after the needed money. I met a friend of mine who I thought was in fine shape financially and said to him I want $10,000. I want you to show me where I can find it. I have the collateral to make one perfectly safe $5.00 to one.

He said: "Uncle Scott it is not a matter of collateral, the money can not be gotten."

I then walked into a bank and said to the banker: "I want $10,000 and have got to have it from some body."

"Why Uncle Scott are you crazy? Take three of the best money men in St. Francis County and they could not raise $10,000 cash. There is no surplus money in this country."

I then went over to the depot and met a railroad man and said: "How do you do?"

"All right Uncle Scott, how are you this morning."

I told him O. K.

We had some little things in common in our past life. We talked and laughed for about twenty minutes. Finally I said to him: "I have got to have $10,000."

"If I had met you last week, I could have let you have it. I am going to Little Rock this morning, and I think I know some one who can let you have it."

"Tell him I will give $5.00 collateral for every one I need."

In a few days I had a letter from this party, stating that he understood I wanted some money and I had plenty of good collateral and would like a loan. If this be true he could let me have about $15,000.

When I read the letter I struck a trail. I was very busy at the time arranging my farming business and in a day or two I started for Little Rock. My aim was to take the train in Forrest City. I met another banker there. This was a gentleman with whom I had had a big law suit, and who was a dear friend of mine, even at the time of the law suit. (I won this suit.)

"Hello Uncle Scott, how are you this morning?"

"All right sir, all O. K. How are you?"

"I am in good shape. By the way, I understood the other day that you were wanting some money."

"Yes sir, that's true."

"How much do you want?"

"I am bound to have $10,000."

"That ain't no little bit."

"You right about that, the way times are now."

"Do you think you can arrange to get it?"

"Yes sir. It is not a matter of thinking with me, I must have it."

"Who have you been trying?"

"I have spoken to several parties concerning the matter. I am now on my way to see a party in Little Rock who has written me. Here is his letter."

He opened the letter and read its contents and said ["]this fellow wants to let you have $15,000."

"Yes that is what he said."

"Well he is all right, he is president of one of the biggest banks in the city of Little Rock."

"That is more money than I want, I just want $10,000."

"When do you want it?"

"Inside of ten days."

"All right, when you get ready just come in and I will let you have it."

"That will suit me. When I get back to my store I will send you collateral; you can examine the records and you can have proper papers drawn at once."

When the papers were all signed and the money received. Theo said: "Pa this is all right. We are now shaped up for another crop. We will double our determination right here and go after it good and hard. Pa I want to congratulate you. You are a dandy."

Now corn and hay, meat and bread, and every body went to hustling. The gravel pit was turning out from 10 to 15 cars a day. The pay roll for the gravel pit amounted to from fifteen hundred to twenty-two hundred a month. Myself and every one else hustled from day break until dark. There was no overflow that year and we succeeded in making and getting a fine cotton crop, made and gathered about 850 bales. Bless the Lord there was another failure after all. The European war came and we could not sell cotton for four cents a pound. Last but not least we made and gathered 15,000 bushels of corn, which was the best of all. Corn means bread which is the staff of life. It also means hogs and hominy. "We killed and put up that year 29 head of hogs. We saved pea hay and other roughage enough to last two years. That year the gravel pit played her part. We loaded and shipped out 1,580 cars of gravel, bringing $23,000. Then and there I doubled my hog crop more than four times. I increased my flocks of sheep 100 per cent. Bought $2,200 worth of cattle and now have 250 head of hogs, have large, well-fenced fields of alfalfa and other grasses, so arranged that I can pasture them at will I am growing high grade registered Hereford cattle with a view of raising the grade of my herds.

You can easily see here, that on account of the war, so far as cotton was concerned and taking into consideration the low prices, was as great a failure as all the balance.

Now, things began to look better. We succeeded in making a good crop of corn and cotton in 1915. This crop was made very cheaply as we had plenty of corn and hay and the mules were all in good shape to start in with. We made and gathered that year 950 bales of cotton and the prices were all the way from 9 to 14 cents. Cotton seed ranged from $30 to $45 per ton. The gravel pit that year ran on time. We loaded one thousand six hundred cars of gravel. Cotton crop and gravel aggregated $58,000.

In the early winter of 1915 I bought a Hercules stump puller and with it removed most of the stumps from a 300 acre field preparing to eventually operate traction plows. This machine was able to pull any stump we could hitch it to regardless of its size or root hold. I then continued my general plan of surface or open drainage (which will later be changed to tile drains) so that when the farming season of 1916 opened I concluded to work this farm with month labor. I got everything in readiness, hired my crew and started plowing and discing. I cultivated 200 acres in cotton and 100 acres in corn. I also had in 49 acres of wheat. The wheat turned out fine. Was reaped and threshed on time and put on the market at a fair price. The corn crop was normal. Cotton turned out wonderfully. The cotton which I grew with month labor, when I sold the seed I found the returns from them had paid the entire cost of the crop including rent, picking and ginning.

This cotton was graded and classed a splendid bender and sold on the market all the way from 22 to 35 cents a pound. I can say that I received as much money this year off of 100 acres in cotton as I had received from 500 acres in many other years. We gathered, handled and sold 1,680 bales of cotton from this year's crop on my several plantations.

I very often stop now and look around and think over the rugged road that I have traveled up to this juncture. It looks almost impossible for a man to overcome the apparently insurmountable difficulties that lay across my way in the years that are gone. The money that we paid out this year, for rebate on cotton seed alone will amount to something over $200,000. We paid as high as $62.00 per ton for cotton seed.

We had counted on ginning about 1,600 bales of cotton, but have up to January 25 ginned 2,680 bales. This cotton was ginned from September 1st up to this date.

There has been more money received from this year's crop than I ever saw come from one crop in any year of my life. Many colored people who had never deposited a dollar in the bank in their life, carried their money to the banks in their overcoat pockets, in their hands and some pulled off their hats and carried their hats full and handed them over to the teller and would say: "I came here to bank my money and I want you to show me how to do it."

MR. BOND VISITS NEW YORK.

Mr. Bond had been pressed by Dr. [Booker T.] Washington to attend the Farmers' Conference at Tuskegee, but owing to pressure of business, did not do so until he received a letter from him urging Mr. Bond to attend, and stating that if he would come transportation and hotel expenses would be paid. Upon receipt of this his son said to him: "Pa, they certainly want you to come and you ought to accept this invitation." He finally decided to go to the conference. When Mr. Bond saw the wonderful work at Tuskegee in his several visits he at once made up his mind that it would be good for the colored people and, in fact, for the whole state, if Mr. Washington could be induced to visit Arkansas. Acting upon this conclusion he began to put forth every effort to consummate this idea. His wish was granted at a most unexpected time and in a way that he had not dreamed of. It came about in this way. The National Negro Business League of which Mr. Bond is a life member was holding its annual session in New York City [in 1910]. Dr. Washington had written him, asking if he could count on his attendance at the meeting. Mr. Bond replied that he would hardly be able to be present. He says: "My reason for so writing Dr. Washington was that as I was uneducated, I did not want to get up before any audience in New York City to make a speech."

The set program included in its numbers some of the leading men of the United States, among whom were former President [Theodore] Roosevelt, Seth Low,[25] Wm. Lloyd Garrison[26] and many other notable men. Col. Roosevelt had just made one of his telling speeches when Dr. Washington, president of the League, said to the audience: "We shall have to vary from the program at this time. I see in the audience a man from Arkansas, Mr. Scott Bond. We are going to ask Mr. Bond to come forward and tell us of Arkansas. Mr. Bond will please come forward."

Mr. Bond, who was in the rear of the hall, says, "You can imagine my feelings as the committee escorted me to the rostrum. All the way I was asking myself what could I say. When I got upon the rostrum and looked over that vast sea of faces I made up my mind to talk just as I did at home."

The files of newspapers of that date quote Mr. Bond as saying:

"Ladies and gentlemen, here stands before you an old one-gallused farmer who never went to school two weeks in his life, but I am in a position to see the difference between the Negro of the north and the Negro of the south. I find that New York numbers in its population 175,000 Negroes. Negroes have no more business here than a rabbit. The majority of the white people here have shown me very clearly that they don't want us here. They also show that they don't need us. They do not come out directly, but indirectly they do. They don't give them employment on the streets, the railroads, the sky-scrapers nor other buildings. I hired a young man yesterday and paid his street car fare to visit all the colored enterprises of the city with me. I have one little Negro to whom I rent a store right along side my store, who is postmaster. I am on his bond for $3,000. I see that that little Negro is selling more dry goods than all the 175,000 Negroes in the city of New York put together.

"Ladies and gentlemen, that shows you at a glance that this is no place for the Negro. The only professions that I see the Negroes of this city have are coachmen for the millionaires, janitors in some of the buildings and a few letter-carriers. Among the 175,000 of my people there are many college graduates. I want to ask a question right here: Is it possible that a young man has to spend eight or nine years getting an education to be a janitor in a flat? I want to say to the Negroes of the north, come to the south, where the greatest commodity of the world is produced, and I will give you a dollar, put you on a farm and give you a chance. (Loud and prolonged applause.)

"Not only can I show you Negroes working in every avenue of industry, I will show you railroads which have Negro section foremen from one end of the line to the other. There are localities after localities that are absolutely owned and controlled by colored people, with Negro mayors, Negro aldermen, Negro marshals, Negro railroad agents, Negro telegraph operators, Negro contractors and builders, and in many other lines. In fact, we can show you Negroes in everything from the pig pen to the white house. It is with much pleasure that this Business League has shown that there are thousands of farms owned by colored people in the south, and very much to my regret it has also shown that there are 63 banks owned by colored people in the south, but not one owned by Negroes in the

Scott Bond and family in their garden at home.

north. My way of looking at things in this country is the south is a paradise for the colored man. I will admit that there are a few white people in the south that from time to time cause trouble and friction, but all broad-hearted people can see that it takes all of one fellow's time to hold the other fellow in the ditch. It has always been a mystery to me why the man who has the greatest occupation in the world is ashamed of his profession. I note that there are a number of farmers who are ashamed to say they are farmers, but call themselves agriculturists. Farming is the only independent living in the world. He only has to depend on nature and the season. There is Mr. Roosevelt who, if the country called him and his wife wanted him, he would have to say, 'Stand still, wife, let me go and see what the nation wants.'

"I want to say to this audience, both ladies and gentlemen, just look at this old one-gallused farmer. If this nation or all the nations should call and my wife should call at the same time, I would say, 'Stand still, nations, I want to go and see what my beautiful wife wants.' The world depends on the farmer. We have the world by the tail and a down-hill pull; we are in position to make all the city dudes pull their hats off to us. We can feed them on whatever we see proper to feed them on. We go to the garden and all the cabbages that are shrivelled up and look like they have snakes in them we can crate up and send to the city for the dudes to eat. We can also go to the hog pen and all the hogs that have their hair growing from the tail to the head or have got the measles and we kill them and send them to the city for the aristocracy and the dudes to eat. (Laughter and applause.) This talk I am making is to call attention to the power the Negro has in his hands if he will use it, to master the entire world along economic lines. As farmers we have the first choice of the products of the earth. This farmer can have beefsteak for breakfast, or ham and eggs, chicken, milk and fresh vegetables of all varieties, fresh strawberries picked while the dew is on, soaked in sugar and served with fresh cream. This farmer can walk in for breakfast and ask for whatever his taste calls for—mutton chop or pork chop—sit down to his table with a large family of boys and girls with a beautiful wife sitting at the head of the table and eat sumptuously and enjoy the comforts of the family circle, get up and put on his hat and walk to the front door and can see the cotton, corn, potatoes and watermelons, fruit growing on the trees, the flowers growing in the yard, the calves and the pigs, the lambs and the chickens, all of which make him know this is home sweet home."

At the close of this address Mr. William Lloyd Garrison stepped over to Mr. Bond and grasped his hand and said: "Little Arkansas man, what you have said amounts to more than all the convention put together."

Dr. Washington then took Mr. Bond's hand and said to him: "Mr. Bond, Arkansas has won the next meeting of the National Negro Business League." Thus Mr. Bond secured the promise of the Tuskegee wizard to visit Arkansas. Turning to the audience, Dr. Washington said: "Are there any questions one would like to ask Mr. Bond?" Hon. J. C. Napier,[27] Register of the United States, Treasury, rose and said: "Yes, I would like to ask Mr. Bond some questions. Mr. Bond, kindly tell us what is your general profession."

Mr. Bond replied: "I have just told the audience I am a real farmer, the greatest profession of the world."

"Mr. Bond, is it not a fact that you handle a large mercantile establishment?"

Dr. Booker T. Washington with Scott Bond and family
at their home in 1911.

"Yes, sir, I ran a store in connection with my farms."

"Do you furnish all the people who work your different farms
from your store?"

"Yes, sir, the hands sell me their cotton and buy what they want
from my store."

"Is it a fact that you own and operate several gin plants and what
is the capacity of each?"

"Yes, I own three, two with a capacity of 50 bales and one with
a capacity of 75 bales."

"What make of gins do you handle?"

"They are all Continental outfits, the greatest gin, that is, the
greatest outfit made."

"Is it a fact that you sell a large amount of gravel to the Rock
Island Railway?"

"It is."

"I would like for you to tell the audience how much taxes you
pay."

Mr. Bond turned to the audience and said: "I believe it is time
for me to stop. Some years ago at a conference in Tuskegee I allowed

them to pull me out, and when I got home the county authorities had raised the assessment on my property $15,000."

"Well, did you pay it?"

"No, I got my attorney and appeared before the board of supervisors and for good and just causes it was knocked out. I will say further that they make me pay taxes on 19 farms aggregating in all 5,000 acres."

At this juncture a lady in the audience arose and said: "I would like to ask Mr. Bond a question. I would like to ask what do you grow on these different farms?"

Mr. Bond turned smilingly to the lady and said: "You have asked a very important question. I grow everything imaginable on these farms: peas, corn, potatoes, cotton, oats, rye, wheat, hogs, cattle, hay, chickens, mules and sheep and the finest boys and girls you ever saw." (Great applause.)

When the session closed Mr. Bond was congratulated for over an hour. So enthusiastic and earnest was the handshaking that Mr. Bond's hand was so swollen the next morning that it looked like two hands.

The following year, 1911, the National Negro Business League held its session in Little Rock, Ark. Here again opportunity was given Mr. Bond to have Dr. Washington speak in St. Francis County. When the National Negro Business League had completed its work, the Arkansas State Negro Business League provided a special train to take the delegates on an excursion to Hot Springs. On the way back Mr. Bond said to Dr. Washington: "I want to offer an apology. It has always been my desire to have you visit my home county and talk to our people. Special arrangements have been made to have the people meet and hear you. All are expecting you. We have provided 150 beeves, hogs and sheep to barbecue and feed the people. The train will stop for you. I have a chauffeur coming from Memphis to drive you and I do not believe you will refuse us."

Dr. Washington replied: "Well, no, I cannot refuse to accept this invitation. I will stop there if the train schedule permits.["]

"We will arrange a special coach for your accommodation and the fast train will stop to pick up your car in the evening," said Mr. Bond.

Dr. Washington said: "Well, Mr. Bond, that is all right if you can do it, but I would rather see that in black and white."

The quisical smile that played over Dr. Washington's face showed that he had his doubts as to Mr. Bond's influence being great enough to induce the railroad people to stop a fast train. Upon the return of the excursion from Hot Springs all retired for a good night's rest. The next morning, bright and early, Mr. Bond was up and went to the offices of the Rock Island Railroad. He only found the chief clerk in the office and addressed him: "This is Uncle Scott Bond from Madison."

The chief clerk said: "Why, this is Uncle Scott. Come in. What can I do for you. I had often heard of you and I am glad to meet you."

Mr. Bond told him that Dr. Washington would stop at Madison and that while he would have no objection to riding in a jim-crow car, yet he and his party would be quite crowded and that if possible he would like to provide a special car for them and have that car placed at the rear end of the train."

The chief clerk told him that would be done and at once dictated messages to that effect to the train dispatcher and gave Mr. Bond a copy of the messages. He then asked what else he could do.

"If Mr. Copeley was here I would like to ask one more favor, but as you do not know me I do not know whether or not it would be all right to ask you," said Mr. Bond.

"What is it, Uncle Scott?"

"I want to ask that the fast train stop at Madison and pick up Mr. Washngton's car that they may make connections at Memphis for Chicago."

"That will be done, Uncle Scott," the chief clerk replied, and he immediately dictated a message to that effect and handed Mr. Bond a copy.

"Now what else, Uncle Scott?"

"Nothing more, sir. I thank you very much for the kindness already shown."

Mr. Bond then had breakfast and when he met Dr. Washington he handed him copies of the messages. He read them and turned to Mr. Bush, President of the Arkansas Negro Business League, and said: "Look at this." Then to Mr. Bond he said: "There are few white men in the state of Alabama who can stop a fast train. You are to be congratulated on your ability to get results."

The train pulled out of Little Rock and arrived in Forrest City on time. The streets were crowded with people and vehicles. Every conceivable kind of conveyance, from automobile to ox cart, was in evidence. When the automobile bearing Mr. Washington, Mr. Napier and Mr. Bond reached Madison, four and a half miles away, the last wagon was just leaving the depot at Forrest City. A larger number of people gathered to meet Dr. Washington than ever before assembled in St. Francis County. The roads leading into Madison from all directions were full, were literally lined with people. So Scott Bond was rewarded for his years of effort to get Dr. Washington to advise the people of his home town. We present on another page a view of Dr. Washington surrounded by the Bond family at their beautiful home, "The Cedars."

NEGRO DEALS WITH NEGROES.

Mr. Bond tells this story of a part of his business experience with his people: I have often heard it said by a certain class of white people that it was impossible for Negroes to join in a business enterprise and succeed, unless they had a white man to manage it for them. This story proves the reverse to be true.

The second gin plant I ever owned had a capacity of forty bales per day, four 70s with elevators, condensers, and a double press; 50 h. p. engine and 75 h. p. boiler. After setting up and operating this plant for two years, I found out that its capacity was not sufficient to accommodate the neighborhood. I was then forced to buy a larger plant. I had often heard my son, Theophilus, speak of a class of people who lived near Cotton Plant, Woodruff County, who were very progressive along business lines. They were all good farmers and owned their farms. I said: 'Now is the time to help others and myself, too.' The principal man of that community was a gentleman of great ability and good reputation named Emmett J. Lee. I wrote Mr. Lee and asked him to come over to Madison and bring with him two or three of his best men. He replied to my letter and set the date he would arrive. I was about closing up my second year's ginning on my plant. The day of their arrival I had a nice day's ginning. The plant was in excellent condition and was doing splendid work. I invited Mr. Lee and his associates to walk out to the gin plant with me. I showed them through the engine room and then up into the gin, which was in full operation, around to the seed house where the seed were being blown directly from the gin into the railroad cars. I said to them: 'Gentlemen, this gin has turned out about 2,000 bales of cotton, but yet it is entirely too small for this community.' When we got back to the office and were seated, I said: 'Now, Mr. Lee, I am ready to explain my object in writing you to come over and bring your friends. I wanted you to see the plant in full operation and the results to be obtained. I am ready to sell you gentlemen this plant.'

"Mr. Lee said: 'Mr. Bond, we need a plant like this in our community, but we cannot buy an up-to-date gin plant like this.'

'Why not?' I asked.

"'Because it is impossible in our community for a colored man to get fire insurance on property.'

"'All right, Mr. Lee,' said I, 'as soon as you get your plant up I will have it insured or it will burn up my property.'

"I sold them the gin on payments, the first to fall due the following November and the remaining payments to fall due each November, the total aggregating about $5,000. On one occasion financial affairs with me were rather stringent, owing to an overflow; I wrote Mr. Lee, explaining to him that inasmuch as they had bumper crops in his county, if he could afford to do so, if he would make me two payments in one I would discount the deferred payment. Mr. Lee did not answer my letter, but in about two weeks to my surprise he walked into my office and laid on my desk a check for $2,000 from the Cotton Blossom Gin Plant. I said to him: 'Mr. Lee, this is all right. It comes in a good time. I will leave my son to calculate the discount and will either give you a check for it or give you credit as you please.'

"'No. Mr. Bond,' was his reply to this, 'we will not accept any discount. It is really a pleasure to meet this obligation. You sold us this plant purely upon our supposed merits without any mortgage or collateral whatever.'

"I had superintended the dismantling and loading the plant for them very carefully myself. It took three cars to haul it. I wanted to be sure that it was properly taken apart and loaded. This is a transaction between Negroes where the whole amount was paid twelve months before it was due. Mr. Lee had insisted when I sold the plant to his company that I keep a one-fifth interest. That interest has paid me 15 per cent annually ever since the deal was made. From this story it can be clearly seen that it is possible for Negroes to succeed along business lines among themselves without outside assistance. At one time I either read or heard that the gin plant had been destroyed by a storm. Some days later I had a letter from Mr. Lee that the gin was destroyed, but all damages were fully covered by insurance. So we are all making money."

SCOTT BOND'S VIEW OF WHISKEY.

"Whiskey has always appeared to me to be the root of all evil."

On the Bond farm in the time of the Civil War, there was an old man named Hardy Bond, who was the "nigger driver." He was in constant contact with the different overseers on the place, which gave great opportunities for buying and drinking liquor.

The farm was located on the east side of Crowley's Ridge, hence the west side of the farm was hemmed in by hills and hollows. The public road, known as the Bay Road, ran right through the farm.

As there were no railroads at that time, steam boats would bring cargoes of goods and discharge at Wittsburg. Wagons would then distribute all kinds of merchandise, including liquor, to points in the interior.

Old man Hardy Bond would buy whiskey from the drivers of these wagons, paying them in corn and fodder. The drivers would raise a hoop on a barrel, bore a hole with a gimlet and draw out as much as they wanted, plug the hole and drive the hoop down again to hide the theft.

These wagons, or prairie schooners, as they were called, were drawn by six and eight yoke of cattle, and were driven by the roughest class of white men that ever cracked a whip.

When the railroads came into existence, the prairie schooners went into discard.

Moonshining then took the place of the liquor provider. Hardy would send me to the moonshine "still" in the hills, west of the Bond farm every morning to get a quart of whiskey. He would send a canteen as he found it to hold three pints. This he could always get filled for a quart. This showed that the liquor had made a thief of him, as he had up to that time been considered perfectly honest. The extra pint for nothing was too much of a temptation for him to resist.

In a little while he got so he would send me morning and evening. A little later he sent for a half gallon twice a day, then for a gallon; then with wallet containing a gallon jug in each end I would have to go twice each day for two gallons.

At last the war ended. Hardy and my step-father rented the Bond farm; they would send to Wellsburg [Wittsburg] for a half barrel and then for a barrel every week.

One time they were to give a Saturday night "festival" in an old store. On the afternoon, before the festival, my step-father received word that his father was dead in North Carolina. He turned the whole thing over to me.

The festival broke up in a fight between two men. Some one put out the lights. I recovered the money which was in the cigar boxes, and, dodging along the wall, found the door, stepped out, rolled under the house and remained there until quiet was restored.

From that day to this, the whiskey purchased by Negroes in Arkansas would float the largest ship that ever sailed the sea; it would pay a fair price for every acre of land in the state; would endow a dozen such schools as Tuskegee.

These experiences and the knowledge of the evil influence and results of drinking liquor, in ruined homes, ruined men, fines, and degradation made me an uncompromising foe to liquor and its attendant curses.

A VISIT TO TUSKEGEE.

Mr. Bond says of his first visit to Tuskegee:

"On a certain occasion I had an invitation to attend the Farmer's Conference at Tuskegee. I finally made up my mind to accept it and pay a visit to the famous institution. I had often heard of Tuskegee and its school. I was naturally expecting to see a nice school.

"When I arrived there and saw the conditions, I was absolutely surprised. I had not believed that there was a school of that class and quality in the world. The only way one could tell the students were Negro youths was that they were black. So far as their demeanor, ability and neat appearance went, it was really superior to anything I had ever seen. The beautiful buildings, the well kept grounds, the many shops, the gardens and farms were indeed a revelation.

In the gardens I found every conceivable kind of a vegetable, the names of many of which I hardly knew. Weeds were conspicuous by their absence. There was perfect order in the planting and so regular was the planting that it looked as if the work had been laid out by a surveyor.

"I was delighted with the appearance of the young men in their military drills.

There were no cigar stumps on the place, nor was there dust and cobwebs anywhere.

The dining room was a marvel of neatness and would accommodate two thousand five hundred.

"The kitchens were as marvelously beautiful and clean as all the other places about the school. One could not see the fire in the cook stoves.

"The bakery was operated by machinery of the latest design and from the ovens came toothsome bread enough to feed an army.

"The silos showed that the students were being taught how to preserve feedstuffs in the highest style of the modern method.

"There was rye and rape for fall and winter pasturage. There were poultry yards and incubators.

"The chemical laboratory was well supplied with apparatus and chemicals.

"The blacksmith, carriage, wagon, cabinet maker, shoe and machine shops were in full operation by the students and their instructors; the same is true of the foundry, draughting room, brickyard, saw mill, dairy, green houses, and departments for live stock which was well supplied with high grade cattle, horses, mules and hogs.

"I also saw a stump-puller in operation.

"The growing fruit trees were in charge of competent orchardists, assisted by the students.

"Nearly every state in the Union was represented in the student ranks.

"A thing that showed the care Dr. Washington took to help the Negro help himself, was that he had provided funds to pay the way of farmers who would attend the conference. By the judicious use of this money he was able to give instructions to many who would not have otherwise been able to be present.

"Tuskegee, the beautiful, Tuskegee the wonderful, a community complete in itself and showing a completeness that urban and sub-urban life is just what we make it, and we can make it what we will.

"There was country life in its highest state of development, and city life, the order of which would be an example for any city.

"And wonder of wonders! conceived in the brain of one born a slave; constructed and governed by this same ex-slave, and with the assistance of others who like himself, had been slaves or by the children of this same class. Negro brains and Negro brawn have in Tuskegee given the evidence that he who says this race is not worthy of every opportunity given any other race is either ignorant or malicious; and perhaps, if studied closely, would be found to be both."

INTEROR OF SCOTT BOND'S GIN.

On another page in this book will be found a picture of the interior of Mr. Bond's cotton gin at Madison, Ark. He stated to the writer that he had spent between $25,000 and $30,000 for gin machinery in the last twelve years, and that the Continental System had given him the results at which he had aimed. The machinery is high-class and the cost of upkeep is practically nothing compared with the work put on it. His experience tells him that no other system will give anything like the sample and turnout of the Continental System. He has built and operated four of these plants: one at Edmondson, one at Cotton Plant and two at Madison. Besides he says that he at all times found the representatives of this company ready to meet him with true business courtesy. He says further that: "I have always found Mr. Dickinson, the general agent of the Continental Gin Company, to be agreeable and helpful and that it seems as if nature had made the southern Negro, the fleecy staple and the Continental Gin people to work together in harmony to get the best results. I have often had my competitors say to me, 'Uncle Scott, your son, Theophilus, is a fine gin man.' I would reply: 'Maybe it is the system used rather than the man, as we use the Continental.' I have often wondered why many people, white and colored, would pass by other gins and haul their cotton a long way to my gin, and I find it is the results obtained by using the Continental System. I make it a rule every year to box my gin saws and send them to the Continental People at Memphis. They put them in the lathe and overhaul the saws so that they always give the same results as new ones.

AVERAGES.

In making a general estimate of a crop in a given field, parts representing good and bad are selected, and from these a general average is assumed. As with this, so in other things.

The public press holds up to the view of the world the many shortcomings of the Negro and but few of his virtues. Hence, it becomes the duty of the Negro chronicler to do his best to call attention of the public to the character and achievements of the men of his race, such as [Frederick] Douglass, [Paul Laurence] Dunbar, Washington, Bond and a host of others, that when conclusions are drawn the general average will not be too low. These men, each in his particular calling, have accomplished much to raise the general standard of the Negro in America, and no fair average could be made without taking into consideration the successes attained by them. Their origin, the apparently insurmountable obstacles they overcame, all bear testimony to the fact "Labor omnia vincit."

The origin of an individual by no means indicates the possibilities of his life. Born in poverty and obscurity, these men have simply done well the things that came up for them to do, striving, always striving to perform each task better than the last, with the result that success came from their efforts and honor crowns their lives. If one will study closely the tales this book contains, he will find that the achievements of Scott Bond did not come from favoritism nor unusual opportunity. Every particle of gain man has made since Adam, either in civilization or material wealth is measured by the number of drops of sweat and blood that it took to produce it. It did not matter about the magnitude of the task, whether minute or vast, that came to Scott Bond, he went in with a will and determination to get the best results. No day was too hot, nor too cold for him to do his best. No night was too dark and stormy for him to do what he conceived to be his duty. It is related more than once in these pages, that in order to accomplish some undertaking he would ride or walk for miles through driving rain, in daylight or darkness to master the situation. If there is one thing more than another that has always commended Scott Bond to public and private admiration, it is the splendid example of a clean life. Wealth, to command or even to be respected, must be backed by sterling character, for without this, wealth and education will not long avail. Every individual of a race who raises himself among his fellows raises the general average of his whole people.

BUSINESS.

"Confidence is the basic of business success; confidence in one's self and confidence in one's neighbor; confidence of those with whom you deal that you can and will 'tote' fair. I was wonderfully surprised after I had entered the mercantile business to learn how broad the commercial world was. The basis of fairness to all mankind that could furnish the intellect and the ability, including the financial part of it. When these things were at hand I found that it was left to the individual to succeed or fail. The poor white man's chances and opportunity along these lines are just as great as the rich white man and the Negro's chances and opportunities are the same as other men's. The commercial world knows no color and has no pets. The great earth, mother of all the people, is acquainted with all her children; she neither knows them by color nor sex. All are left to draw from her at will and the mercantile is but the clearing house for the different treasures gathered from her bosom. In order to keep alive the mercantile business it is necessary to feed back to the soil in the same ratio that we draw, and to get a favorable standing in this great clearing house one must be ever on the alert to see that the balance sheet of one's integrity does not have a deficit in one's standing in his commercial conduct. If those who sit on dry goods boxes and street corners and complain about their chances would get busy and try to do something they would soon find that legislation is not against them, but for them and in their favor. They would also find that there is no room for complaint if one would use his brains and energy. The seasons and climates come to all alike. There is no discrimination. Where one fails it is largely chargeable to himself. If the black man had the mental vision to perceive it he would find that his chances along spiritual and material lines are as great as any one's else, so that in the commercial world if he will deliver the goods he can get the money."

THE ST. FRANCIS BASIN.

"The rich alluvial lands of the St. Francis Basin, when brought into cultivation, could produce in foodstuff sufficient to feed the entire population of the United States. The climate is exceedingly mild. The strip of land forming this basin will average about 46 miles and extends north and south nearly 375 miles. So mild is the temperature in the southern half of this basin that stock can get a living in the open for twelve months in the year. On the top of Crowley's Ridge at the south end, vegetables may be grown in the open from March to December. The writer has gathered English peas, snap beans, lettuce, mustard, Irish potatoes, radishes, beets, turnips, rape, cabbage, salsify, parsnips, carrots, parsley and sage from Mr. Bond's garden in the Christmas week; this, too, in open ground.

The average small farmer can clear above all expenses from $500 to $1,000 per year. More Negroes own land and automobiles in St. Francis County than in any county in the United States. The mineral resources, coal, salt, marl and kaolin are untouched. There are still vast tracts of virgin forest awaiting the woodsman. Wheat, rye, oats, corn, alfalfa and cotton are at home in St. Francis Basin. This land will with good season and proper cultivation produce a bale of cotton to the acre, which at present prices of seed and cotton is worth $163, which gives an idea of the intrinsic value of this land. $163 is ten per cent of $1,630, and as the ruling rate is ten per cent the land is worth $1,630 per acre. Do you say this valuation is too high? Well, deduct $38 per acre for cost of cultivation, gathering and

Registered O. I. C. hogs.

marketing and you still have $125 left, which is ten per cent or $1,250 per acre. But this is still in favor of the above conclusion, because the cost of making and gathering a bale of cotton will reach no such high figure. All the crops mentioned are equally valuable and besides these, Irish potatoes, sweet potatoes, sorghum and ribbon cane will produce as much. Six crops of alfalfa a year. It is for these reasons we want the world to know that the man who wants to do may, and the man who does not wants nothing.

MR. BOND IN NEW ORLEANS.

In 1911 I received through Mr. R. E. Jones, president of the Louisiana Negro Business League, an invitation to visit New Orleans. The League paid my expenses, as they wanted me to talk to the League. This trip to New Orleans was my first and it proved to be a great source of pleasure and information. The audience was large; in fact it was said that the meeting was one of the best that they had ever held, as they had representatives from all parts of the Pelican State. I gave them the best talk along business lines that I was able to give in a common, horse sense manner. My hearers seemed to be highly elated over my discourse. Mr. Robinson, who succeeded Mr. Jones as president of the League, was a noble gentleman and a fine specimen of our race. He was one of the leading contractors in New Orleans and was a large holder of Crescent City real estate. There was a typical southern banquet given in my honor at the home of a leading doctor, where everything was up-to-date. I was positively surprised to find that I was known to every Negro business man in New Orleans. I passed the spot where Abraham Lincoln stood watching an auctioning of slaves, and is said to have declared that if ever he had a chance to strike slavery, he would strike it hard. The loading and unloading of vessels at the wharf with modern machinery was a revelation to me. I looked at Negroes engaged in different capacities around the landings and when I thought of the vast quantity of merchandise of one kind or another that was annually exported from New Orleans, and that by far the greater part of it was produced by Negro labor, it seemed to me that if the Negro knew his power and his value he would soon become a mighty factor in the commercial life of the south.

CHICKENS.

If the Negro stands convicted of one thing more than another, it is his love of a nice, juicy chicken. However, he is not by himself for the chicken is found domesticated among all civilized people and this domestication is far from modern. I have always believed in living at home, and as chickens are not only a source of food for home consumption they also supply many needed pennies to meet the picayune expenses of the home in the course of the year.

My son, Theo., found a neighbor who had a large flock of white brahmas with which he was quite successful; so he purchased a "start" of this breed of chickens, and now our yards are well supplied with this toothsome fowl. I have found it better to have one good variety of chickens than half dozen mixed and inferior grades. Any farmer can make this industry pay, if he will devote a few of his spare moments to the work.

My wife has always done her full share to make my home a real home. She has up to this time made my milk cows a source of pleas-

Mrs. Bond and her pets.

ure and profit. She has also taken upon herself at all times the care of the poultry and the accompanying picture shows her in the midst of her "Biddies."

SHEEP GROWING.

I am in no sense a large grower of sheep, yet I have tried my hand at it. I have always been a great lover of sheep. A few years ago I bought three and from them I have grown my present flock. I purchased a ram at the Tri-State Fair and turned him in with my other sheep. The result was a raising of wool production, from two pounds to three and a half pounds. I paid $50 for the ram and thought the price exceedingly high, but the increase in wool product and the improvement in the size and vigor of the lambs the following year showed me I had made no mistake. Sheep are not expensive. They can survive nicely in the open nine months in the year. They will eat many things in the pasture that no other animal will eat. A lamb is at his best at six months, for he is worth more then than he will ever be again. Any farmer can easily care for a small flock of sheep. One can soon learn how profitable sheep growing is and how little it costs to care for them. Besides it is a real pleasure to look at a flock of sheep and to watch the lambs as they gambol in the springtime.

CLEARING LAND.

Clearing land is not play. Most of the smiling fields now owned and cultivated by Scott Bond were wrested by him from vast cane brakes and trackless forests.

Clearing land is no child's play. In addition to removing the timber, cutting the cane, vines and undergrowth there follows years of sprouting, grubbing and stump pulling, there comes in the lowland region, a continual battle with poisonous reptiles, insects and perhaps worst of all, myriads of malaria carrying mosquitoes. Then the occasional overflows make new ground cotton crops very uncertain by shortening the season, and apparently creating or at least encouraging the crop devouring cutworm.

The writer has cleared thousands of acres of swamp lands, such as Scott Bond owns in the St. Francis Valley and knows the thousand and one things that must be done before the work is complete.

Add to the clearing, the fencing, the draining, the building of houses, barns and shelters of one kind or another and it will be found that the cost is several times the original cost of the land.

It has been estimated that where a man starts, without capital, except his own labor and buys 40 acres of land, clears it, gets it paid for and properly improved his life is fully spent. It has on the other hand been proven that where one with small capital and that capital be stock, tools, feed and food needed for the work, enters upon the same task, with courage, economy and perseverance will soon become independent. It was by this last method that Scott Bond climbed. He share-cropped and rented until he acquired some capital and then started his land purchases, by paying cash for the land and then with his remaining capital improving it.

It will no doubt be interesting to one not acquainted with this particular line of endeavor to know something, in a general way, of just what is done to make a farm out of a jungle.

Let this illustrate: Not many years ago the land lying between the Mississippi river and Crowley's Ridge was a dense swamp, covered with virgin forest in which cane, briars and vines grew so thick as to be almost impassible. The cane grew twenty-five and thirty feet high, the vines grew up and festooned the forest giants of oak, gum, elm and cypress, and among all this wild vegetable life, there thrived the bear, the panther, the wolf, the deer and many varieties of smaller game. Here and there were found deep lakes and bayous teeming with fish and different amphibious reptiles. It was a paradise for ducks and geese.

As civilization pushed westward, an occasional pioneer would start a clearing and be later joined by another. The hardy sons of toil would cut and burn a place in the cane and undergrowth on some spot on the bank of the Mississippi or the St. Francis. Then they would girdle the trees by taking out a chip all round the trees about three feet from the ground. Then wherever possible, corn, garden seed and cotton would be planted and cultivated for the first year. The second year the same land would be cultivated again and the clearing extended as before. The tent or bark house would give way to a substantial log cabin with a chimney built with sticks and mud.

At this stage the pioneer farmer's work had just begun. The coons and bears would attack his corn, the birds and squirrels would assist their comrades in foraging on the growing grain.

All this was but the beginning. The second year, the limbs from the deadened trees would begin to fall on the farmer's crop. The third year the deadened trunks of the forest giants would begin to fall and then for three or four years there would be an annual cutting, piling and burning of logs until at last the clearing became an open farm.

It is thus, step by step, Scott Bond carved his way as told in this book and this description is given, that the reader may have some idea of the gigantic task he set for himself and how well he accomplished it.

It would be hard to determine the value of timber that has been destroyed, absolutely wasted in the Delta country between Crowley[']s ridge in Arkansas and the hills in Mississippi. Nearly all this vast stretch of lowland was shaded by a magnificent growth of valuable timber, such as oak, ash, popular, maple, tupelo, hickory, cypress, cotton wood, hackberry, walnut persimmon, elm and gum.

For many years the saw mills that began to utilize these forests would not use the gum, tupelo, elm, cotton wood and hackberry. In fact only the very best logs from the other varieties were used.

Before the coming of the saw mills, all kinds of timber would be deadened and left to rot and fall. If all the timber that was destroyed in that period was standing today, its value would be greater than the land upon which it grew.

Now the cut-over lands of the St. Francis basin are selling for all the way from $25 to $40 per acre.

Great dredges are at work cutting canals all the way from twenty feet wide and ten feet deep to fifty feet wide and fifteen feet deep, to drain the swamps into the St. Francis and Mississippi rivers. When this system of drainage is completed and the land is underdrained with tile, every acre of it will be worth from $225 to $250 per acre.

A LOOK INTO THE FUTURE.

With the incidents of these pages clearly before us, it is not difficult to see what will be the condition of the under race, one hundred years hence, should the young of our people improve the opportunities that are theirs, and make use of the things that come to hand for the weal of our common country.

The development of a people must come from within. They must either advance or go backward. That the Negro race will not retrograde, is certain from the evidence given by his progress in the first half century of his citizenship.

That the elements that go to make any people great, has become a real, living entity in the Negro's heart, is proven by the success attained by hundreds of the race in every walk of life in which the energy of man avails to conquer.

To close one's eyes to the things that are not agreeable is, but like the ostrich to bury one's head in the sand.

Look up. Look into the future. See the twin stars of hope and promise ever beckoning us, leading us upward and onward in the march of civilization. To what heights they will lead us depends entirely upon ourselves.

(a) What does the Negro think of the conditions under which he lives, moves and has his being?

Scott Bond's office. Theo. Bond, U. S. Bond, and H. S. Bond.

(b) How does he compare with the Negro of the last quarter of the 19th century?

(c) How do these things affect him in his thoughts of the future?

(a) In answer to the first question: He knows the laws of the land guarantee to him the right to life, liberty and the pursuit of happiness. He knows that the laws of many states, made and provided, in devious ways, contradict the spirit of the Constitution of the United States. He knows that in courts of justice, he does not get fair play, neither as a witness nor as an attorney practicing at the bar, because he must submit to being addressed as "nigger" and other equally [un]pleasant names, by small minded practitioners of other races and that any attempt to have this evil corrected, would bring down upon his devoted head, the wrath of opposing counsel, should that counsel be of the stronger race. He knows that the laws of the states guarantee him equal accommodations on the railroads and other public carriers. He also knows that these laws are not enforced. He knows that the public school laws provide the same educational facilities for his children as are provided for the children of other races. He knows too that these same laws are all too often ignored and that as mentioned elsewhere in these pages amount almost to a dead letter where the education of the Negro child is concerned. He knows that every child of every citizen of this great democracy has a right to aspire to every position that is open to the child of any other American citizen and he knows that aspiration is crushed beneath a wall of prejudice that he cannot scale; certainly not at present. Hence he thinks he is not being fairly dealt with. He also thinks that if like Scott Bond, he can show a clean character and a good bank account, backed by large holdings of real property he may then look forward to those things guaranteed by the laws of his country. It is in this spirit this book is written. Let us look conditions full in the face, accept them as they are and strive with might and main to better them.

(b) How does he compare with the Negro of the last quarter of the 19th century?

In the last two and a half decades of the last century, the American Negro was trying to get his bearings. He had just emerged from the cloud of slavery that had enveloped him for 250 years. He was like a bird just out of a cage. Such leadership as he had was carefully feeling the way. Many of his leaders were of the idealistic school, having been thrown into the spotlight, by the catapult of circumstances, they were not sure of their ground. Over zealous friends had crowded them too fast and reaction had set in. Yet the progress made was marvelous along the lines of wealth and general education. In that period two schools of thought had the race divided; one led by [W. E. B.] DuBois was clamoring for classical education of the race. The other, led by Booker T. Washington insisted upon industrial training as a prerequisite to higher things. Neither was well understood by the masses yet both were in a measure right.

DuBois was like the great Douglass an idealist. Washington was intensely practical.

An illustration might not be amiss. Douglass, when speaking of the United States, said, "separate as the billows, one as the sea."

Every one had not seen the sea and could not comprehend the majestic figure of Fred Douglass' idealism.

Booker T. Washington, when speaking at the Atlanta Cotton Exposition, of the black and white races in America said: ["]For all things social they are separate as the fingers; in all things for the

"Robert," registered Hereford bull at five months.

moral and economic development of the southland, the races are
one as the hand."

Every one had seen the hand and understood at once the practical application.

From that day all eyes were turned to Booker T. Washington as
the Moses who would lead the Negro to the promised land, where
he would enjoy the fullness of American manhood rights and bask
in the sunlight of democracy's perfect day. Be it said to the credit of
Booker T. Washington, that so intensely practical was he and so much
in earnest, that he revolutionized the educational methods of the
world. Besides, with his National Negro Business League idea, he
started the Negro up the ladder that has led him to industrial and
commercial fame. So that to compare him with then and now, the
race has grown in wealth from $200,000,000 to away beyond
$1,000,000,000, owning lands and houses, urban and suburban, fac-
tories, mills, gins, banks, mercantile establishments, great newspapers
and printing offices, drug stores, oil mills, oil wells, coal mines, telephone exchanges, cities and towns. He has his own physicians and
pharmacists, D. D.'s and LL. B.'s, in fact everything that other
people have, finds representation among Negroes. They have a

civilization within a civilization. The comparison is: He started with nothing and has made good.

(c) How do these things affect him in his thoughts of the future?

The great strides made by the Negro in these first fifty years, has opened his eyes to the possibilities of advancement and convinced him that merit can and will compel its reward. It may appear tardy, but its arrival is certain. They have quickened his pace and lifted his eyes above the petty annoyances that used to fret him. They have taught him self-reliance and a desire for team work. They have taught him thrift. They have given lessons in integrity and high moral purpose. They have prepared him for the struggle in the climb up the rugged mountain of excellence, and make him think that in the not distant future, he will take his place among his fellow citizens as a man wherever manhood and sterling qualities count, and that he has a message for the world i. e., "If a man will he may."

We will ask the reader to turn back to page 28 and read the trenchant paragraphs of Scott Bond's philosophy.

Enthusiasm, eager and earnest is the crying need in rural districts today. It would bring undreamed of progress, if the young men and women of the race would use for self-development, the time they spend in idle gossip and some other less respectable things.

It is a trite saying that "the young of today is the adult of tomorrow." It is by no means desirable nor beneficial to forgo all innocent amusements. What is suggested is, a systematic effort for self improvement; a determination to do something worth while; to be somebody in the community in which one lives.

When the states, led by the National Government, was making an enthusiastic and determined effort to increase food and feed production in the south, a visit was paid to our town by prominent speakers. Scott Bond was called on by these gentlemen to get into the speakers automobile and express his views and thereby encourage the farmers of St. Francis County (a vast majority of whom are Negroes) to do their bit to prepare for the World War, that had at last drawn this country into the maelstrom.

Mr. Bond accepted the invitation and climbed into the auto. He spoke of the opportunity offered to encourage diversification and showed that the program outlined by preceding speakers was not only good for war times, but would work equally well in times of peace; and showed that it was by this method that he had built up his own enterprises.

He then, as he always does when talking in public, had a little heart to heart talk with his own people. He told them among other things that greater than the conservation of food and feed is the conservation of character, and greater than all these is the protection of the home.

He said: "In Europe they have kings and queens. In this country all the women are queens and all the men are kings; each equal to the other in the eyes of the law, having a right to use that invincible sword of democracy, the ballot. The man who will not protect his queen and his ballot with even his life if necessary, is unworthy the matchless blessing of American citizenship. In short, protect your women and your homes with the ballot, yes, even with your life.

["]Educate your children. Educate heart, hand and mind. Take your place in the ranks of men who do the world's work."

RACE PREJUDICE IN AMERICA
AN ECONOMIC LOSS.

The repressive race prejudice exhibited in the United States is an economic loss. Figures that would state the loss in dollars, from this cause would far exceed in amount the billions this country has poured into the mighty stream of money needed to win the world war.

We ask you to read the fourth paragraph on page 21 of this biography. Then with that paragraph in mind, follow us to our conclusion; remembering the while, that these are cold facts that arise from no sentiment, other than the material and intellectual loss the nation has sustained, and that will continue to grow, on the wrong side of this country's economic ledger, as long as these unfair civic conditions prevail. Because of his poverty the Negro could not be other than a laborer in the first years of his freedom. He would long since have been of far more service to his country, had there not been a wall of prejudice built across his pathway by his white brother worker in the fields of skilled labor. There seemed to be a determination to keep the Negro laborer a hewer of wood and drawer of water. Here and there, by some fortuitous circumstance, one of the race would find a position in some machine shop, foundry or other place where skilled labor found employment; these isolated instances being rifts in the cloud.

Labor unions were formed and one of the basic principles upon which they acted, seemed to be, "no nigger need apply." This was repression with a vengeance.

On the farms where the larger numbers of the race found employment, there was no attempt made to teach the Negro worker the reason why a thing should be done a certain way. He was simply told to do this or that without being taught the reason why.

He was not trusted to do a piece of work and given to understand, that his reward would be measured by the amount and excellence of his work.

He was left in charge of an "agent" who was in all too many cases prejudiced against him; with the result that he learned little under this kind of a task master. He labored under the baleful crop mortgage system that took from him his self-reliance and made him a dependant indeed. On top of all this was opened a way to the unscrupulous, whenever it was so desired, to short change the renter or cropper in the annual settlement.

Jim Crow and other segregation laws were put upon the statue books which seemed to the Negro to tell him at every turn that he was hardly human. He was excluded from the public parks and breathing place in urban communities, frequently facing at the entrance to these places, signs reading, "Negroes and dogs not admitted."

If he visited churches of his choice denomination, Christian (?) churches, of the dominant race, he was tolerated but told to stay "way back and sit down" or was relegated to the gallery.

The Negro's child-like mind told him that what caused all this was the spirit of prejudice.

For years, all this had the Negro at a stand-still. He was wondering if after all democracy and Christianity really meant what their definitions indicate.

This was not all, these things caused the country an enormous loss in efficiency. It has been estimated that the loss to progress thus caused averaged not less than $100 per capita per annum of the total Negro population, financially and an equal amount in the morale of that part of the citizenship of the United States.

As costly as all this has been, it has given the Negro a chance to get hold of himself, and after all, has been a blessing in disguise. By compelling him to flock by himself, it has taught him to take an introspective view of himself, to see that to whatever heights he may aspire, the force to get him there must come from within.

WHAT IS THE NEGRO FARMER DOING?

Read the fourth paragraph on page 52.

But little notice is given to one phase of the Negro's progress. It is common to hear people, who travel over the country on the railroad trains, say they are well informed about the Negro and the things he is doing.

The truth is, the usual traveler, draws his conclusions from wrong premises. He sees the usual idlers at the railroad stations he may pass or porters, waiters and servants in the towns where he may sojourn for a few days. If he is so disposed, he studies his group as typical of the whole race and concludes, that as they are so are the other Negroes.

Nothing could be farther from the truth. The station idlers, hotel waiters and car porters, no more represent the Negro than the whites of these same labor groups of white people, represent the best there is in the all-conquering, dominant race in this country.

To localize: The community where this book is published is composed of both races, about three Negroes to one white. Both races are in the main hard-working and industrious. Yet in this place as in most others there are idlers who loaf about the town and the railway station. They are not representatives of the best in either race.

Those who count for anything are engaged in the various manufacturing and mercantile concerns that thrive here, or they are on the farms near and remote. Here as elsewhere, by far the most progressive part of the race is making good in the agricultural pursuits. There are places where one can walk for miles and miles on joining farms owned and operated by Negroes. The only way one can make a reasonably fair estimate of the progress of the race in rural communities, is to study this group for it is among them that will be found the thrifty farseeing men of the race, who look into the future and see that one who rules the land will be the one who owns it. This class of men has bought thousands of acres of land in this county in the last two years. The white people, know from experience, that the more they do to make the Negro a land owner, the more will be the rate of increase in wealth to all. The man who buys land gives a bond to society for his good behavior.

The quiet thrifty Negro farmer, is laying the foundation of an economic structure, that will be the best fortification in the commercial and industrial battles of the future. He now owns more than $500,000,000 worth of farm property in the United States and is increasing this at a rate of 10 per cent in each decade.

If that part of the race that is now entering the other fields of industry, heretofore closed to him, will but make efficiency, continuity and thrift his watchwords thus keeping pace with the farmer, the whole of America's colored citizenship will be able in a few years to demand rather than plead for a place in the sun.

CONDITIONS CHANGING.

Little more than fifty years ago the Negro was a slave. Now he is a citizen, counting his wealth in millions and has representatives in the Alumni of the best colleges and universities of the world.

Fifty years ago people of the United States did not agree that Lincoln was worthy the highest niche in the temple of fame. Today in the south and the north in the east and in the west, Washington, Lincoln and Wilson are honored alike in the pictured representations of the nation's greatest presidents.

Fifty years hence there will be an equal change of sentiment toward the Negro. It will hardly be conceivable that present conditions ever existed. He can well afford "to labor and the wait." His reward is as certain as the flight of time.

As noted in the opening chapter of this book, tremendous changes have come in America, since the birth of Scott Bond, in 1853, and all these changes have in some way affected the Negro. He has come out of each of them, violent though they may have been, better off than before.

This book would not serve its purpose, did it not call attention to the steady improvement in the condition of the Negro as represented by the achievements of Scott Bond.

Scene showing cotton field in July where cane grew
thirty feet high a year before.

The Negro was the bone of contention in the Civil War. Yet he proved faithful in the care and protection of southern white women and children on the one hand and did valiant service as a soldier of the union on the other. He won the plaudits of the men who wore the blue and the undying praise and gratitude of the men who wore the gray.

Out of that struggle came emancipation, which like anything else new, was not understood by either the master or his former slave. It took time for both to adjust themselves to the new condition.

Thoughtful men were watching, to see what the emancipated race would do with its new found freedom.

Some suggested that they be left to care for themselves. Others thought the ballot should be placed in the hands of the Negro as his surest means of protection. The idea of enfranchisement prevailed. The friends of the Negro did not take into consideration the fact that the ex-slave was not fully prepared for that advanced step. They expected too much in so short a time. Hence it was soon found that the ballot in the hands of the ignorant, was not a panacea for the ills that beset the country in the years of reconstruction.

Then followed a period, in which by violence as well as legal subterfuge, the ballot was literally taken from the Negro in a large part of the country. It is to the credit of the Negro that in the few years he had the opportunity, he gave to the service of the nation and of the several states, many men who in point of ability and integrity were prophetic of the future.

Disfranchisement rolled a cloud, black and portentous, across the roseate dream of the Negro. So dangerous did it appear, that it looked for a while as if all the fruits of the awful struggles of the Civil War were to be swept away.

From this travail a new star of hope was born, twinkling and dim at first, it grew brighter and brighter as time sped by. A new era dawned for the Negro. Men like Booker T. Washington, seeing the demand for efficiency in doing the world's work, began the effort that should have been started with Lincoln's Emancipation Proclamation. Men like Scott Bond, knowing that to erect a building, a foundation must be laid, and if the structure is to endure the foundation must be on solid rock; began by precept and example to teach the race to educate the hand as well as heart and the mind. This school of men taught that efficiency and thrift would be the proper foundation upon which to build; that the ownership of some of this world's goods would go a long way towards removing the stumbling blocks from the pathway up. So insistent and persistent was this school of men that today, efficiency, character and wealth are dispelling the cloud of despair and doubt that hung so low, only a few years ago. The Negro is coming into his own.

The question arises: Has he kept pace with the growth of intelligence, with the material and spiritual advancement of other groups that make up American citizenship?

We will see.

In electricity, great strides were made, appliances that annihilated distance and used the subtile fluid for communication between distant points, and harnessed this same mysterious force to the wheels of manufacture and transportation. Not to be outdone, the Negro, Granville T. Woods, of Cincinnati, in the early 80's invented a system by which he could sit in the moving trains of the Pennsylvania railroad, and without visible connection hurl his thoughts through the impalpable ether to wires strung along the tracks of that great

Interior view of Scott Bond's store.

system of roads and by the same method receive dispatches from distant points—wireless telegraphy.

In mechanics, [John T.] Hancock, with his inspirator, [Elijah] McCoy with his lubricator and a host of other[s], divided honors with their brothers of the fairer skin in the most wonderful age of mechanical development the world has ever known.

In art, the form, perspective and color-blending of [Henry Ossawa] Tanner is considered an honor upon the walls of any salon in Europe.

In letters, [William S.] Scarborough's Greek text book was long ago adopted by Harvard.

In literature, the songs of [Paul Laurence] Dunbar have wrung tears and laughter from the people of two continents. Oh! the shame of it! All this while the race to which these men belonged, was being held back by the repressive attitude exhibited by too many of their fellow citizens.

The higher spiritual advance of the Negro, up to this time is one of the most remarkable things in his history. He is numbered by millions in the several Christian denominations and counts his missionaries to foreign countries by hundreds. He has kept pace with the growth of civilization, and it may be that the present world war will produce the heat that will fuse the people of this country into a common agreement, that the law shall protect those who protect the flag of our country.

APPLICATION.

Racial movements all have basic causes.

The present exodus of Southern Negroes to the north has causes based in many things; among them perhaps the greatest of all is the repressive attitude assumed in almost all parts of the south toward him. By this we do not mean segregation in the cars, the schools, the hotels, and places of public amusement. So far as the Negro is concerned he had rather have it this way if he got what the law plainly says he must have, "equal accommodations." It is the repressive spirit behind these things that makes for discontent.

There are few places on the railroads, except in the larger cities of the south, where the Negro passenger can get a lunch without having to accept an offence with it.

The impotency of the law to protect him, the injustice he meets in many places, in settlements for his toil or his crops, the limited opportunity he has in numerous parts of the country, for the full and free exercise of the franchise, the storm that would gather about him should he ask the suffrage of his neighbors for public office, have their repressive influence upon the Negro and serve as a cause for unrest.

The Negro is no more a saint than his white neighbor; nor is he more of a devil than his white neighbor has taught him to be.

It is not the purpose here to urge the Negro to strive for public office nor to put up a whine or an excuse. What is desired is to find a way to better conditions and make the future safe, prosperous and happy for all the people.

To be hurt by the point of a pin is trifling in itself, yet if this slight irritation be continuous it would become unbearable.

To hear some opprobrious epithet applied, such as "nigger" or "negress," and that with malice, thoughtless or aforethought, is never pleasant; but when this is a continual thing, it is to say the least annoying and offensive so much so that the worm turns at last as in the Houston [race riot] incident. Had the police officers in that town been prudent men, the Negro soldiers would not have been driven in maddened frenzy to violate the law.

To be defeated for public office is trifling in itself, yet when one knowing he is a citizen and has a right to aspire to these things sees a wall of repression rising higher and higher before him and this in the face of the law made and provided for all alike, sees the aspiration for these things crushed in embryo and the door of hope forever closed in his face, he is not likely to be a contented laborer in such circumstances.

The states have upon their statute books, laws providing for the education of the young in public schools. In most states the law directs a per capita expenditure of funds collected for the public schools without discrimination as to race, creed or color, except that there shall be separate schools for blacks and whites. This is excellent. But when the Negro finds that there is from $12.50 to $15.00 per capita expended on the education of the white child and only $2.00 to $2.50 per capita in the provision for the education of the Negro child, he can only make these balance with the difference. Hence, when he hears of another part of the country, where the enforcement of the school law gives his child an equal chance for education with that of the white child, he becomes restless and eventually moves into that part of the country where his child will get the benefit of public school education.

No state in the Union has better school laws than Arkansas, and were they enforced in spirit it would be an example to less progressive states.

The proof that the Negro is doing well, in nearly all parts of this great state, is that so many are coming into this state to better their condition.

The days grow brighter as the years go by. The Negro is being advised to pay his poll taxes, to register and to vote in school and municipal elections. We are happy to know that this advice and these coachings come from men of the highest standing in the dominant race.

You have read the story of Scott Bond. We have tried to give it as nearly as possible in his own words, using quotation some times, and at other times, letting him speak directly in the first person.

This story is prophetic of the future. The millions of Negroes who have lived and died in America, the millions who live in the great republic and the countless millions who will be here in the ages to come are a part of the great procession of humanity that is passing through the melting pot of evolution must reach at last the higher, brighter light of the perfect day.

Oh, Southland, the land of Dixie, the land of the moss, the cypress and the pine, the land of flowers and of sunshine, the land of the mocking bird, the land of corn and cotton, the Negro loves thee.

By the sufferings, the tears and the prayers of his foreparents in the 250 years of his apprenticeship in Columbia, he has earned the right to full citizenship.

Why repeat here tales of faithfulness to his master in the years before the Civil War, the honor with which he acquitted himself of caring for the families of the soldiers in gray while they were fighting to hold him a slave and seal forever the doom of freedom and democracy, with the warm red blood of the south's bravest and best sons?

What need of retelling the story of pushing back the forests to make place for smiling fields of grain and cotton, building cities and then building roads of steel to connect these cities and bear to them and to the outside world the products of mine, field and forest?

All these things the Negro has done and will continue to do. Why tell of the Negro's valor upon land and sea in the nation's battles for birth, for existence and for honor? These things are written so high upon the firmament of glory that angry worlds of prejudice can not eclipse the light of true history that shines now and will shine forever.

The Negro's salvation is in his own hands.

These pages tell the achievements of an individual. If each Negro will do one one-hundredth part as much as the one about whom we write, the Negro's place in the sun will be larger. Individual effort he must have, yet he is not measured as an individual nor judged by individual conduct but as a race responsible for each infraction and refraction by the individual. Hence he needs to learn team work. When individual effort is melted into team work, racial solidarity in economic action will be the outcome and the Negro will take his proper place in the commercial and civic life of the nation he clothes and helps to feed.

We will "let down our buckets where we are," for "if a man will he may."

Whatever may be the apparent difficulties, the south especially Arkansas, is the best place in the world for the poor man; and as the Negro is the poorest man in the world, it is the best place for him. Will the south apply the balm herein suggested?

SUMMARY.

As the printers are setting the last chapters of this book, Scott Bond is finishing the first of a number of silos that he has planned for his different farms. He believes in cotton. Yet when the boll weevil threatened to put an end to that industry he began to look in other directions for money crops, and now, with hundreds of head of cattle, hogs and sheep, he is ready to meet the emergency. Should it become necessary to stop growing cotton, other things equally as profitable would take its place without serious inconvenience.

It is this foresight and resourcefulness that has made him successful and gives reason for writing the contents of this book.

Think of it. A little slave boy. Then the kaleidoscope turns and we see the dawn of freedom and the slave transformed into a dutiful and respectful stepson.

Another turn and we see a young man starting out on his own account to tickle the bosom of mother earth that she might bring forth abundant harvest.

We turn the kaleidoscope again and we see an embryo merchant in Forrest City. Capital was too small.

The next turn and the pent up energy of the young man is found again exerting itself on the Allen Farm and this picture is colored with the roseate tints of a happy marriage and the exhibition of that wonderful industry that has sent by leaps and bounds, the once slave boy to the ownership of lands, gins, storehouses, stocks in various corporations, brick yards, saw mills, excavating works, herds and flocks in the hills and valleys, educated children, a happy Christian home, the friendship and respect of black and white, a clean, moral character and while without attending school his success as a farmer is attested by the certificate of Tuskegee Institute, conferred on him in 1917 for his knowledge of agriculture.

Scott Bond.

APPENDIX.

Since this book went to press I learn of a land deal Mr. Bond has made of three of his farms, twelve miles north of his store at Madison, on the St. Francis river.

One of these farms, Mr. Bond sold twenty-six years ago for $8.00 an acre and was well pleased with the profit he made in the sale. The man who bought it kept it five years and did some improvement. He then sold it to a northern man for $18.00 an acre. He, also, was well pleased with the profit he made in the deal.

Mr. Bond then rented the farm for two years from this northern man for $500 a year and then bought the farm again for $22.00 an acre and was delighted and called it a wonderful bargain. He kept the farm for three years; cleared and brought into cultivation forty additional acres and built one new house. There is 150 acres in cultivation. This farm consists of 266 acres. To this farm he added two other adjoining farms, making in all 1,140 acres, which he has just sold for $114,000. He reserves 800 acres in the same neighborhood which he is now using as a cattle ranch.

This is another evidence of the wonderful opportunities in Arkansas. I understand that Mr. Bond intends to invest the net proceeds of this sale in Liberty Bonds and for Y. M. C. A. purposes to help the soldiers of the nation to win the war for this our great republic and for the liberty of the world.

He has always said that the only way for one to be happy is to make all around him happy. This is one way he hopes to do his bit to help make the nation happy. It will be remembered that Mr. Bond has already contributed $200 to the Red Cross and $2,000 in Liberty Bonds.

Notes

1.   Granville T. Woods (1856–1910), a versatile African American inventor, patented about thirty-five inventions "that were vital to the development of electrical and mechanical equipment," including those related to the steam boiler furnace, telephonic transmission, railroad telegraphy, galvanic battery, and automatic cut-out for electric circuits, among others.

2.   The battle of San Juan Hill in Cuba during the Spanish–American War occurred on July 1, 1898, and the battle of Carrizal occurred in Mexico on June 21, 1916, during the Punitive Expedition sent there by the United States. Both were well-known military engagements in which African American troops were involved.

3.   Mrs. Bond refers to Mary Frances Mebane Bond, who was the wife and later widow of John W. Bond, both natives of North Carolina. The Bonds settled in the St. Francis River Basin in eastern Arkansas, where they owned a large plantation. Mary Frances (Fannie) Mebane Bond, who was often referred to as "the widow Bond," inherited slaves from the Mebane family who continued to be called the "Mebane slaves." Mebane is consistently misspelled *Maben* in this work. On the Mebane family history, see http://www.sallysfamilyplace.com/Wheeler/mebane.

4.   Magnolia Nash, a native of North Carolina, had been a slave of Leila Nash of Forrest City, Arkansas, prior to emancipation.

5.   Celia Mebane Allen was the proprietor of the large plantation rented by Scott Bond. She was the first cousin of Mary Frances Mebane Bond and the widow of John Abijab Allen. The Allens had lived in Forrest City, Arkansas, but after her husband's death, Celia Allen moved to Knoxville, Tennessee.

6.   The Mr. Allen mentioned here was Celia Allen's son, John Mebane Allen.

7.   Ralph Block refers to Raphael Block, co-owner of the mercantile establishment of R. and B. Block of Wittsburg, Arkansas.

8.   L. Rollwage and Company was a large store in Forrest City owned by two brothers, Louis and Otto Rollwage, natives of Cincinnati, Ohio. Scott Bond was a close friend of the younger brother, Otto.

9.   Thomas O. Fitzpatrick was a politically active and widely

respected Republican in Cross and St. Francis counties. He served as circuit judge, county clerk, and postmaster of Forrest City. He was also a farmer and a cotton gin owner.

10.　The Mrs. Manning mentioned here is the wife of William Manning, a prominent farmer and stock raiser who represented St. Francis County in the state legislature. She was a native of Pennsylvania.

11.　John Hope (1868–1936), born in Augusta, Georgia, was a graduate of Brown University who became a prominent educator. He began his teaching career in Roger Williams University in Nashville, Tennessee (1894–1898), then joined the faculty of Atlanta Baptist College and became the institution's president in 1906. Its name was changed to Morehouse College in 1913. Under Hope's leadership Morehouse became one of the outstanding black colleges in America. In 1929 Hope became the president of the newly created Atlanta University. Active in the NAACP and numerous other organizations, he challenged Booker T. Washington's philosophy of race relations.

12.　The Captain Stearns mentioned here refers to Captain J. G. Stern, who grew up in Illinois and served in the Union army during the Civil War. He fought in various battles in northern Virginia and was captured twice by the Confederates and escaped twice. He returned to the South in 1872 and piloted a boat on the Mississippi and St. Francis rivers prior to settling in Madison, Arkansas, about 1883. Here he established and operated a timber and lumber business.

13.　William H. Goodlow refers to William H. Goodloe, an antebellum planter of considerable wealth, who lived a few miles from Canton, Mississippi. Both Goodloe and his wife, Elizabeth Mebane Goodloe, were natives of North Carolina. Mrs. Goodloe may well have been a relative of Scott Bond's owner, Mary Frances Mebane Bond. There is considerable confusion about William H. Goodloe's birth, but the most frequently cited year is 1822.

14.　"Plunder room" was a storage room in which cast-off furniture, old clothes, and similar items were kept.

15.　Mrs. W. S. Graham was the daughter of Dr. George T. Stull, a native of Nashville, Tennessee, who became a prominent citizen of Crittenden County, Arkansas. Stull later moved to Memphis. Mrs. Graham's husband, W. S. Graham, was a prominent merchant and cotton ginner in Forrest City, Arkansas, and the owner of a large cotton plantation. After her husband's death Mrs. Graham contributed $95,000 toward the building of the W. S. Graham Memorial Presbyterian Church in Forrest City.

16.   The Tennessee Separate Coach Law mentioned here refers to the legislation passed in 1891.

17.   Anthony Stanford was an important figure in the Liberian migration movement in the 1890s. A minister in the African Methodist Episcopal Church and a physician, he actively recruited blacks in St. Francis County to settle in Liberia.

18.   Captain James Fussell, born in Trenton, Tennessee, moved to Forrest City in 1875 and joined the firm of Pollock, Fussell and Company. He was elected president of the Bank of Eastern Arkansas in 1889 and in 1902 became director of the Bank of Forrest City. He "occupied a high plane in business and social circles of Forrest City."

19.   Otto B. Rollwage, born and reared in Cincinnati, Ohio, moved to Forrest City, Arkansas, in 1874 and joined his brother Louis in a mercantile business. He served on the city's board of aldermen and as mayor. Under his leadership as mayor, Forrest City became "one of the best governed cities in Arkansas." He later became a lawyer.

20.   Bishop Abraham Grant (1848–1911) was born a slave and educated at Cookman Institute in Florida. He joined the African Methodist Episcopal Church in 1868, was licensed to preach in 1873, and rose rapidly in the church hierarchy. He was first elected bishop in 1888. From 1904 until his death he presided over the district that included Missouri, Kansas, Colorado, and California and resided in Kansas City, Kansas. He was active in Republican Party politics and supported Booker T. Washington's approach to race relations.

21.   Philip Van Patten, a physician, was born in Schenectady, New York, but grew up in Iowa and graduated from the Medical University of Iowa. In 1861 he married the daughter of Colonel John Miller of Batesville, Arkansas. During the Civil War he served first as the surgeon of the Thirteenth Arkansas Volunteer Infantry and ultimately became division surgeon. He was elected to the Arkansas legislature from Poinsett County in 1860 and later served as secretary of the Arkansas State Board of Health. He settled in Forrest City in 1885. Van Patten acquired an enviable reputation as a physician.

22. On Ravenden Springs, see Lawrence Dalton, *History of Randolph County, Arkansas* (Little Rock, AR: Democrat Printing and Lithographing Co., 1946[?]), 231–34.

23. This name should probably be Blackshear rather than Blackshire. The Blackshear family figured prominently in the history of Ravenden Springs.

24. Front Row refers to the area in Memphis where the offices of numerous commission merchants were located.

25. Seth Low (1850–1916) was a successful businessman who, born into a wealthy New York family, was involved in a wide variety of reform activities. He served as president of Columbia University and as mayor of New York City. He was an important supporter of Booker T. Washington and the Tuskegee Institute.

26. The William Lloyd Garrison mentioned by Scott Bond obviously refers to the grandson of the famous antebellum abolitionist leader. Like his father (1838–1909), he was also the namesake of the abolitionist leader. This third William Lloyd Garrison (1874–1964) was an investment banker who was identified with various reform efforts, including anti-imperialism, free trade, pacifism, and sexual and racial equality.

27. James C. Napier (1845–1940), born free near Nashville, Tennessee, was an attorney, banker, government official (Register of the Treasury), and civic leader. Active in Republican Party politics and a strong supporter of Booker T. Washington's approach to race relations, Napier served as president of the National Negro Business League in 1915.

Index

(Note: Roman numerals in the index refer to pages in the Introduction, and arabic numerals refer to pages in *From Slavery to Wealth*.)